The Meaning of the Middle Ages

The Meaning of the Middle Ages

A Sociological and Cultural History

Norman F. Cantor

Distinguished Professor of History
State University of New York at Binghamton

Allyn and Bacon, Inc., Boston

A society, like a mind,
is woven of perpetual interaction.

Marc Bloch

7-18-73

to Mindy

CONTENTS

CHAPTER FIVE: CREATIVITY AND REBELLION   203

CHAPTER SIX: THE CRISIS OF MEDIEVAL
    CULTURE   249

EPILOGUE: BEYOND THE MIDDLE AGES   283

SUGGESTIONS FOR FURTHER READING   311

PREFACE

This is not narrative history; I have already written a narrative history of the medieval world (*Medieval History. The Life and Death of a Civilization*. New York: Macmillan, 1963; second edition 1969). Nor is this book simply an intellectual history of the Middle Ages. It is rather a cultural history in the functional-social tradition of Maitland, Bloch, Huizinga, and Southern. I have attempted to work out a model, or pattern, of medieval thought and attitudes in relation to social, economic, and political change. I have tried to show what the leading ideas of the Middle Ages really signified in terms of social life and individual behavior. I have tried to reveal how these ideas and life-forms came into existence and were altered under the pressure of social change. I have tried to show where the medieval traditions came from and how they were molded and adapted under the impact of political and social circumstance. At the same time, I have tried to demonstrate the significance of medieval ideals for the shaping of social and political institutions.

I wish to acknowledge the valuable assistance of Mrs. Clarissa Atkinson, Miss Zane Berzins, and Mrs. Beth Lawrence in preparing this book for publication. Part of section II of the Prologue was originally published in the *Journal of Contemporary History*, Vol. III, no. 2, April, 1968, and it is used here by permission of the editors. I am grateful to Mr. Tom Huber for preparing the index.

NFC
Binghamton, N.Y.

Prologue

PERCEPTIONS OF THE MEDIEVAL WORLD

I. The Relevance of the Middle Ages

With the recent rage for "relevance" in the universities, it is natural to wonder why we study the history of a society so vastly different from our own as that of medieval Europe. Medieval history may be enjoyable, it may tell a good story, but can an understanding of the Middle Ages help us to confront twentieth-century problems? What use is our knowledge of medieval thought and medieval people?

Paradoxically, medieval history is "relevant" primarily because the society it describes was indeed so very distant from our own—was, in fact, pre-industrial and non-democratic. Before there were huge cities, mass populations, factories, or democratic governments there was the Middle Ages, with its very different systems and styles. Nowadays there is a widespread feeling that industrial democratic society has failed somehow, that we are dehumanized in a society which produces "one-dimensional" men and frustrates the liberation of human nature. We no longer are optimistic about our society; we are aware of the profound defects of industrialism, bureaucracy, and democracy. Various pundits envisage a new post-industrial era in consequence, among other things, of communications technology, mass consumption, and population boom. They claim that this new society will supersede the industrial, democratic world of the last 150 years. It is essential, if all this is true, to seek alternatives to modern society—to industrialism, democracy, and bureaucracy—and historians point to such alternatives in the medieval world.

History will not solve all our social problems (it may not solve any of them), but it can provide alternative social models. We study history in order to examine the cumulative experience of the human race in any particular endeavor, and the study of the Middle Ages offers us a look at a non-industrial, non-democratic world in which bureaucracy developed late and was never very effective. It was a world where ideas and ideals counted for a great deal, where values and commitment were emphasized above everything—if ever there was a society based on commitment, it was the medieval. The warnings and denunciations of certain contemporary critics of modern society have a medieval ring; their words and tone suggest the reactions of a medieval monk transplanted to our world from his own idealistic, committed society. There is, apparently, a spiritual tie or at least parallel between alienated twentieth-century man and his medieval ancestors.

The medieval world preceded the era of the nation-state, the modern bureaucratic state of the western world. It was for a long time an extremely pluralistic society, broken into very small units within which people associated and communicated. The nation-state was only one of these units, and it developed very late in the medieval period; its hold on people was always limited. There is much talk today about the possibility of the "global village," hoping that modern communications and technology may enable us to pass beyond the era of nations and states into a world in which people may live in small communities and still enjoy the benefits of modern culture. Medieval people did live in such units, quite unlike the modern Leviathan—the all-encompassing, monolithic modern state—and it might be interesting to find out what their lives were like. No one advocates a return to the Middle Ages—God forbid!—but the medieval world does offer a contrast, a backdrop, an alternative model, a distinct civilization unlike our own. The study of medieval history may make us more or less hostile to our own civilization, but it cannot fail at least to offer us provocative ideas.

Incidentally, the study of a non-modern society may help us to understand Africa, Asia, and Latin America, where many of the things that happen follow the parameters of a pre-modern society. Even when modern technology is introduced in these parts of the world, the results are different from what we see in Europe or

North America. The recent history of China, with its Red Guard and cultural revolution, represents a distinctly medieval situation, inspired by intense idealism (misguided, perhaps), of fanaticism expressed in violent student rioting. As Europe and North America begin to slip into the post-modern period, we see similar phenomena in the West.

It is obvious, too, that we may discover in the medieval world the first clear formulation of many of our ideas and institutions. First of all, the idea of love is largely a medieval invention. Erotic love—sexual love—became fully articulated and conceptually significant for the first time during the Middle Ages. Sexual love had always existed, obviously, but medieval men were the first to think about it extensively. They were also the first to think of women in some sort of equality with men. The romantic ideal was born during the Middle Ages.

The medieval world also invented representative, parliamentary government. Liberal political theory was largely, if not entirely, a product of the Middle Ages. Ultimately, of course, the Middle Ages produced the nation-state—perhaps out of desperation.

It should be obvious that understanding of the medieval world is essential to an understanding of the Roman Catholic Church, the Church of the past and the Church in this century. What is happening in the Church today represents a struggle between its surviving medievalism and attempts to go beyond medievalism. Moreover, what is happening today is also a recurrence of the medieval situation, where bishops and priests (or bishops and pope) and the clergy and laity were frequently at odds.

The older, more traditional reason for assigning relevance to the Middle Ages was the assumption that the "origins" of certain ideas and institutions central to western civilization could be discovered in that era. A more recent criterion for ascribing significance to the Middle Ages is the belief that the pre-industrial Middle Ages can be contrasted with modern industrial society and also that certain parallels are evident between the moral and millennial attitudes and doctrines of medieval men and the post-industrial or sometimes anti-industrial ideological radicalism of the late 1960s and 1970s. A special relevance of medieval history to present-day concerns involves the Catholic Church, whose recent history has centered on the struggle between the perpetuators of medieval Romanism, on the one side, and on the other the anti-Romanists who seek a more modernized liberal institution and the radical millenarists who yearn (like radical sixteenth-century Protestants) for the democratic spiritual community they discern in the apostolic Church.

These are all reasons enough to find meaning in the Middle Ages. None are fantasy; all are motive enough to seek understanding of the pattern of medieval development. Yet the Middle Ages are complex; we shall not prejudge the issue by proclaiming at the outset the themes that give meaning to the medieval era. We should take note, however, of the patterns that academic scholars have perceived in the medieval era and the assumptions by which they have interpreted the medieval centuries. This will allow the lay reader and student to become initially acquainted with the great scholars whose studies I have built upon in arriving at my understanding of the meaning of medieval history.

II. *The Modernity of Medieval Historiography*

Each era in the past conjures up a certain image in the minds of modern men. Each era stands for certain things, has a particular meaning in modern consciousness. And this meaning changes, partly as a result of scholarly research—that is, greater familiarity with the past era—but partly also as we change, as the standpoint (social, political, intellectual) from which we view the past itself alters.

Historical scholarship has advanced to its present state of knowledge and sophistication in large part because of the critical examination of primary sources. Twentieth-century scholarship has benefited from the exhaustive labors of scholars sincerely convinced that the particular questions which they were moved to pose of the past were the most meaningful and instructive to mankind. Serious historians—the men who have helped us to illuminate the past in all its richness and perplexity—have seldom been vulgar apologists for the contemporary establishment, either intellectual or political. Neither have they, on the whole, been conscious propagandists for some existing or hoped-for social order. Nevertheless the study of

medieval history has always been strikingly condition
temporary social needs and intellectual fashions, in th
century as in previous eras.

It is well known that the image of the Middle Ages which —
tained at any given period in early modern Europe tells us more
about the difficulties and dilemmas, the intellectual commitments
of the men of the period than it does about the medieval world itself. The Renaissance thinkers who first branded the Middle Ages
as "barbaric" and "dark" were men in rebellion against certain
aspects of scholasticism and clerical authority. To justify their own
departure from prevailing intellectual orthodoxies, they found it
psychologically necessary and didactically useful to project their
disdain backwards in time and pronounce a thousand years in the
history of European man as boorish and intellectually retrograde.
Similarly, the sarcastic opprobrium of the Enlightenment towards
the medieval world was in large measure dictated by the guerrilla
warfare which the *philosophes* waged against the power and pretensions of the Church in their own day. Monsieur le curé was
personally obnoxious to Voltaire, who found him bigoted, narrow-
minded, parochial, and ignorant. Voltaire proceeded to apply this
unflattering stereotype to an entire historical epoch.

At the hands of nineteenth-century Romantics, the Middle
Ages suddenly received a good press. The Romantics disliked the
excessive rationalism of the Augustan world and sought comfort
and refuge in the medieval period as an age more congenial to the
values of the heart and the imagination. A great number of the
most sensitive minds of the nineteenth century were repelled by
the crass materialism of their own societies, by the ugliness of the
factory and the sterility of the counting house. Simultaneously,
they discovered and idealized the great spiritual values of the Middle Ages.

This highly subjective quest for the true identity of the medieval period continues into the twentieth century. The historiography
of the Middle Ages, perhaps inevitably, has been conditioned by a
response to various twentieth-century needs and aspirations.

It was only in the nineteenth century that the study of history
became in some measure emancipated from the literary elegance of
belles lettres and the didacticism of moral philosophy. Modern
historical study of the medieval world began in Germany in the

1820s, with the establishment, under the auspices of the Prussian government, of the *Monumenta Germaniae Historica*. To this institute was entrusted the task of editing and publishing German medieval texts on a scholarly, critical basis. For a hundred years the German school was consistently the greatest school of medieval scholarship. Especially in medieval intellectual history, the pre-eminence of the Germans remained unchallenged until the 1930s.

In the nineteenth century, historical scholarship began its development, utilizing the tools of classical scholarship and the ideas and assumptions of classical humanism. The nineteenth-century German scholars who compiled, edited, and interpreted the major primary sources of medieval history were humanists reared on Greek and Latin, men who shared the heritage of Goethe and Kant. Conscious of their role as innovators and committed to the integrity of the new discipline, they believed that it was possible to realize the full autonomy of the new subject. The truths and values of history came to be regarded as independent and manifest in the subject matter of history itself, unrelated to politics and society, and free of the intellectual presuppositions of other disciplines.

History, however, can never exist as an autonomous discipline, so long as historians are men and not data-processing machines. The autonomy of history is not only an illusion but a socially damaging one. While it is understandable that the men who struggled in the nineteenth century to extricate the facts of history from the precepts of philosophy and religion may have believed in the full emancipation of the new discipline, the persistence of this idea into the twentieth century is both curious and suspect.

The historian who speaks today of so-called autonomous history is merely rejecting the theoretical incursions of the social sciences into his field, in favor of the ideas and concepts of classical humanism. Avowed adherence to the autonomy of history usually signifies an unwillingness or an inability to apply the tools and resources of modern psychology, sociology, and economics to the study of the past. This may arise either from the historian's insecurity in coping with the new disciplines, or alternatively, be the result of his fear of perpetrating anachronisms by the free extrapolation of modern sociology and psychology into a historical past innocent of such preoccupations. But these historians who refuse recourse to the social sciences are, if only by default, governed by the older, traditional assumptions of classical humanism regarding history and the historian's task. Among these, we may isolate two as pre-eminent and tenacious into our own day.

With the partial and ambiguous exception of Herodotus, classical historians to a man believed in the state as the vehicle of history. The *polis*, the Roman republic, and later the Roman Empire, were the arena in which the drama of human life was staged. Classical history was political history, often of the most narrow sort. Thucydides, Tacitus, Livy are all but mute on the family, the religions, the social structure of the ancient world. They write of the organized power vehicle that is the state and of its struggles to attain ascendancy over other states.

The second governing assumption of classical humanism in historical thought is the concern with the personalities of great men, believed to be the instruments of the state's prosperity or its downfall. The words and the deeds of Augustus Caesar, and later of Charlemagne and Henry VIII, determined whether the state would rise or fall, experience war or peace, misery or ease and joy.

The mystique of the state, coupled with the overriding importance attached to the great leader, produced among historians committed to classical humanism, whether in the fifth century B.C., the first, sixteenth, or nineteenth centuries A.D., endlessly detailed accounts of political intrigue, dynastic power struggles, and a completely lopsided emphasis on the fortunes of a myriad of petty politicians and office seekers. Consequently, the fortunes of the state and the personality of great rulers dominated German historical thinking in the nineteenth century. The efflorescence of German nationalism following the invasion of Napoleon's armies reinforced the inherited assumptions of classicism. The result was that medieval history became a search for the first incarnation of the German Imperial state with Otto I, Frederick Barbarossa, and Bismarck cast in strangely similar roles. Europe in the nineteenth century appeared to be full of great personalities marching at the heads of nations. From Napoleon to Cavour to Bismarck, the myth of the soldier-statesman seemed to be confirmed. The impact of the intellectual climate on the writing of history was predictable. Medieval German history became a long series of struggles, near triumphs, and deplorable reversals in the attempt of one after another great prince to unify Germany. A century of German scholarship, conditioned by the assumptions of classical humanism as fortified by the yearnings of nationalism, culminated in the 1920s in the work of Karl Hampe and Heinrich Mitteis, and was neatly summarized by the English historian Geoffrey Barraclough in his meticulous and brilliant synthesis, *The Origins of Modern Germany* (1946). The relentless search for the man who is to be the creator of the mighty German state is here the underlying theme. Otto I, Frederick Barbarossa, Henry VI, Frederick II, each in his turn devotes all his wit and power to the gargantuan task of state building. Just as the final stone in the great edifice is to be cemented, the entire structure is toppled by the ruthless designs of some nefarious rival potentate (usually the pope), or given a severe setback by the selfish particularist schemings of petty princes.

The great difficulty in these histories lay not in their execution but in a basic conceptual error. Having assumed a substance—the German state—professors set about writing its history. One of the more unfortunate results of this ceaseless quest is the very large lacunae which to this day have remained conspicuous in German medieval history. We do indeed know much of the political history of Germany, particularly the idea of Empire and the actions of individual rulers. Of the social institutions of this would-be Empire we know almost nothing. Medieval German economic, religious, and (somewhat surprisingly) administrative history, have been grossly neglected. How people made a living, how they worshipped their God, paid their taxes, and treated their neighbors—of all these we are largely ignorant.

That this strangely one-sided history should have flourished in Germany in the era of Bismarck and Kaiser Wilhelm is not surprising. Like all nationalisms, the German needed a history, needed its folk heroes and its precedents. These could hardly be sought in the disunity of the early modern period when the nation, unlike France and Britain, consisted of a myriad of competing petty states. Only the Middle Ages could plausibly provide the Germans with their much desired national and imperial heritage.

Beginning in the years before the first world war, German historiography underwent a gradual shift. Under the influence of the neo-Hegelian philosophers, and under the leadership of Friedrich Meinecke, German historians began their brilliant work in the history of ideas. For a brief period in the 1890s, before the ascendancy of Meinecke became irreversible, it had appeared as though German historiography might take a different course. Karl Lamprecht stood at the head of a nascent school of history which attempted to analyse and understand society through the construction of social models. This approach gave promise of producing a humanistic, sociologically based history. Meinecke, however, rejected Lamprecht's efforts as an exercise in ultra-rationalist system building, a methodology derived from the Enlightenment. His own most important books, *Weltbürgertum und Nationalstaat* and *Die Idee der Staatsträson in der neueren Geschichte*, are both studies in the growth and development of an idea without consideration or judgment of the specific social and political conditions with which these ideas were inextricably bound up. The first examined the transition from cosmopolitanism to nationalism in German thought, while the second traced the progress of political Machiavellianism and the concept of *raison d'état* in European history. Meinecke's history of ideas was thus bound up with an extreme form of moral relativism disguised beneath the prestigious badge of "historicism." Ideas, so long as they were considered apart from their social bases, could be left as devoid of moral judgments as mathematical propositions. The historian's task became exclusively one of exposition and empathetical understanding.

Meinecke dominated German historical writing during the critical years 1910 through 1945. Although himself a student of modern history, he had an enormous impact on an entire generation of medievalists, who found his approach particularly congenial and fruitful for their own period. The scholarly achievements of German medievalists of the 1920s and 1930s were vast. With great subtlety and imagination they revealed to us the enormous complexity and variety of medieval intellectual life. Drawing on art and literature, they were able to carry intellectual history beyond textual analysis and to show the intricate connections between the social, political, and artistic imagination of the Middle Ages.

While admitting that scholarship has been enriched by the work of German medievalists in the twenties and thirties, it is imperative that we do not ignore the social and political climate which proved so congenial to this approach. The study of rather abstract ideas was a most comfortable one to pursue in post-Versailles Germany, for it removed the historian from the obligation of forming judgments on social systems in a way that no other historiographic approach could do. It is instructive to look at the academic careers and the personal lives of the leading historians in Germany during the era which wtinessed the rise of nazism. The three most distinguished German medievalists of the period were Percy E. Schramm, Ernst H. Kantorowicz, and Carl Erdmann.

Schramm's early work was a study of imperial ideas in the reign of Otto III (*Kaiser, Rom, und Renovatio*). Making extensive and pioneering use of iconography, Schramm reconstructed a great intellectual world in which Otto and his ally Pope Sylvester struggled to renew the Roman Empire. From Otto, Schramm proceeded to a more general examination of the symbols of rulership. He devoted his great intellectual powers to examining the emblems, the iconography, the coronation rituals of medieval kingship throughout western Europe. The actions of the men who wore the crowns of royalty were apparently of no interest to him. The influence of kings for good or evil, for the sickness or health of the society over which they ruled, remained unassessed and unevaluated. It is difficult to avoid the suspicion that this concentration on the symbols of power—at heart a study of form at the expense of substance—facilitated Schramm's collaboration with the Nazis, his more than tacit acceptance of Hitler. Schramm, a scion of a leading Hamburg mercantile family, was official historian of the *Wehrmacht* during the second world war and the editor of Hitler's war diaries and table talk, volumes which no doubt have a certain usefulness for historians interested in the *Ideengeschichte* of the Third Reich.

The early career of Ernst Kantorowicz is at least as interesting as that of Schramm. Kantorowicz served as a captain in the German army during the first world war. Although a Jew, he moved easily in the elegant aristocratic circles of post-war Germany. He was closely associated with the influential anti-democratic group which congregated around Stefan George. He was a member of at least one proto-Nazi organization, and his first book, published in 1928, was inspired by right-wing romanticism. The work itself described the struggles of Frederick II of Hohenstaufen, by now a well known German superman, against a motley assortment of political and ecclesiastical underlings conniving against the interests of the German state. Implicit all through the book, and explicit at the end, was a summons to Germany to produce a great and fitting successor to the medieval giant. Perhaps it was the manifest intellectual fascism of this book which enabled Kantorowicz to remain comfortably in Berlin until 1938, when he departed for Oxford.

From Oxford Kantorowicz moved to Berkeley and—after achieving suitable celebrity as a liberal during that university's loyalty oath crisis—in 1951 to the Institute for Advanced Studies at Princeton, where he became a colleague and devoted friend of another eminent American liberal, Robert Oppenheimer. His last book dealt with *The King's Two Bodies*, a subject of enormous importance for English constitutional history. In this work Kantorowicz traces the separation of the king's person from the office and instiution of kingship. With great erudition and imagination, Kantorowicz pieces together a vast array of precedents, drawing on everything from the ancient Near East to Shakespeare to document the gradual divergence of the two ideas of the king's natural body and the king's political body (the crown). Significantly enough, Kantorowicz pursues his theme from every aspect but the practical. The book is vague or silent on how this idea was actually worked out in English society and law.

Kantorowicz's death was a great loss to medieval historiography. Perhaps this explains the excessive delicacy of those American scholars who wrote his obituaries, discreetly omitting all mention of his Nazi associations.

Perhaps the most subtle mind among German medievalists of the inter-war period was that of Carl Erdmann. Erdmann was among the few dissenters from nazism in the German academic world. His great contribution to medieval history is a detailed study of the rise of the crusading ideal in the eleventh century (*Die Entstehung des Kreuzzugsgedankes*), a work whose significance has been largely lost on those American medievalists who have devoted entire careers to writing the history of the Crusades. Erdmann examined the development of the crusading ideal and found its origins in the militant devotionalism of eleventh-century Christianity. Superficially the work appeared to be a great ode of praise to the brave and devout knights who sought to free Jerusalem from the infidels. In fact the book traces the slow corruption and perversion of the crusading ideal by its gradual involvement in militarism at the hands of a vicious and degenerate aristocracy. The point was not lost on the Nazis. In 1942 Erdmann was conscripted and sent to certain death on the Russian front, where he in fact perished.

In the early years of this century, as an alternative to Meinecke's apolitical *Ideengeschichte,* Karl Lamprecht had tried to establish a German school of sociological history. Meinecke prevailed, and Lamprecht's much more critical and far-ranging analysis was shunted aside. But since the collapse of the Third Reich with which so many German academic mandarins collaborated, a sociological school of medieval German (and Austrian) history has begun to emerge. The work of the dean of post-war German medievalists, Herbert Grundmann, on heresy still suffers from hesitancy and vagueness in dealing with the social matrix of medieval piety. But Heinrich Fichtenau's study of the Carolingian Empire represents a radical departure in German scholarship: Fichtenau attempts a functional analysis of the significance of Charlemagne for ninth-century society, and in so doing deflates eighty years of German hero-worship of the Emperor Karl. The analyses of feudal society by Otto Brunner and Karl Bosl are contributions of the highest quality to the forming of an historical sociology of medieval Europe.

As in Germany, the study of medieval history in France was launched in the middle years of the nineteenth century partly as a response to nationalist needs. The French government founded the *Ecole des Chartes* to promote medieval studies. Unlike their German counterparts, French historians of the nineteenth century tended to be liberal republicans. Hence nationalism asserted itself somewhat differently in French historiography. French medievalists faced a dilemma: committed to belief in the early national existence of France, they were nevertheless as good republicans reluctant to stress the role of the monarchy in the creation of the French state; it was notoriously difficult to admit that medieval France was the creation of the Capetian kings when they had a profound distaste for the institution of monarchy. Partly as a consequence of this paradox, French nationalism tended to express itself historiographically in a reverent mystique of the land and the people. The distinction between the nation and the state appeared early in French historical writing. The great monument of this scholarship, at once republican and nationalistic, was the multi-volume work edited by Ernest Lavisse at the turn of the century, in whose pages the great moments of French history inevitably center on the efforts of the nation to repel a foreign, usually German, menace.

After the second world war, the struggle-of-the-French-people-against-the-German-menace motif again inevitably loomed large in French medieval historiography. In the 1920s and 1930s the Austrian scholar Alfons Dopsch (later a strong adherent of nazism) and the Belgian historian Henri Pirenne had both argued that the German invasion of the fifth century did *not* represent a cultural disaster, since the Germans were at a level of civilization little, if any, below that of the Roman Empire—the barbarian invasions were really a quite peaceful, *gemütlich Anschluss*. In the late 1940s Robert Latouche, Pierre Courçelle, and E. Salin were all contending that Gibbon and Montesquieu were right after all—the fifth century Germans were primitives who brought low a superior culture and committed atrocities on the conquered population.

Besides its own form of nationalism, French history has been continuously under the influence of positivism. The French academic mind has consistently insisted on a rigorous, precise empiricism as the foundation of all historical studies. At its worst this approach has tended to produce narrow, anti-humanistic works dedicated to the scientific examination of minutiae. While positivism tends to cramp inspired flights of the historical imagination, it has also had the very salutary effect of curbing the kind of abstract intellectualism characterisic of German scholarship at its worst.

The foremost French historians of the twentieth century were Lucien Febvre and Marc Bloch, colleagues in the late 1920s and early 1930s at the University of Strasbourg. Both men had received their training in the positivist tradition. Perhaps because their personal backgrounds were rather atypical (Febvre was a Protestant mystic, Bloch a Parisian Jew), both transcended the limits of positivism and expanded the historical consciousness by involving history in the social sciences. Whereas Bloch was attracted to the prospect of integrating cultural anthropology and sociology into history, Febvre was fascinated with the application of modern psychology to an understanding of the past. He anticipated much later work, notably that of Erik Erikson, with a biography of Martin Luther which sought, for once, to understand him not as a German or Protestant folk hero, but as a struggling man rent by psychological contradictions. By modern standards Febvre's book has its shortcomings, but it remains a milestone in French scholarship, one of the very few crucial works which helped to produce a revolution in historical methodology.

Marc Bloch, Febvre's colleague and friend, was the greatest medievalist of his generation. But it is his life as much as his scholarship which has earned for him, in the twenty odd years since his death, the reverence of almost the entire historical profession. Instinctively, historians have recognized the unity between the accomplishments of the scholar and the life of the man.

In *Feudal Society* (1940) Bloch at last produced the great work of synthesis towards which positivists had always claimed they were moving. Bloch's great sensitivity and intuitive grasp of the spirit of his sources enabled him to apply the discoveries and techniques of sociology, economics, and anthropology to the medieval world. The result was a vast and vivid panorama of an entire social system. Bloch's work indeed stands at the extreme antipodes of German scholarship of the period. He produced an integrated, critical evaluation of an entire social system. Both kings and peasants were the subjects of his detached but compassionate scrutiny. Bloch never forgot that the end of any social system, the standard by which it had to be judged and evaluated, was its ability to provide for human happiness.

There can be no doubt that Bloch, like his German colleagues, was a man conditioned by the tortured, frightening experiences of the thirties. But he gave his fervent allegiance to liberal republicanism with all its faults, and to his own vision of an open democratic society. The commitment to the secular humanism of western civilization is evident throughout his work and received its final testament in his personal life. In 1940 Bloch, then professor of economic history at the Sorbonne, joined the underground rather than flee to the safety of England or the United States. He was killed by the Gestapo in 1944 while at work on *The Historian's Craft*, an examination of the nature and responsibilities of his profession. It is illuminating to read even today Bloch's published reviews of German medieval scholarship of the thirties. His anxiety and dismay at the extreme moral relativism displayed by the German school are quite apparent.

After the war an institute under government auspices was founded in Paris as a monument to Bloch. Headed by Ferdinand Braudel, it aims at promoting the new methodology in which Bloch and Febvre pioneered. Its success can be measured by the fact that the leading school of medieval history today is French. Bloch's influence has extended to the United States: the general history of medieval society by the Yale scholar Robert Lopez, *The Birth of Europe*, follows directly in the Bloch tradition. Unfortunately, some of the recent work that has come out of the French institute has lost the breadth and scope which characterized the work of Bloch himself. The narrower, drier side of the positivist tradition, excessively enamoured of statistical compendia, has tended to reassert itself. The institute has produced work—scientific to a fault—exact, exhaustive, but too often unreadable. The positivist spirit of the lab technicians, fundamentally antithetical to that of Bloch, persists in French historiography.

The other constant of French historical writing also remains conspicuous in the work which has emerged from the institute. The great hesitancy and ambivalence of the French about powerful central government, coupled with the perpetuation of strong regional affections, have produced a plethora of works on the social structure of the most remote French towns and provinces, while French medieval government has not been sufficiently studied. The old republican yearning for the "people" in the countryside and small towns is reflected in the passionate regionalism of Georges Dubuy, Bloch's ablest disciple. The propensity of modern liberal nationalism to idolize the "people" in the medieval past, as against the power elite, also inspires the long and tiresome series of encomia on the glories of the Flemish bourgeoisie turned out by Henri Pirenne early in this century.

The study of medieval history in England began considerably later than on the Continent. The long tradition that envisaged the writing of history as a gentleman's leisurely after-hours pursuit was slow to give way to the rigors of modern scholarship. Neither Oxford nor Cambridge had a distinguished historian on its faculty until the latter decades of the nineteenth century. In the 1860s the Cambridge Professor of History was Charles Kingsley, known to posterity as the author of *Westward Ho!*, a schoolboy's novel.

Unlike France and Germany, England created no institute to promote the study of medieval history. This may be a comment on the greater complacency of English nationalism in a century when England was pre-eminent among European nations. In lieu of an institute, funds were made available for the collection and editing of medieval source material. This job, potentially of enormous value to future generations of historians, was unfortunately entrusted mainly to Anglican clergymen, gentlemen scholars not noted for their critical insight. The result was the Rolls Series, a miscellany of chronicles and other texts most of which are badly in need of re-editing today.

Nevertheless the first important medievalist was in fact an Anglican clergyman. William Stubbs's work on English constitutional history was heavily influenced by German methods and ideas, borrowed, as we have noted, from the tenets of classical humanism. Stubbs tended to view British law, so chaotic and haphazard in its beginnings, as nevertheless containing the seeds from which would grow the future magnificence of the British constitution; it was an organic view and inclined to the presupposition that the grandeur of the nineteenth-century constitution was predestined in the remote medieval past. British law was nurtured from tiny acorn to mighty oak by a succession of great personages who from time to time assumed command of government.

Despite these classical and Germanic prejudices, Stubbs had an extremely subtle mind. A careful examination of his writing shows that he was able to envisage alternative approaches. These he rejected partly because he was sincerely convinced of the superiority of his own assumptions, and partly because he was in a hurry to finish his book. Stubbs had long entertained hopes of being made a bishop. When this, his dearest wish, was realized, the church's gain became history's loss, since Stubbs took the opportunity to cease his historical writings altogether.

Following Stubbs there appeared in England the isolated titan of English medievalists, F. W. Maitland (1850–1906). It is ironic that the greatest of English medievalists had no precursors and virtually no successors in his native land. Indeed, Marc Bloch seems to be the closest disciple Maitland ever had.

Maitland rejected all notion of predestination in English constitutional development. The English constitution was to him a chancy, difficult, sometimes random product of men's day-to-day struggles with society and their fellow man. He saw no unbroken line of development in the making of the English constitution. He pointed out a thousand apparently insignificant turning points which, cumulatively, had shaped the constitution to its present form. Maitland implies that at any moment things might have turned out very differently from what in fact they did. Nothing in the English constitution was irreversible or absolute. Particular specific circumstances, not grand design, created the English system of government and law. Maitland's approach was purely functional and pragmatic and in its implications it was radical. Liberty was not something received from on high but something which men had to struggle to secure and consolidate each day of their lives. Although in his published works he remains consistently laudatory of Stubbs, his illustrious predecessor, his private correspondence shows his deep differences with the venerable English Tory.

Maitland received his training in Cambridge at a time when that university was the dynamic hub of a new radical secularism. He was a product of the same climate which produced, somewhat later, the Bloomsbury group, the new sensitivity of Virginia Woolf and the liberal radicalism of Keynes. The lack of English followers to Maitland's radical functionalist approach remains puzzling. A partial explanation may be sought in the fact that Maitland was formally a professor of law, not of history. If historiographic influence is to be sustained from teacher to pupil, the study of history must be institutionalized. It is not really surprising that the would-be lawyers in Maitland's classes were left largely unmoved by the broadest dimensions of his work.

The work of T. F. Tout in the 1920s shifted the focus of English medieval studies from the problems surrounding the origins of law and constitutionalism to the narrower issues of administrative history. Maitland's latent radicalism became a latent conservatism in the works of Tout and the Manchester school of historians, who devoted themselves to studying the techniques of government. The study of administrative history is at heart the study of how the existing powers perpetuated themselves and hence, as A. J. P. Taylor has remarked, has a fundamentally Tory bias. Maitland's greatness as an historian lay in his ability to relate the development of law to the actual day-to-day life of Englishmen. His work constantly sought to show the interaction of government with the mores and customs of society. The feedback from Yorkshire and

East Anglia conditioned and modified in practice the statutes and writs emanating from Westminster. In the work of the Manchester school the social base of English government was eroded. Administrative history became a study of how the rulers ruled.

It is not accidental that the golden age of administrative history came in the 1920s and 1930s—a period not distinguished in England for the vitality of either its political or its intellectual life. The drabness of Stanley Baldwin has its parallel in English historical writing. With the optimism of the pre-war era vanished, the historical vision grew narrower, atrophying into a punctilious and bland Toryism.

When the reaction against administrative history came, it tended to be extreme. The next generation of English medievalists abandoned the study of English institutional history almost completely and concentrated their sights on the cultural and spiritual life of the Middle Ages. The new men in English medieval history sought to write the history of modes of feeling. After the second world war, F. M. Powicke, a product of the Manchester school, who dominated medieval scholarship at Oxford for three decades, published *King Henry III and the Lord Edward*. Nominally a work of political history, Powicke's book is in fact a study of the changing self-consciousness of the English nobility and marks a radical break with the Tout tradition. David Knowles's publication in 1940 of the first of four volumes on the monastic and religious orders of medieval England was one of the outstanding achievements of the new history. The book sets out to be an account of English ecclesiastical institutions, but Knowles constantly transcends institutional history by a superb evocation of the attitudes and ideals in the minds and hearts of his medieval monks. His recreation of the conflicts and perplexities, the faith and devotion of their lives, is a masterpiece of intuitive understanding and historical artistry. It is the best book on medieval history ever written by a Roman Catholic.

The greatest of the post-war books which sought to explore the devotional, idealistic side of medieval life was R. W. Southern's *The Making of the Middle Ages*. Southern's theme is the transformation of medieval society in the eleventh and twelfth centuries through the impact of the "new learning" and the "new piety." The eleventh and twelfth centuries were a period of rapid innovation and development in medieval political and social life. Southern argues that the transfiguration of the medieval world order began with the transformation of the Christian experience. In this period, Southern finds man humanizing God and Christianity becoming a faith charged with personal passion and pain. This change in the spiritual life of medieval man promoted the political and social upheavals of the period.

This post-war English preoccupation with the beautiful and idealistic side of medieval life did more than redress the imbalance between institutional and cultural studies of the Middle Ages. The world evoked by Southern was perhaps too much one of tranquillity, chivalry, and grace. The disorder, the violence, the corruptions of the medieval world receded far out of sight. The ugly side of medieval life is certainly not ignored, but rather highlighted in the book that stands beside Southern's work as the most powerful evocation of the medieval imagination—Johan Huizinga's *The Waning of the Middle Ages*. But Huizinga was from another time, another place: this Dutch scholar was a member of that same fin-de-siècle generation that produced Freud and James Joyce, and he positively revels in exposing the sickness and terror of the medieval mind.

The deliberate immersion of the English medievalists of the late forties and the fifties in the richest, most emotionally satisfying side of medieval life was itself a response to a tired and disappointing world where political and economic realities were harsh and threadbare. Frustrated idealism, finding itself supremely irrelevant in post-war Britain, searched the past for a a New Jerusalem so clearly missing from contemporary English life. While it is true that in the past few years a critical functionalism has appeared in British historical writing, in the work of such scholars as G. R. Elton, Lawrence Stone, and J. H. Plumb (dealing with the period 1485–1760), so far this tendency has not appeared in medieval historiography.

The writings of Catholic historians on the medieval period have always been susceptible to the dangers of special pleading. Most nineteenth-century medieval studies done under Church auspices unfortunately assumed a grossly partisan approach, inspiring a great deal of romantic nonsense celebrating the glories of medieval Christendom. In the twentieth century some very learned and

high-minded clerical scholarship on the Middle Ages has been produced. Its chief limitation—not a small one—has been an inability
adequately to account for the evolution of the medieval Church.
The primitive Church under the Roman Empire was in fact a small
and outcast band of believers; the Church of the High Middle Ages
a complex hierarchical power structure splendid with rich and powerful bishops and abbots. Church historians rationalized the latter-
day development of the Church by reactivating the old organic
explanation, so popular with English constitutionalists, in a new,
more metaphysical guise. It is claimed that the Church, with all
the secular and religious powers at its command at the height of its
dominance of the medieval world, existed—in potential (or in the
mind of God)—from the very start. Its potential growth and development, like that of the English constitution, was predestined from
apostolic times. The linear continuity of development was never
interrupted or reversed.

The line of reasoning reached its apotheosis in the 1930s and
1940s in the multi-volume history of the Church edited by Fliche
and Martin, at the University of Louvain. In Fliche's own account
of the Gregorian Reform, the great eleventh-century pope is no
longer the radical innovator he appeared to himself and his contemporaries. Gregory VII is seen as a good-hearted, moderate moral
reformer. Similarly, J. J. Ryan of the Pontifical Institute at Toronto
finds the sources for the teachings of Peter Damiani, another
Gregorian radical, in traditional canon law. The Gregorian Reform
is held to be part and parcel of an inevitable progressive development and constitutes no major break in the evolution of Christianity. This view does a great injustice to the critical turning points in
the history of the Church. They are either disguised or denied, and
hence of course unexplained.

The belief that nothing drastic or unexpected ever happened in
the history of the Church is not peculiar to clerical historians. The
present Cambridge medievalist, Walter Ullmann, has been much
enamoured of this view and has in fact found its secular application. Just as clerical scholars believe that an adequate understanding of the medieval Church can be obtained from the study of
canon law and papal decretals, so Ullmann assumes that the medieval state is best understood by the careful examination of Roman
law. The actual patterns of Church and state development, in so
far as they diverged from prescribed legal formulas, are ignored, or

at best explained as unfortunate, ephemeral deviations from the mainstream of development. In his book on *The Individual and Society in the Middle Ages,* Ullmann disdains even to mention Peter Abelard, the prime medieval spokesman for radical individualism.

Clerical historiography has not as yet mirrored the left-wing radicalism apparent in certain sections of Catholic thought. Present-day radicals within the Church are seeking to promote a less doctrinaire, more flexible attitude towards canon law. Should this impulse appear in historical scholarship, the results promise to be very fruitful. A full-scale exploration of the conflicting ideological and social movements within the medieval Church would almost certainly be the result. The sociology of heresy as well as an elaboration of the variety and richness of medieval Catholic thought can certainly be hoped for.

It is rather difficult to isolate the main trends in American medieval scholarship, since so many American historians have been influenced by various European schools of interpretation. The study of the history of ideas was launched in America in the 1930s by the influx of German (usually Jewish) refugees into the American academic community. Scholars such as Kantorowicz have influenced two generations of American graduate students. Similarly Bloch's social and economic analysis has found some response in American schools.

On the whole, native American medieval scholarship has centered on the study of the institutional side of medieval life. The most influential American medievalist of the early twentieth century was Charles Homer Haskins, professor at Harvard from 1910 to 1932. Haskins in many ways typifies the preoccupations of American medievalists. His approach is extremely pragmatic and functionalist but at the same time highly conservative. He was a student of Norman institutions and society; his work is a detailed and erudite examination of the Normans' ascent to power. The moral and spiritual dimensions of Norman statecraft are left wholly unexamined while the techniques by which they consolidated and expanded their strength in the medieval world are appraised with realism and thoroughness. The pursuit of power as it expressed itself in the creation of the medieval state is also the theme of Joseph Strayer of Princeton, Haskins's ablest student, and probably the most prominent American medievalist of our own day.

The spiritual and emotional issues with which medieval men wrestled appear to have a peculiar unreality for American historians, whose excessively hard-headed realism shows an inadequate appreciation for the extreme idealism and emotionalism of the medieval world. American scholarship has been strangely deaf to the terrors and the majesty of medieval religious and spiritual life. The neglect of this side of medieval history certainly reflects the strong secularism of American life. It may also be an expression of the latent hostility to the intellect which so many foreigners have seen as a characteristic of American civilization. The American historian's persistent fascination with the manipulation of power for its own sake may also be a dismaying comment on American society today.

Medieval history in American universities has failed to develop a flourishing, distinctive school. The institutional analysis that Haskins inaugurated could have, with the admixture of functional sociological analysis and cultural anthropology (both strong movements in the American academic world) have developed into vital and creative historiography. Unfortunately, the reverse happened: the institutional school in the four decades after Haskins became more pedestrian, narrow, and genteel. For this, the leading scholars in other fields of history (usually United States and modern European) in the dominant graduate departments must shoulder part of the blame. Somewhere along the line—between 1930 and 1950—eminent scholars who would not tolerate intellectual conservatism and dullness in their own historical fields became convinced that medieval history was per se pedestrian, narrow, and genteel and that holders of chairs of medieval history—unless they were interesting emigrés like Kantorowicz or Lopez—had to be marginal antiquarians whose communications about the medieval world inevitably had no significance or relevance to anything an educated or intelligent man would care about: in other words, it was decided that medieval history was nonsense and it was suitable to appoint professors of medieval history who talked nonsense.

In consequence of this cynical attitude towards the medieval era in many prominent history departments, situations like this one developed: the professor of medieval history at Harvard University for three decades after Haskins was a tweedy-looking gentleman who in his whole career published two insignificant articles (on medieval tax collection). To those who believe that the study of history is socially valuable, and who perceive usable meaning in the Middle Ages, such an outrageously absurd academic situation must reflect criminally irresponsible conduct on the part of a great university.

The prospects for the serious study of medieval history in American universities are slowly—too slowly—improving today. For example, Karl Morrison at the University of Chicago, a highly prolific scholar, appears to be moving away from his starting-point in the tradition of *Ideengeschichte* to broader social and cultural analysis. Gene Brucker at Berkeley, one of the many assiduous miners in the rich lodes of the Florentine archives, has advanced from political narrative and institutional description to something approaching urban sociology. Another Florentine miner, Marvin Becker at the University of Rochester, is attempting a provocative and important psycho-social analysis of the late medieval Italian culture. Yet on the whole, the current generation of senior American medievalists do not seem much more lively than their teachers, and the young scholars coming out of the graduate schools (perhaps because they have often been repressed and ruined by tyrannical and narrow-minded teachers) are not particularly promising as creators of new interpretations. Not fortuitously, the three most subtle and original minds in medieval studies in this country today are not holders of history chairs, but are teachers and scholars in the humanities—D. W. Robertson (Princeton) and Robert Hanning (Columbia) in literature, and François Bucher (SUNY-Binghamton) in art history.

The approach to history which is the most productive, and from which I have learned most, is neither political nor social, economic nor intellectual. It can be called cultural history, or social-intellectual history. It is an appreciation of the complexity of life and of human experience, an attempt to describe how things really were—for example, how religious values related to the economic situation, how the political structure related to the organization of the Church: the relationship of saint and warrior, pope and king. This attempt to work out the complex nexus of a given society is sometimes called sociological history, but it has no special sociological jargon or social theory. It describes how society actually functioned, how thoughts and values were related to the institutional structure.

The sociological understanding of medieval institutions began with Maitland. He was a historical genius, and geniuses in the field of history have been rare indeed. Maitland was one of the very few first-class minds to be applied to the writing of history, and he analyzed the formation of English law in a completely new way. Not content to describe what the laws were and when and how they came into existence, he tried to show how law responded to social need and how the law courts of medieval England were a function of the general social situation. When people made their money a certain way, had a certain kind of educational system, class structure, and religious values, it followed that they would have a certain kind of legal system; and the legal system, in turn, would affect other aspects of society and culture. Law is not laid down from on high, nor is it simply created by great lawmakers, great personalities. It is a response to a special social situation, and it functions in accordance with social need.

Maitland was a pioneer, a creator, on a par with those other great creators of the early twentieth century (Freud, Weber, Einstein, Joyce) whose intellectual capital we still spend. Contemporary historians did not understand Maitland's book; they admired his learning, his footnotes, his understanding of Latin, and his discovery of new manuscripts in the British Museum, but they were too accustomed to narrow political history to grasp the essence of his contribution. Only slowly, under the impact of the social sciences and the shift in cultural values, did historians begin to appreciate the functional approach and the sociological emphasis.

Another pioneer in the sociological-cultural history of the Middle Ages was Huizinga, whose *The Waning of the Middle Ages* is a sociology of late medieval aristocratic life, an account of the social and intellectual and cultural values that existed in the courts of chivalry in fifteenth-century Flanders and France. Huizinga used literature and art as sources for history, and he did it very well. He was not much appreciated by academic historians in his own day but has been much admired in the last 25 years.

The third great pioneer in the new approach to history was Bloch, whose *Feudal Society* is a frustrating book; it was not really finished, and it is not quite what Bloch wanted to write, or what he would have written if he had lived. Parts of the book misfire; they are incoherent, or even dubious—but despite these weaknesses, it gets closer to the complexity of medieval life than any other book.

If the criterion of great history is the ability to related widely-separated phenomena (religion and government, art and war, class structure and prevailing philosophical schools), then *Feudal Society* is great history. It is a beautiful book, an attempt to bring together a variety of complex ideas and impose order and symmetry on a rich variety. Bloch's French style is unusual and very difficult: his French is full of allusions, of overtones of the high liberal culture of the Third Republic. The English translator did not attempt to capture all of the richness and subtlety of Bloch's language, but in either language, it is the single most valuable book on medieval history.

The fourth great mind in recent medieval historiography was Southern. *The Making of the Middle Ages* provides a somewhat sentimental veneration of medieval piety combined with preciously subtle insight into the facets of medieval personality and the role of religion in the shaping of the medieval world. Southern portrays convincingly the central importance of Christian dogma and piety in medieval society. He shows that for many of the best medieval minds the qeust for God and salvation conditioned all other aspects of their lives.

Drawing upon the insights of Maitland, Huizinga, Bloch, and Sotuhern, I have tried in the following pages to analyze the main forms of medieval thought and feeling in relation to social change. Just as these scholars drew upon the newer ideas circulating in the intellectual world of their time, I have adapted and applied some of the more significant and valuable concepts of the culture of the 1960s and 1970s. If a knowledge of the past helps us to understand the present, so do the ideas of the present enable us to make sense of the past. This view is regarded as radical and untenable by many academic historians. But the history of medieval historiography in the twentieth century (as also the historiography of any historical field) sustains my view. When academic historians reject the attempt to understand medieval culture in terms of the ideas of the 1960s and 1970s, they are merely expressing their contentment with the consciousness of the 1950s, the 1930s, or (in some cases) the 1880s.

Chapter One

THE BURDEN OF THE ANCIENT WORLD

I. *Politics and Society*

THE ANCIENT NEAR EAST

Medieval civilization emerged out of the union, synthesis, and adaptation of certain aspects of the ancient Mediterranean world. It used to be thought that European history, like Caesar's Gaul, could be divided into three parts: ancient, medieval, and modern. This division was first made by the humanists of the fifteenth century for ideological reasons, and we tend to use the same divisions in our terminology and our college courses. It is an absurd system, really: it gives far too much importance to the fall of the western Roman Empire. Medieval civilization was not produced by any one event or series of events, but by the absorption by western Europe of certain ways of life, ideas, and religious attitudes that had prevailed for many centuries in the Mediterranean world. These ideas and values were pulled northward into western Europe —into northern France, southern England, and the Rhine valley— and in the process, certain aspects of Mediterranean culture were adapted and changed. (It is perhaps even more significant that many aspects were *not* changed.) Before the Middle Ages then, there *was* a Mediterranean culture and society that was adopted and absorbed. An understanding of that civilization is absolutely essential to an understanding of the medieval world.

The culture that was eventually absorbed by medieval western Europe made its first appearance in the Mesopotamian Tigris-Euphrates valley late in the fourth millennium B.C. and perhaps a little later in the Egyptian Nile valley. That is the point where civilization began, if we define civilization primarily as structured society, organized government, and specialized economy over a large area. No longer were men all herdsmen or all hunters; they became kings, priests, soldiers, farmers, merchants, or craftsmen.

The earliest civilized communities of the ancient Near East were dominated by a small, self-sustaining aristocracy as early as 3000 B.C. The nobility, or elite of these Egyptian and Mesopotamian societies controlled nearly all of their economic resources. One of the noble families became the ruling dynasty. From the same families, and from the ranks of the bureaucrats who served the monarchy, were drawn the priests who controlled the temples. Thus the ideology of the ruling religious group sanctioned the prevailing government and social structure.

In these early societies there were in essence only two social groups or "classes" (to use a term that has been central to historical thought since the nineteenth century). There was the elite: the aristocratic group which controlled both rural and urban wealth and dominated the religious institutions, the government, and the bureaucracy. The other class was a mass peasantry who may or may not have been slaves, but in any case were bound to till the soil in the interests of the ruling elite. We have no reliable statistical information about these early societies—indeed, it is difficult to give social statistics for any period before the later Middle Ages—but a safe estimate would be that the elite comprised no more than 10 (at the utmost, 20) per cent and no less than 5 per cent of the total population. The vast majority of the population, somewhere between 80 and 95 per cent, belonged to the working class and peasantry.

In the cities of the ancient Near East, particularly in Mesopotamia where there were a few large urban centers like Babylon and Ur, there was an urban working class comprising perhaps 10 or 15 per cent of the population of the whole state. Even in these ancient societies there was a merchant class, maybe 2 or 3 per cent of the total population, whose function was to engage in international commerce and to serve as adjuncts or assistants to the aristocracy. The merchants played an important role in the economy, but they had scarcely any more political or social power than the peasants.

It is said in the Hebrew Bible that the Hebrews were slaves unto Pharaoh in Egypt. The point here is that almost everybody was a slave (legally or empirically) unto Pharaoh and a very small elite. It could be said indeed that these were one-class societies; only the aristocracy had any real consciousness of its identity, its rights, or its destiny. The aristocrats held a monopoly of power, learning, and culture, and the aristocrats alone had a sense of their special and privileged place in the world.

In the long run, the existence of this intensely elitist society in the ancient Near East was of enormous importance to the history of western civilization. At late as 1700, the prevailing European social system was still one in which vast power, the greater part of landed wealth, and the prime control of political life belonged to the hereditary landed aristocracy. In the social history of pre-modern western civilization—whether the modern era is designated as beginning in 1500 or in the eighteenth century—a series of aristocracies perpetuated the control over the resources of society held by the ancient Near Eastern elite. It is a history in which successive challenges were made on moral and ideological grounds, to aristocratic control of society and its resources. Obviously, there is a substantial pattern of change and development in pre-modern social history, and these changes are highly significant and deserve close examination. Nevertheless, the factor of continuity—of the perpetuation down to the modern industrial world of a one-class social structure, or, in another phrasing, of the domination of a landed aristocracy—is one of the fundamental facts and continuing conditions of the history of western civilization.

It is natural to wonder how the Near Eastern aristocracy came to gain its dominant position, but it is not a question to which any certain answer can be given. Literacy did not begin in Mesopotamia and Egypt until the late fourth millennium B.C., and in the first written records the aristocracy had already emerged and the forms of government and social control had already been established. Historians speculate that these societies assumed their fundamental structure during the so-called prehistoric (i.e., preliterate) period— that is, somewhere around the middle of the fourth millennium B.C. However, we can only guess from archeological evidence at the process by which the aristocracy came to dominate society, and although the evidence is substantial and has been carefully examined by scholars, it provides at best only an approximation of the truth. Archeologists work with material objects, and the process of prehistorical social change has thus been established on a materialistic bias. They are bound to attribute social changes to alterations in the means of production because their evidence only discloses such alterations. Artifacts alone, without written records, cannot reveal great changes in human values or ideological upheavals which may have determined social change. Some historians have postulated a great intellectual revolution, some tremendous shift in human consciousness, behind the emergence of the first ancient civilizations; but in the absence of written records, this explanation can be no more than a happy guess.

The first important scholar to examine the archeological evidence of the fourth millennium B.C. with the intention of accounting for social changes was V. Gordon Childe, who was a rather doctrinaire Marxist and applied with considerable relish the materialistic interpretation supported by the evidence. Nevertheless, scholars who are not ideological Marxists, such as the American archeologist Robert Braidwood, have also explained the beginnings of Near Eastern societies in terms of change in economic organization, although not exactly the changes that Childe perceived. Childe believed that the most important development in the fourth millennium B.C. was the use of metal, particularly bronze, which created a revolution in the forms of production, and allowed the group of people who controlled the metal resources to dominate the rest of society. This, of course, fits the Marxist paradigm that those who control the important means of production will become the dominant class in society. The rise of the Near Eastern aristocracy, as seen by Childe, parallels the triumph of industrial capitalists in European society in the nineteenth century.

Subsequent scholars have given us much more complex explanations. Braidwood has pointed out that large-scale farming was first undertaken in the dry outlying plateaus of Mesopotamia in the fourth millennium B.C., and that this farming economy was carried out more extensively later in the fourth millennium in the Tigris-Euphrates Valley, where extensive irrigation was both necessary and possible. The land in Egypt is very fertile; it is rescued from the desert by the annual flooding of the Nile. In both instances, therefore, an abundant food supply could be produced in natural or man-made irrigated areas. Those who placed themselves in control of the irrigation resources controlled the substance upon which everybody depended; eventually they dominated the whole society. They established a centralized government in order to maintain the irrigation resources and to distribute food, and they established cities—or at least populated centers, palaces, and temples—to serve as the military and administrative centers of this organized community. Karl Wittfogel has described such societies as irrigation despotisms; he sees the Near East as the prototype for the social structure and government of all oriental societies in the Far as well as the Near East.

Archeology, then, offers change in economic forms as the explanation of the rise of a narrow elite, with control over all the resources of the society (intellectual as well as material, religious as well as political). Whether this change was in the nature of new forms of production through the use of metal, or new forms of agriculture through the use of irrigation resources, the people who initially got control of these revolutionary economic forms immediately monopolized the key economic resource of society. They could do anything they wanted thereafter, provided that they remained a relatively homogenous and peaceful group. By and large they did remain homogenous and at peace among themselves. They decided how to divide up the power, how to divide up the wealth, who should be king, and which family should become the royal dynasty. The instability in these societies usually came not from within but from external invasions by new people—in the case of Mesopotamia, from the north, and in the case of Egypt, from the sea or the desert—who at various times pushed into these wealthy river valleys and gained control. Their control usually collapsed or was overthrown a few generations later by the old native aristocracy or by later invaders. But all the invaders perpetuated the existing social structure, taking over the prerogatives of the old aristocracy.

The social structure of the ancient Near Eastern societies, once established, was perpetuated in the Hellenistic empires which replaced the old Near Eastern dynasties after the conquest of the Near East by Alexander the Great in the fourth century B.C. The Hellenistic empires were conquered in turn by the Romans in the second and first centuries B.C.; by and large, the Romans also perpetuated the Mediterranean social structure they had found.

The exploitation of serfs by their lords was, then, not an invention of the Middle Ages. Medieval people inherited the rule of lords over peasants; they knew no other way of life or alternative organization of rural society. It was natural to them that a few lords should own all the land while the mass of peasants toiled their lives away—that was the very nature of society. Medieval people did not give this social structure a second thought; just as twentieth-century westerners for the most part take middle-class society for granted, so medieval Europeans took for granted the aristocratic-peasant organization of society.

The social system of lord and peasant was not questioned, but medieval men had to justify it and to organize it and they did this in a number of ways. Variations in social patterns between the ancient Near East and medieval Europe are not fundamental changes; they are simply various in theory or methods of organization. An Egyptian lord mummified in 2500 B.C. and revived in France in 700 A.D. would not have been upset by the social system he found. It was a little looser, perhaps, a bit more liberal, but it was based on the same assumptions and facts. The ancient social structure was elaborated or varied in different places at different periods, but mainly it was simply perpetuated for thousands of years.

In order to understand medieval people one must understand the burden of the enormous past of Mediterranean society. We do not feel such a burden today, but it was heavy upon our ancestors even in the eighteenth and nineteenth centuries. Until the twelfth century, at least, medieval people were not even conscious that it could ever be thrown off. Their way of life had always been there; to reject it was to disappear into primitivism, into the void of barbarism. Under these circumstances, it is remarkable that anything ever changed in the Middle Ages—for their heritage *was* extraordinary. If a Frenchman of the fifth century A.D. had travelled up the Nile and seen temples, Sphinxes, pyramids—greater constructions than anything that his own people could possibly build —he would wonder at the splendid accomplishments of ancient society, and it would never occur to him to think that it was wrong! Medieval social theory, at least before the twelfth century, was entirely a question of justification of the existing system, and even in this respect, medieval people inherited a tradition from early Mediterranean civilization.

In the ancient world, in Egypt and Mesopotamia, the social structure was justified on religious grounds. It was God's plan for the world—God's will—and acceptance of the social forms was a religious duty. Medieval men inherited that attitude and built upon it. They had more difficulty than the Egyptians, however, because there were certain strains within Christianity that were incompatible with the ancient system. There is an egalitarian strain in the Bible (particularly in the New Testament) that runs counter to the ancient traditions of exploitation and domination. Medieval people had to relate these two traditions, and they came out heavily (before the late Middle Ages almost exclusively) on the side of the ancient, class-dominated, authoritarian society.

In a sense, then, the heritage of the ancient world set the conditions for medieval society. Although it is true that in many respects the Middle Ages (from 300 to about 1500 A.D.) was a distinct and separate civilization, still medieval men were not able to create just the world that they chose: they had to work with what they inherited. They began with a definite set of social forms, political and economic institutions, and ideas and attitudes.

One of the most important patterns, or conditions inherited by medieval men from the ancient Mediterranean civilization was that of political functioning, of rulership. The monarchical political system that came to exist in Egypt and Mesopotamia by 3000 B.C. did not change substantially during the Middle Ages; indeed, in some parts of the Near East it is still unchanged. The social and political forms of 3000 B.C. were handed on to the Hellenistic empires created in the Mediterranean basin between 350 and 100 B.C., then these were absorbed by the Roman Empire, which took on the ancient political forms and much of the Hellenistic ideology. From Rome, forms and ideology alike were passed on to the medieval world.

The first political ideology, and the most essential, was that of kingship—of monarchy, and particularly of theocratic monarchy which is God-centered and God-ordained. It is obvious to any student of medieval history that kings were all-important, and in the twentieth century we are apt to wonder why this was so, why so much emphasis was placed on the ruler. Again, medieval men worked within the system of divine monarchy mainly because they had no clear consciousness and scarcely even an awareness of any other; theocratic monarchy was not only the orthodox political form but, as far as they knew, the best-functioning form. The king represented God; he represented the divine forces in this world; he was the image of God on earth. His subjects obeyed him not only because that was the useful, virtuous course of action, or because his soldiers enforced his wishes, but because they believed that that was what God wanted them to do. This was an essential fact of western history from 3200 B.C. right down to the eighteenth century.

We do not really know why theocratic, autocratic kingship established itself as the dominant political system of the ancient Near East. We have no written documents from before the time of kings; the pharaohs were already rulers at the time of the first records, which describe how the rulers operated but not how they came into existence. The beginning of monarchy is usually explained functionally, on the basis of archeological evidence. Historians make an educated guess that in a society whose food supply and very life depended on irrigation, an autocratic system was required in order to maintain the irrigation system. A democracy is always fragile, perhaps too fragile for these harsh circumstances, and a dictator was needed who had the power to command the peasants to work on the canals or do whatever was necessary to maintain the irrigation. A king in the image of God would have had enough power over agricultural society to get the job done, while peasants in a free commune might have argued endlessly. Other systems may have been tried—we do not know—but finally one family or one group under the leadership of a great warlord got control of the society and organized everyone else under their leadership. The belief that the king represented God on earth began in the fourth millennium B.C. and was derived from the needs and experiences of that period.

However the system of divinely ordained monarchy came into existence, it was well established throughout ancient civilization. Medieval men knew of no form of government (or no successful form) except kingship, and without experience of alternatives they could not envision any other system. By the time the Christian Church came into existence and medieval culture was in its formative period (during the second and third centuries A.D.), the rare alternatives to theocratic monarchy had disappeared from the

Mediterranean world. The Church with the prime agent of communication between the ancient and the medieval worlds, and by the time of its formation, only the old Egyptian system remained. By the fourth century A.D.—the swing century, the gateway to the medieval world, the last ancient and the first medieval century—the old oriental system had prevailed and was well established in the Roman Empire. Constantine, the first Christian emperor, was described by his friend and biographer Eusebius as the "image of Christ," God's representative in the world. This is the old Mesopotamian ideal of divine monarchy, which had driven out the various, short-lived attempts at alternative kinds of political systems.

Other systems of government had indeed existed in the ancient world. Fifth-century Athenians participated in a direct democracy, and Spartans of the same period were governed by a military oligarchy, as (for all practical purposes) were Romans of the Republic. These are well-known alternatives to theocratic monarchy (and there were others), but none was long-lived or successful enough to serve as a model for the medieval world.

In the Athenian *polis*, or city-state, all citizens participated in government. They argued in the marketplace, chose committees by lot to run the business of the state in ordinary times, and elected leaders to see them through crises. The system resembled the town meeting government of New England, but it was much more ambitious: Athens was not a village but an international commercial center and the capital city of a vast empire. Direct democracy worked very well during the first half of the fifth century, less well in the second half, and disappeared in the fourth century. This was partly because Athens was defeated and conquered, but also because the system itself ceased to function. In its last fifty years of independence before conquest by Alexander the Great, the Athenian government became extremely unstable and the community suffered from frequent upheavals and violent disruptions of all kinds.

Direct (as opposed to representative) democracy is extremely cumbersome; with so many citizens participating actively in government, endless debate made decision-making difficult. When representative democracy is working as it should, elected legislators and officials are more intelligent and experienced, by and large, than the electorate, and less apt to be swayed by passion. Direct (or "participatory") democracy is easy prey for demagogues and is inclined toward radical, simplistic solutions to complex problems. An Athenian jury, for example, had six hundred members—and an Athenian jury condemned Socrates. Furthermore, the Athenian system was basically too simple for the burdens of empire. It failed to develop a bureaucracy to deal with problems of war, administration, and taxation. The Near Eastern monarchies, with no legislature and no community participation, developed vast bureaucracies, but Athens was operated by short-term officials. With an endless turnover of new generals, new tax collectors, and new ambassadors, the system was functionally inadequate as well as unstable. Also, direct democracy presupposes strong communal feeling. In the early days, Athenians lived frugally and lived for themselves and their own community. As the Empire grew there was more money to be made; public office (which had once demanded self-sacrifice) became lucrative, and greed and ambition corrupted the officials. Factions and parties emerged, tempted by the prospect of large profits, and the late history of Athens is an endless story of dispute and dissension.

Democracy was discredited in Athens, largely because Athens was beaten by the Spartans, by Alexander the Great, and finally by Rome. The ancient world had great admiration for Greek achievements in art, literature, historiography, and so on, but not for the Athenian political system. Not until the fourteenth century A.D. was Athenian democracy given any credit for the artistic and intellectual achievements of the Periclean Age, and even then not very clearly.

A second alternative to divine kingship was oligarchy, or aristocratic government. Oligarchic systems existed in Sparta and in republican Rome, but the Roman system was perhaps a little looser and broader-based. Essentially, Sparta was a fascist state in which the entire community was organized around the army. State and army were one, and everyone served in the army or contributed to its support. Sparta was admired by a great many contemporaries (including Plato, in certain moods) for the very qualities that often make fascism attractive. There was "law and order" in Sparta; the state was efficiently run and in certain respects very successful. Spartans were respected, largely because their army was powerful out of all proportion to the resources of the country in wealth or population. In an armed camp in which everything was organized for war (there was no Spartan art or literature), the army did very well indeed.

The Spartan system required enormous discipline and constant attention to detail and organization. It is an exhausting, taxing form of government; regimentation is absolutely essential and yet very difficult to sustain. Sparta was a small, poor country and the Spartans remained a stern, ascetic people for whom the system of military oligarchy worked well. They had no empire, no wealth or territory to divide.

The Spartan system worked well in a military camp but not as well in the center of a great empire. Rome rose to power under a system very like the Spartan—in republican Rome of the fourth century B.C. there was also very little art or literature. The Romans were soldiers or farmers who led crude, simple lives—tough, brutal military men. The Republic was dominated by twenty or thirty or forty families whose sons commanded the army while their fathers controlled the Senate. Senators (mostly retired generals) ran the domestic affairs of Rome while the younger men conquered the world. The world and events described by Livy present a simple, Spartan picture of conquest and militarism, and Sir Ronald Syme (a great modern authority on Roman history) characterizes the Republic in that style.

However, the republican system broke down in the first century B.C. when the Romans tried to use it to govern a world empire. With a vast territory to exploit, the prizes of power became enormous and the leading families could no longer arrange equitable division of power. They began to quarrel, and the history of first century B.C. Rome is essentially the story of struggles for power within the oligarchy. No longer willing to share the great rewards of military command, imperial office, and control of the Senate, each family tried to eliminate its competitors. Eventually, of course, one family succeeded in attaining supremacy—the family of Augustus Ceasar, the Julio-Claudian line. At first the emperors called themselves simply "first among equals," and indeed, although the royal house controlled the army and controlled the treasury, Rome was rich enough to allow members of all the old families to share the wealth. Over the first two centuries A.D., however, the ruling family transformed the Roman state into an imperial, oriental-style monarchy. Augustus Caesar was proclaimed a god after his death, and the whole imperial family acquired a divine character. By the third century, the emperor regarded his own person as divine; the emperors of Rome had come to resemble the ancient pharaohs.

Dramatists have drawn a picture of Rome corrupted by Egypt, of honest republicans seduced by oriental wickedness into a corrupt imperial system. This is the impression left by Shakespeare's *Antony and Cleopatra,* and by Shaw's *Caesar and Cleopatra.* Some historians agree, but in fact the Romans were not really corrupted from the outside—it was perfectly natural for them to fall into a similar peculiar style. After all, autocracy is the most obvious, the simplest form of government. Democracy is not at all simple or secure—a basic fact of political science best illustrated, perhaps, by the Russian attempts to escape autocracy. (Despite all the talk and all the efforts of the nineteenth-century Russian revolutionaries, Russia had only a few short months of liberal, democratic, constitutional government in 1917 before falling back to an autocratic system.) Democracy is very, very difficult to achieve and maintain, and one of the great themes of medieval history is the gradual tempering of the autocratic system of government inherited from Rome. Yet the Roman tradition stayed alive (although changed and moderated) right down to the eighteenth century: the Declaration of Independence is Jefferson's protest against the remains of divine kingship. Divine, autocratic monarchy was the political legacy of the ancient to the modern world.

Medieval society inherited a social tradition as well as a political system from the ancient Mediterranean civilization. It is widely believed that no group is a genuine social class unless it has a sense of identity—class-consciousness. Some historians describe the ancient social structure as a one-class system, because outside of fifth-century Athens (always a significant exception), only one group—the ruling elite—had such a sense of identity. Only the aristocracy had a distinct life-style, justified its own existence, loved itself as a class. Not until much later did the bourgeoisie (and later still the workers) begin to develop class-consciousness. In the ancient world, only the elite knew things, knew how to do things; the ruling class was the only literate, conscious group in society.

Who was included in the ancient elite? Its members and size varied, of course, from place to place and time to time, but it always included government officials, bureaucrats, and army officers. In the great cities of the Hellenistic empires, wealthy merchants or businessmen were members of the ruling class, or hoped to be: they were literate, rich, and powerful, and generally they were accepted into the elite. However, the most important group within the ruling class was that of the landlords, whose role as suppliers of food was absolutely essential. In the ancient Near East (and today), not much was needed in the way of shelter or clothing; with a secure food supply the land could support a large population. Some of the subjects of the pharaohs (or of Nasser) might live miserably, but they survived as long as the food supply was maintained. Landlords were essential in pre-industrial society, and as the dominant group within the elite they set the tone of the ruling class. Land was the great source of wealth until the nineteenth century; it is still a great source of wealth, and even in the twentieth century land ownership retains its mystique as a symbol and a satisfaction.

The ancient elite varied greatly in numbers, and in size proportionate to the rest of the population. In ancient Egypt the elite may have numbered 5 to 10 per cent of the population; in Rome of the third century B.C., perhaps 40 per cent; in Rome of the third century A.D., between 10 and 15 per cent. In Athens of the fifth century B.C., perhaps 40 or 50 per cent of the population could be counted as members of the dominant group Through all these variations, landlords remained as the necessary ingredient of the ruling elite.

THE ROMAN WAY OF LIFE

The life style of the "one class" of the ancient world is a very important part of western history because it was perpetuated in the educational curriculum right down to modern times as the only model for the good life. Until the twentieth century, the Greek and Latin classics were the staples of the educational system of the West, and these writings comprised the literature produced by and for the ancient elite. Classical literature set up a model of what the ancients believed about good living, about the "right" attitudes and style, and this survived throughout the Middle Ages and grew even more influential after the renaissance of the twelfth century. During the early Middle Ages, puritanical churchmen had serious reservations about classical culture; they disapproved of various pagan ideas and attitudes, including the eroticism of much of ancient literature. However, the classics were never seriously threatened as educational tools, largely because no acceptable alternative curriculum could be found. After the twelfth century, however, and even more after the Italian Renaissance, the classic ideal and model became completely dominant and remained so until about 1900.

The ancient aristocratic mode was developed partly in the Greek world and partly in the Hellenistic civilization of the eastern half of the Mediterranean during the last three centuries B.C., but it was particularly a product of the Roman Empire. The Romans started out as a band of warriors bound together for purposes of conquest and exploitation, but as they conquered the world and developed a distinctive political system, the process of humanization began to operate. Roman life became more temperate and easy-going, less exploitive. Conquered peoples were brought into the Roman world and given the extensive benefits of Roman citizenship; in 222 A.D., all free-born people of the Empire were made citizens.

The Roman way of life, adapted from the style of Rome's leading families, was carried over to the medieval world. It is true that the style of the Germanic invaders of the fifth and sixth centuries was very different, but after a period of initial cultural shock the Roman mode prevailed. Over the very long run (the Middle Ages down to the fourteenth century), the Roman aristocratic style became the dominant mode of Europe, and it has not yet been replaced by any lasting alternative.

The style which prevailed was that of the Roman aristocracy of the first and second centuries A.D.—the Golden Age of Rome. Our knowledge of the Roman way of life and attitudes is not based on precise ideology, on the writings of any ancient social theoretician, but on extrapolation from the works of writers, mainly rhetoricians and poets and notably Cicero, Vergil, and Horace. Not even Cicero, whose work came the closest to ideology of any Roman writing, presented any consistent social theory. The Romans were intensely practical people who lived their ideology without writing about it. A life style, in any case, is a matter of experience rather than theory; it is complex and existential, and political and social theory seldom comes to grips with the realities of how people think and feel. What we know we have learned from the classical authors, from historians such as Livy and Tacitus, and from Roman law—perhaps the single most valuable source of information about how the Romans lived and what they believed.

Devotion to the family was a major aspect of the Roman aristocratic life style, which became the upper-class European style after a brief period of Germanic predominance in the fifth and sixth centuries. The Romans had a strong sense of the importance of family and of family honor, and they worked continually for the betterment of their own families. Indeed, family honor and family unity are still extremely important among the very rich and the very poor: only among the deracinated bourgeoisie has the family become a secondary institution. A Roman senator or consul used his term of office to improve the fortunes of his family, to find jobs for his relatives and add to the family wealth, and this was considered natural and proper.

Another important characteristic of Roman thought was intense devotion to the state—to the *res publica*, the state as a separate entity from the individuals within it. The Romans had a deep sense of the viability of the state as an institution, as an organism with its own birth, growth, and maturity. This concept seems obvious because it became a basic element of European political thought, but the Germans had no such idea. They had a concept of kingship; they followed warlords who provided booty and protection; but when a warlord died, his band died with him and the members went off to find a new protector. There was no distinction between the individual king and the state. To the Romans, on the other hand, consuls and emperors come and go but the state goes on forever.

The Romans assumed, too, that their own state was eternal. Perhaps because Rome had existed for so long and had become so powerful, Rome became the world itself. *Res publica, imperium, saculum, civilitas*—state, empire, world, civilization—all of these entities were coexistent with Rome by the second century A.D. All of the ancient peoples (except the Jews, who believed in Creation) thought that the world had existed forever and would exist forever; by implication, Rome itself was eternal. This belief, of course, was shattered by the disintegration of the Roman Empire in the fourth and fifth centuries, which brought about one of the great intellectual crises of all time. In doubt, confusion, and bewilderment, people looked around for an alternative eternal institution, and in the Middle Ages it was the Church rather than the state that was identified with the world. Since the thirteenth century we have returned to the Roman view of things: not that any one state is eternal, necessarily (although nineteenth-century Englishmen and twentieth-century Americans might believe this), but that the institution of the state is eternal. The Romans taught western society that there is no way to live outside the state, no other way to organize society and increase the commonweal, and this has become so essential to western thought that anarchists have great difficulty projecting an alternative.

The Romans believed in force, in militarism; they were among the least pacifist of all peoples. In fact it is unlikely that any ancient people were pacifists—certainly not the Jews, who concentrated on fighting throughout the whole era described in the Pentateuch. The Romans worshipped Mars, the god of war, and they believed that war was good, was necessary, brought public benefits. Whatever else a man might be in the Roman Republic, he had to be a fighter. We really know very little about the early Republic (before about 250 or 200 B.C.); our only source is Livy, who wrote in the time of Augustus Caesar. Whether or not we can believe Livy (and Syme and other scholars are skeptical of Livy's accuracy and veracity), his work is a wonderful projection of Roman beliefs and attitudes. To Livy (and presumably to his contemporaries), the mark of a good citizen was his readiness to leave his plow when summoned to fight and die for the *res publica*. The Romans throve on war and believed in it, and this despite the *Pax Romana*. It is true that after the Romans conquered the Mediterranean peoples they called a halt to expansionist war in the mid-first century A.D. They did so partly because they were not sure there was anyone left worth conquering, and partly because the task of defending such a vast frontier was more than enough of a military burden. After about 50 A.D. the conquered peoples did enjoy the benefits of peace, but Roman violence did not disappear when the expansion ended.

The Roman aristocracy remained violent in tastes and behavior; it had a bloodlust, and when that lust could no longer
be sated in conquest it was sated in the circus. It is difficult even to
describe the horrors that went on in the Colosseum in the first
three centuries A.D. The Romans believed in public torture, rel-
ished public execution, and paid to see humans massacring each
other or being torn to pieces by animals. They watched these spec-
tacles regularly; violence was an accepted and necessary part of
everyday life, and the Romans remained aggressive and violent
long after they ceased to fight expansive wars.

Violence and aggressiveness were important aspects of Roman
sexual attitudes; in fact the attitude of the typical Roman aristocrat
toward sex and women was grim and sordid. Romans had a poor
opinion of women in general. Prostitutes and courtesans had some
influence, but only in a sexual role, while other women were not
considered. Roman poetry is full of pornography of a distasteful,
base variety studded with dirty jokes and vulgar anatomical references. A great deal of this kind of material survived (assumed)
censorship by the medieval monks who transcribed it, and the
chances are that the worst of it was not preserved. The Roman
attitude was not only sordid but heavily masculine—a characteristic of aristocratic and of proletarian societies. Women are regarded
as playthings in the first; as housekeepers and breeding animals
in the second. Medieval people inherited the Roman attitude, but
softened it during the centuries into a more gentle, egalitarian
attitude toward women—one of the main contributions of the
Middle Ages to western civilization. The triumph of the bourgeoisie in the nineteenth and twentieth centuries did still more for
female emancipation, but the medieval people did at least shake off
the worst horrors of the Roman "male chauvism."

The aristocratic life is a physical life, and physical signs of
wealth and position are essential to the aristocrat. An upper-class
Roman (and other aristocrats after him) had to have a large house
in town and a splendid villa in the country. He had to have servants
and a fine wine cellar, to give lavish parties and wear beautiful
clothes. The paintings on his walls were regarded as evidence of
wealth and status, as were the musicians he could hire. As far as we
know, it was the Romans who developed these long-lived symbols
of aristocracy. We do not know very much about the private life
of the ancient Greeks, but the evidence is that their leaders lived

frugal, simple lives. No private houses have survived from ancient Athens—only public buildings—and we believe that Pericles and Plato lived in wooden houses much like those of the ordinary citizen. In Rome, on the other hand, a major tourist attraction is still Hadrian's villa—the emperor's private country house, with vistas, gardens, and works of art to rival those of any public edifice.

The Romans started the tradition of private splendor, and it continues still. Even under communism, when a man achieves power and wealth he builds a large, expensive house and dresses and entertains in a manner designed to reflect his station. Historians often comment on the supposed immobility of Byzantine or Chinese ruling society, but the western aristocratic mode is also strikingly permanent—and when the bourgeoisie did emerge as a class, their ambition was simply to imitate this aristocratic style. Their large houses, fine clothes, and grand manners were a continuation of the age-old way of life. A peculiar exception to this pattern was made by some of the wealthy English bourgeoisie of the first half of the nineteenth century, one of the few groups in the West that did *not* live like the old Romans when they had the opportunity. Perhaps because of religious Puritanism, they gave away large amounts of money and made an effort to live simply, to dress simply, to be moderate in food and drink—a rare exception to the pattern set in ancient Rome.

The Roman aristocracy took great care in the education of the young; they were much more conscientious in this field than any earlier elite. It is true that the Romans learned a great deal from Athens and from the Hellenistic world, but they also believed in themselves as educators, as trainers of the next generation in a specific order of civilization. They developed a tough, aggressive educational system that took no notice of individual talents, of feelings or emotional development. Children were regimented, and physical force was used to make them learn. Boys were turned over to tutors (often slaves, and frequently frustrated, sadistic men) at the age of six or seven and forced to learn their letters. There was no room for art or music within the system; all boys were forced to become little grammarians, as language and literature were, in fact, the whole of their curriculum. Higher education was simply higher studies in language. A society dominated by an aristocracy is one in which the rulers need to learn nothing but language; they do not need science or the arts, they do not need new knowledge of technology or sources of wealth, but they must communicate—they already have power, which they will exert through communication. Through narrow concentration the Romans did do marvelous things with Latin—basically an awkward, inflexible language. They ignored the sciences, studied almost no mathematics and very little history, but learned Latin superbly well. Intellectual experimentation was sacrificed to rigid literary education.

The Romans were psychologically damaged by their educational system, as evidenced by their violence, aggression, sadism, hostility to women, and other unattractive characteristics. Children were treated very badly indeed, and many of them grew up to be sadomasochists. The system was modified, of course, but vestiges have survived into the twentieth century. The educational system of the medieval Church was based upon the Roman and there were a good many neurotic educated adults within the medieval Church. Later western systems were based on the Roman; educators read Cicero and Quintilian and found their model convincing and acceptable. It is a natural system for an aristocratic society, which needs only to train its young people to accept the power handed on to them—a similar system existed in Confucian China.

The Roman aristocracy had a great talent for law, and this is not surprising. In an aristocratic, militaristic, landed society, the interests of the ruling class can be expressed in terms of law. Law cannot deal with perceptions and emotions—with love, beauty, joy, or sadness; it deals very well with family property, state power, class privilege, and military force. A familial, paternalistic state is very rule-conscious, and its inmost meaning is expressed in rules—little wonder that the Romans were the greatest lawyers the world has known. The dominant legal tradition of Europe is Roman; every western country (outside of England and its former colonies) has a legal system based on Roman law.

Roman law was influential because it was excellent law. On the highest (theoretical) level, law was believed to be a reflection of reason, or of "natural law," which is not the law of animal life, but quite the contrary. The concept of natural law (taken from Stoic philosophy) assumes that the world operates according to rational principles, that there are universal principles of reason. The law of the state was regarded as the positive, detailed implementation of natural law, and any law that was repugnant to reason had to be a bad law. The problem arose, of course, over the question of who had the authority and the wisdom to decide whether the law conformed to reason. Who could make law accord with the principles of reason? That was the great question of Roman political history.

Under the Republic, Romans believed that the people had the authority, collectively, to decide what the law of the state should be. The history of the Republic is the history of the argument over who belonged to the "Roman people"—certain leading families, all the men in the army, everyone who lived in Rome? By the first century B.C. the Romans had an awkward, cumbersome system in which everyone had some vague share in government. The system failed because the Romans of the Republic were unable to settle on a workable system of popular sovereignty, and this failure doomed the republican form of government. By the early Empire, law-making power was shared between the emperor and the Senate, which consisted at that time of elder statesmen—members of distinguished families who had retired from active military or official life. As time went on, the role of the Senate became less and less important, and by the late Empire the law-making authority belonged to the emperor alone. At this point, Roman jurists proposed a legal theory, the *Lex Regia* (Royal Law), which stated that the legislative authority of the state resided in the Roman people, but that the latter had surrendered this authority, irrevocably, to the emperor. The will of the emperor had the force of law.

The development of Roman law from an awkward kind of popular sovereignty to dictatorship or autocracy was an extremely significant fact of medieval history, because the medieval world inherited the autocracy of the later Empire. Roman law was codified in final form in the fifth and sixth centuries A.D., and it was codified in the form of autocratic, royal law. Subsequent European society was heavily devoted to Roman law, and that law favored absolutism of all kinds, from the absolute power of the pope to the divine right of kings.

The principle of equity is a major aspect of Roman law, and it is a logical corollary of the belief that law must conform to reason. If in a specific case the law seems to work against reason —to work an injustice or absurdity—then the judge must have the power to overrule the law in that instance. Roman jurists had wide powers, and judges in all Roman systems can set aside the law or make exceptions on behalf of the greater principle of justice. English law did not develop an effective principle of equity until the fifteenth century, and it never was integrated completely into the common law—although the American legal system has some measure of equity through the Supreme Court and the practice of loose construction, which allows judicial review of the law in accordance with equity. Equity as it developed in Rome is basically a reflection of an aristocratic system in which members of the ruling class can trust the judges (fellow-members of their own group) to make decisions according to the principle of equity. In a democracy, judges might not be trusted to make law or make exceptions (they might favor one group over another), but where everyone—including the judges—belongs to one class, this system is possible.

Process is a most significant aspect of law, and the procedures of Roman law were very different from those of the common law that developed in England in the Middle Ages. The common law operates on the adversary system, in which opposing attorneys contend against each other while the judge acts as an impartial referee. He pronounces on points of law and he passes sentence on the convicted criminal but he may not impose his own opinions on the jury. In Roman law the very opposite is true: the court belongs to the judges, who make all the decisions. A panel (usually three or five judges) acts as investigator whose job is to establish the truth. Common law pleading is mostly oral, but in Roman law courts the attorneys submit long, written briefs (again, this is suitable for an aristocratic system in which everyone who matters is literate and skilled in the use of language) some time before the trial begins. The judges study the briefs, and very often they are able to announce their decision without any further investigation at all. However, if the "truth" is not obvious from the briefs, the judges summon witnesses, interrogate them, and torture them—if necessary—to get the truth. Torture was called "putting the question," and it was part of Roman legal procedure for many centuries. Vestiges of the Roman procedure survive even today on the Continent, although the more liberal countries now have juries. The jury is a recent innovation in Continental law, however, and it is distinctly subordinate to the judge; judge and jury retire together to come to a decision.

The Roman system works well, on the whole, particularly in criminal cases; the judge is very often able to get at the truth through close analysis of the facts without a jury to be swayed by popular pressures and demagogic attorneys. The Romans were extremely proud of their legal system: it provided justice, permitted the rational to operate in human affairs, and allowed men to live together peacefully. When St. Paul was arrested in Asia Minor, he claimed his rights as a Roman citizen to demand a Roman trial.

The Roman legal system was, then, a beneficent aspect of aristocratic society; law is always an important part of the machinery through which a ruling class orders its affairs and perpetuates its power. Roman law perpetuated the idea of autocracy, and the principle of equity, and it was responsible for the idea that there should be a legal system at all. The Germans who invaded Rome had no such system; indeed, they really had no law as we know it. The medieval idea of the necessity of a legal system, of legal education, of a legal framework for society, was part of the heritage of Rome.

II. *Philosophy and Religion*

Classical Philosophical Systems

Certain systems of thought within the Greek and Roman world had enormous impact upon the medieval consciousness. Until the seventeenth century, in fact, almost all western systems of thought tended to operate within the framework of Platonism, Aristotelianism, or Stoicism. These systems had an incredible hold upon western intellectual history, and when they finally were abandoned or rejected, it was not because they were replaced by more satisfactory systems (in fact we are still searching for replacements), but because modern science and technology had provided new experiences, or revealed aspects of human nature, on which these ancient systems could shed no light.

A system of thought is a group of ideas or theories with some integrating principle or basic attitude which can be worked out in every aspect of thought or life to provide a unified, integrated world view. The modern system which best fits this definition is Marxism, and this may explain its wide appeal. It is a subtle, adaptable system with a broad and comprehensive view of history, of society, of human nature—in fact, of reality. Marxism can absorb new ideas and data and keep going, and adaptability is essential to the success of any intellectual system. Attempts have been made in this century to make Freudianism into such a world-view, but they have as yet not been very successful. Liberalism, which is now in trouble, never developed a sufficiently wide and adaptable philosophy. It was effective in politics and in certain ethical problems, but it never really came to terms with industrial civilization and it failed to develop an esthetic. Like Stoicism, liberalism was too narrow to become a successful world-view. Of the ancient systems, Platonism best fits the definition of a thought-system; it is unified and adaptable and can be applied in a wide variety of directions. Aristotelianism is too sophisticated, too abstract and scholarly for wide appeal; Stoicism is not sufficiently intellectual, and too narrow.

The most influential philosophical system of the ancient world was, then, Platonism. More has been written about Platonism than any other system of thought, and even today—when modern linguistic analysts reject Platonic metaphysics—it is still influential in many fields, including social anthropology (as interpreted by Claude Levi-Strauss) and linguistics (as interpreted by Noam Chomsky). Plato has been neglected and rediscovered again and again, but his influence has never vanished completely. He was that rare combination: a great thinker and a great writer. Rarely visibly dogmatic, he was resolute in devotion to certain basic principles, and Plato was one of the great masters of Greek prose —a rare facility for a philosopher. His style is leisurely, elliptical, and paradoxical, and his writings can be interpreted in various ways. Platonism is an entire philosophy of life; along with St. Augustine, St. Thomas Aquinas, Descartes, and Hegel, Plato produced a philosophy that could be lived. He discussed love, birth, death—all the concerns of humanity.

We know very little about Plato himself. He came from a

wealthy Athenian family and was well educated—a member of the elite. He was involved in the government and political life of his time, but he never achieved his ambition to be a political leader. Perhaps he was too intellectual to be successful in politics; intellectuals often suffer from their ability to appreciate complexity, to see the other side, to find the common base among arguments. Plato lived in a bad period, in any case. Athens had been defeated by Sparta in the Peloponnesian Wars, and a radical democratic bourgeoisie was taking over from the old elite. Plato was too aristocratic for that era, and he was associated—to his misfortune—with the traitor Alcibiades. He never did get a political position in Athens, and may have been embittered by the failure.

Plato travelled widely, perhaps as far as the Near East. There has been speculation that he came into contact with Hebrew prophetic thought and that this contact was responsible for the strain of mysticism within his philosophy. This may be true, but rationalism and mysticism are not necessarily incompatible, and Plato might have arrived at the same point without travelling to the East. He did go to Sicily, where he evidently had an opportunity to exercise some political power under one of the tyrants, or dictators, of the Greek cities there. It is generally believed that he made a bad job of it and had to leave the city. Plato went back to Athens and opened his famous Academy in the hills outside the city. The Academy was very much the kind of place that students want a modern university to be—not primarily a place for instruction or research but a center for inquiry, for dialogue, for the pursuit of intellectual pleasures. Plato and his students (rich young Athenians) led a pleasant life and discussed such questions as: What is truth? What is beauty? How do we know anything? Is there an after-life? Plato worked very hard, and over a period of many years he molded these discussions into great works of art, affirmative philosophical statements. *The Republic*—the most important of these *Dialogues* of Plato—is one of the most significant works of western civilization.

Plato did not choose to speak as himself in the *Dialogues* but chose Socrates as his mouthpiece. He reports that it was Socrates' death at the hands of an Athenian jury that caused him to leave the city in outrage, but we do not know whether this is true or whether any of what he says about Socrates is true. We do know that there was a Socrates in Athens during the fourth century, and that he was a professional nuisance, a stonemason who used to wander into the Agora (market-place) and try to involve his fellow-citizens in argument and debate. He asked such questions as "What is justice?" and annoyed his fellows by pointing out why their answers were wrong. It was a period of speculation in the Greek world; in Asia Minor a group of philosophers (now known as the pre-Socratics) had been speculating for half a century on questions about the nature of reality. One of them—Heraclitus—came close to a dialectic like that of Plato or Hegal. Eventually some young Athenians (of whom Plato may have been one) decided to take Socrates seriously, and because some of these young men (including the notorious Alcibiades) were involved in political life, Socrates got in trouble with the authorities. He was tried for sacrilege, or treason, convicted, and died by forced suicide. His death is described by Plato in the *Apology of Socrates*, which presents Socrates as a paragon of wisdom and virtue, although it is likely that Socrates said little or perhaps nothing of all that is ascribed to him.

In Plato's *Dialogues*, Socrates or someone else asks a question which is answered by a student or guest. The answer is demolished at length by Socrates, who usually turns around at the end of the argument to discover the grain of truth within his opponent's answer. Some of these *Dialogues* are short and some very long; as Plato got older, his writing got more didactic and less literary. The idea that Plato took from Socrates (if anything) is that it is necessary to analyze the real meanings of the words we use. (In this sense, Plato was the first analytic philosopher.) Terms are concepts, and in order to answer such questions as "What is love?" we must find out what we mean by "love." General terms like "faith" or "love" or "justice" predicate a concept, and in discussing terms, we are discussing ideas.

To Plato, ideas, or conceptual forms, were not idle fantasies but essential realities. When we refer to "justice" or "the state" or "love," we are actually referring to something that has independent existence outside our minds—this is translated into philosophic jargon in the phrase: "universals have reality." A student might say "I have a table in front of me; is it not real?" but Plato would reply "What is a table?" A table is a structure of plastic or metal or wood in a particular form, but without that particular form, there would be a shapeless mass of material and no table at all. The table would not have come into existence without the idea of a table; it is the idea that gives it shape and reality. Pure, ultimate reality is pure Idea, and the physical world that we touch and see has reality only insofar as it participates in or is formed by pure Idea. Reality requires recognizable form, and the physical world has no form unless it is shaped by Idea.

Plato believed that anything real must be eternal—and this may be the weakest part of his philosophy. He thought that reality was identical with eternity, that when we speak of reality we mean something perfect, permanent, secure, definable—nothing transient or indiscriminate. This seems plausible when we realize that the concept of a table in Plato's time is a concept still while the particular tables of Plato's time have moldered away. In our own lives, our bodies die and decay while our ideas survive. This fundamental fact of human nature probably helped to inspire Plato's theory and certainly in part accounts for its ever-recurring popularity.

To Plato, reality is purely conceptual and the terms men use refer to eternal forms and pure independently existing ideas. The purpose of dialogue or communication is to clarify our ideas so that we can bring them to full consciousness and refer to them with understanding. Two men refer to "justice," but unless they can agree on the meaning of the term, they cannot discuss it effectively. The purpose of education, of thought—of life, even—is to clarify our ideas so that we can develop knowledge instead of opinion. Knowledge, in Plato's sense, is an idea thought out and critically examined; it is achieved only through the painful examination and rejection of unclear, unreal concepts.

Plato's theory of knowledge is as good as any theory ever developed, but he was more than an epistemologist. Having concluded that reality is pure Idea and that we know it by defining and purifying our concepts—by reason and critical thinking—Plato went on to develop a whole philosophy of life and of the world, perhaps because he was forced to examine how man gets ideas in the beginning.

Is a child born an animal, in whom, as time goes on, accumulated experiential responses add up to consciousness or mind? If so, then consciousness is created by experience. This is (roughly) the position of the modern psychological behaviorists. Plato, on the other hand, believed that the mind exists when the child is born, that experience serves only to modify and develop consciousness. There is a world of pure Ideas somewhere in the universe—a world of reality—from which the child at birth received the impress of images and thoughts. If he is correctly educated (and Plato was the first adherent of progressive education; he realized that the childish mind could be irreparably damaged by bad education), then in adult life he will receive the fullest possible perception from the world of Ideas. We cannot get the complete perception of reality (one cannot convey a three-dimensional fact in words or images), but with proper education and rigorous training we can better our understanding.

Plato's philosopher-king was a man whose understanding was refined beyond that of other men. In the end, a fortunate few go beyond thought in words or images to "the flight of the soul"— what we might call a mystical experience, an ultimate illumination. It is possible to go beyond any particular idea to the One Idea, the ultimate of the universe—the Good, God, or X—"the source of all things beautiful and right." This does not happen to many people or very often; it is a rare and beautiful illumination which comes only after excellent education, constant thought, and fine training of the mind.

Plato wrote about death at great length, about what became of the marvelous mental equipment developed in a lifetime of thought and study. At this point Platonism can become a religion of sorts, which explains why it was attractive to the early Christians. Christianity was built as much on Plato as on the Judaic tradition, and for that matter, there has been a great deal of Platonism within Judaism since the Middle Ages. Plato pointed out that the human being has two aspects. He agreed with the Greek dramatists and artists who portrayed men as half-man, half-god; half-man, half-animal. Man decays like an animal but lives forever like a god. This recognition of the polarity of human life is the origin of the long-lived and crucial philosophical distinction between soul and body. Hebrews did not distinguish between soul and body (except in mistranslation); it was Plato who emphasized and even inaugurated the distinction. The human body is material, transient, corruptible, and therefore unreal. Bodies are usually ugly —on the rare occasions when they are beautiful we worship them —but their importance is as temporary resting places for the soul.

Plato does not convincingly tell us why the soul bothers to use a body at all, but he does point out that human life is valuable because the soul grows and matures in the body, and the soul of Socrates the philosopher is very different from that of Socrates the infant. Through study and insight and love and dialectic and—finally—mystical experience, the soul can ascend, can become one with the Idea. If the soul has been rightly educated, if it is beautiful and just and good, it will return to Beauty and Justice and Good after death. Quite obviously, this concept entered into the Christian view of immortality, of ascension into heaven at the end of a good life and descent into hell at the end of a bad one.

The Platonic philosophy leads, fairly obviously, into a social and moral theory. Good conduct is the pursuit of the intellectual life. A man must cultivate the finer things of the mind, must study and refine his taste to get as close as possible to pure Idea. The just man fulfills as much as possible of his potential for beauty and truth, and the just state allows each individual to fulfill his potential. To Plato, the first criterion of a good society would be: What kinds of schools does it have? How does it clarify the minds of young people? How does it liberate their souls?

Plato's theory can thus be elaborated to explain much more than epistemology and educational theory; it can tell us who we are, where we are going, and how we may escape the limitations of death. His solutions to questions of knowledge, of human personality, of society, are not final answers but they are plausible answers.

The philosophical system of Aristotle was very unlike that of Plato, and it had little influence until the twelfth century. Aristotle himself was a brilliant, hard-working scholar who came from northern Greece and studied for a time at Plato's Academy. The two men were very different in temperament—Aristotle wanted to collect data and to categorize while Plato wished to sit still and to reflect—and eventually they parted. Aristotle founded his own school, known as the *Lyceum,* and his disciples are generally known as the *peripatetic* (walking around) philosophers. Aristotle was too busy teaching, lecturing, and advising statesmen to write down a coherent body of doctrine, and what remains of his work is generally believed to be a collection of lecture notes put together by students after the philosopher's death. The result is unattractive as reading matter, as it is full of repetition, of answers to students' irrelevant questions, and of confusing and impenetrable material. Aristotle was more a pedagogue than a poet, and his best-known pupil was Alexander the Great. Philip of Macedon called on Aristotle to educate his son, and from what we know of Alexander, his tutor did a very good job.

To understand Aristotle we have to appreciate his temperament of mind, his belief that if one investigates, examines data, collects information, and does research, one can set out all the gathered material and come to a decision. His was the first scientific mind, and he believed that if all the data are collected and put together, a pattern will emerge. This is a very different theory of knowledge from that of Plato; it assumes that the human mind is an active, conditioning receptacle for experience, that the mind reacts with its environment and receives sense data. On the basis of that data the mind discriminates, generalizes, and develops universal concepts. Our concepts are generalizations from experience and not necessarily parts of the divine order of the universe. This is basically a scientific, academic attitude.

Aristotle was very poorly received for many centuries after his death. His philosophy was too dry, too theoretical and abstract, not total or emotional enough to satisfy the needs of the time. It was difficult to popularize, and with the exception of his work on logic (still the best textbook on the subject), his works were little considered until Arabic and Jewish scholars in Spain began to study them around the year 1000. From about 200 B.C. to 1000 A.D., Platonism was the dominant philosophical system.

Stoicism, the third influential philosophy of the ancient world, was an offshoot of Platonism diverted into practical ethics. Stoic philosophy was a day-to-day guide rather than a theory of ethics, and it was enormously important in the Greco-Roman and Christian worlds. It is the moral philosophy of the "inner man" and the "outer man," and its chief proponents were a Roman emperor (Marcus Aurelius) and a Greek slave (Epictetus). These philosophers urged men not to commit themselves too much to the outer world or to material things, to remain in tune with the joy and reason and harmony of the universe and not to be swayed by the temptations of passion or the corruptions of power. This became a code of privatism, of the nine-to-five man who keeps back the best part of himself for his private life of feelings, of the arts, of family and beauty. His real life takes place after five, when he can concentrate on the emotional, esthetic, intellectual pleasures available to everyone. Nature, music, and family life can be enjoyed by everyone, and material blessings are not worth a struggle.

Stoicism is well suited to a society which could not control or explain ravages of nature such as plague, fire, war, or holocaust, and therefore convinced itself that the physical world was not important. It was well suited too to the Roman Empire, where political life for many years was either in the hands of a tiny autocratic group or dispersed in a violent, unstable kind of situation. Political life offered little, because at one time one could not get into it and at another time it was dangerous and frightening. The reigns of crazy emperors and the murders of emperors were not reassuring. Apathy, fear, and disillusion with public life encouraged concentration on private life, which is a recurrent pole in human history. At the other extreme are the periods of millennial, apocalyptic fervor, times when men believe that they *can* create a great society and make everyone happy, and that they must sacrifice everything to improve society. From the time of the decline of the Athenian polis, around 430 B.C., the political life of the ancient world was corrupt and despotic or violent and unstable, and those who could retreat were glad to do so.

Stoicism is a wonderful philosophy for aristocrats who have made their money and do not need to worry about the competition for material things. They claim to find joy in simple things, in nature—a recurrent theme of this long-lived philosophy. Revolutionaries and even social reformers can obviously not be satisfied with Stoicism, but it was a crucial element in medieval thought, and before there could be social revolution or unrest, the conservative Stoic cast of thought had to be broken. Stoicism is a powerful thread in the New Testament, in the writings of St. Paul; it was central to the medieval social ethic. The Stoic thread in medieval Christianity may account for the scarcity of social upheavals in the Middle Ages, and it is still reflected in the attitude of upper classes toward their social inferiors.

THE HEBRAIC TRADITION

Medieval culture was a culture of the Book, and in the Middle Ages, the Book was the Bible. It might be said that the primary task of medieval universities, when they were first established in the

twelfth and thirteenth centuries, was the explication of the relation of Biblical thought to secular culture; in fact, this was true in
some sense of all educational institutions down to the late nineteenth century. The Biblical tradition brought special problems,
ideas, and beliefs—religious, historical, moral—to the medieval
world, and these were quite unlike the legacy of the classical philosophers. It is not surprising that medieval scholars were able to
spend their lives studying and arguing over the Bible. It is an extremely difficult book, and we can sympathize with scholars who
claimed that it was beyond reason—that God's word could not be
understood without faith, that belief was essential to comprehen-
sion.

Before entering into any discussion of the content of the Bible
we should attempt to understand its source, to find out who were
its authors and why they wrote as they did. Who were the Jews,
and why were they unlike all other people? There is no certain
answer to these questions, and perhaps the old description of a
"chosen people" is as satisfactory as any explanation. Scholars used
to speculate that Judaism developed an immaterial and universal
god because the Jews (Hebrews) were originally a wandering, pastoral people. Egyptians and Babylonians could worship material
deities who resided in special temples or palaces, but nomads
needed a god they could carry around with them. (However, the
desert Arabs were as nomadic as the Jews, but it took them many
centuries to develop a monotheistic religion—and even then, much
of Islam was derived from Judaism and Christianity.)

It has also been said that the Jews learned monotheism from
other Near Eastern cultures. There are similarities between certain
Mesopotamian religious ideas and stories and those of Judaism:
the story of the Flood, for example, is a common Mesopotamian
myth, and the Jews may have originated in Mesopotamia—Abra-
ham was supposed to come from Ur of the Chaldees. One of the
pharaohs (Ikhnaton) evidently practiced a kind of monotheism,
but the Egyptian priests objected, and his experiments did not
survive him. The Persians worshipped a spiritual, immaterial god,
but they were not monotheists: their god of light and spirit battled
a twin god of darkness and matter, and if the Jews learned their
religion from the Persians, they did not learn it very thoroughly.
Elements of a monotheistic, universal, religion existed in the an-

cient Near East, but even if the Jews had picked up every available fragment, these could not have amounted to more than a small percentage of the religion of Moses.

The great questions of Old Testament scholarship have always been: When was the Hebrew Bible written, and who wrote it? To put this another way: Who founded Judaism—the patriarchs, Moses, or the prophets? (The phrase "Old Testament," which is offensive to Orthodox Jews because it implies the existence of a later and higher revelation, is used in this context as a convenient label for the Hebrew Bible.) In the nineteenth century, the so-called Higher Criticism began to supply answers to these enduring questions. In the Higher Criticism, the Bible was examined as a socio-literary document and not accepted at face value as divine revelation. This kind of criticism was not entirely new in the nineteenth century: the approach was used in some of the work of the Church Fathers, in the Talmud, and in some medieval criticism. The first critic to take a genuinely historical approach to the Bible was probably Benedict Spinoza, the Dutch Jewish philosopher of the seventeenth century, who treated the Bible as a social document and eventually was excommunicated. However, like every other kind of modern scholarship, Higher Criticism really began in nineteenth-century Germany, where philologists (usually Protestant ministers) applied the tools of classical scholarship to Biblical studies.

The greatest of the German philological critics was Julius Wellhausen, whose books are still unsurpassed in the field of elaborate, literary criticism of the Bible. Wellhausen believed that the Old Testament, and Judaism as expressed therein, appeared quite late in Hebrew history (after the seventh or sixth century B.C.): Jewish theology was a product of the age of prophets and scribes. Fragments of the pristine, early Judaism of the age of the patriarchs and of Moses may be incorporated in the Bible, as well as old myths and legends and (especially in the book of Deuteronomy) laws, but most of it was written after 700 B.C. The sixth century was a period of great stress, of constant turmoil, of struggle for national survival, and eventually of exile, which provided contact with other cultures. Wellhausen's argument depends for proof on sophisticated literary and philological inquiries, and during the late nineteenth and early twentieth centuries it was widely accepted among secular and Protestant scholars. Orthodox Jews never accepted this view, and Roman Catholics, until very recently, tended to ignore the entire controversy. Wellhausen's thesis has the ring of historical truth; it is plausible to a secular historian that new religious ideas would appear in an age of crisis and of communication with other cultures.

Despite its plausibility, Wellhausen's arguments have been bitterly attacked in the last forty years. Archeological evidence from new sites in the Near East has been used to support a new theory of the origins of Judaism. One leader of the new movement is an American Protestant, William Foxwell Albright, who published in 1940 a vehement and widely accepted rebuttal of Wellhausen's views: *From the Stone Age to Christianity.* Another leader is Yecheskel Kaufman of the Hebrew University, who has published several works on this subject. In their view, Judaism in its fundamentals was a product of the age of Moses, and Moses was its chief founder. Most recent scholars believe that the accounts of Moses and his teachings in the canonical text of the Hebrew Bible are fairly accurate—not word for word, necessarily, but acceptable. The Bible dates approximately from the time of Moses, which means that Judaism was founded five or six hundred years earlier than Wellhausen believed. The archeological evidence goes back to the time of the migrations, and to that of Moses and the early kings of Israel, and it tends to confirm a great deal of the Bible. In this view, the Hebrew Bible is based not on myth but on actual history: making allowance for embellishments, the Bible can be taken almost at face value as a narrative of the early history of Israel. This interpretation is now dominant in Biblical scholarship.

According to the new scholarship, then, the age of Moses was the founding period of Judaism. The prophets who appeared in the years between 700 to 500 B.C. did not create Judaism, although they may have developed or reinforced certain teachings. Scholars like Albright and Kaufman claim that the prophetic tradition is continuous in Jewish history, that Moses was the first and greatest prophet, that Samuel was a prophet, and the men whom we call "the prophets" should really be identified as the "later prophets."

The fundamental tenet of Judaism is the belief in an immaterial or spiritual god who created the world and is omnipotent and omniscient. God is everything good, everything great, everything true—He is everything that *is*. The second essential of Judaism is the belief in a god of Israel who is also a god of all people. It is true that the universality (or international character) of God is emphasized more strongly in the later books of the Bible and the writings of the prophets than in the Pentateuch, but universality was one aspect of Judaism from the beginning.

The third essential of Judaism is particularly significant to a historian: the Jewish God is a god of history, and the important things that happen in the world happen in time. The Greeks wrote history, but they did not believe in its importance: to Plato, man's excellence—or salvation, or security—depended on his realization of perfect forms, and his ability to unite with the timeless Idea. In the static Greek view of the universe, perfect forms had always existed and would always exist, so that real change was not possible. In the Hebrew view, on the other hand, God existed before the world began (He created it), but He acts in our lives through history. God set up a drama in which men participate; He directs the course of human history—and He does all this in order to give man a chance to love Him. In the drama of history, which had a definable beginning and moves toward a definable end, man has the freedom to love God or to reject Him. This last point has proved profoundly mysterious to Jews and Christians alike, and many medieval thinkers struggled to reconcile belief in human freedom with belief in an omnipotent and omniscient God. If God is omnipotent He can direct man to love Him; if God knows everything, then He knows whether men will love Him, and therefore men are not free. Medieval Christian theology can be regarded as a series of attempts (perhaps futile) to solve this ancient problem.

The first book of the Bible deals with Creation, the next books with "sacred history"—the history of God's actions in the world and of man's struggles to accept Him. Later books (*Daniel* in particular) speculate on the end of the world. The Jews believed that the end would come when God judged all men, and the prophets speculated on its meaning—would it bring joy or terror, stress or peace, or all of these? The Jews were not certain what the end would be like, but they were confident that there would be an end—*eschaton*, in Greek: the Hebrew Bible becomes increasingly eschatological in its later books.

As a whole, then, the Bible posits a created world, with human society established as a setting for the continuing drama of the choices of various societies, particular communities, and individuals, to love or to reject God. Finally, the Bible posits a definite end to human history in a time of terror and peace, joy and suffering. This is a very different view from that of the Greeks, who believed that things were as they had always been and would always be. The Jews believed in perpetual change. States have come and gone, and people; even the pharaohs have disappeared into dust. Man transcends his past and moves forward, and human society perfects itself as it moves through history.

The Hebrews had a continuous tradition of political and social upheaval, presumably directed by God toward some great moment in the future. The reforming spirit of the West, the western belief in change and reformation, can be understood as a perpetuation of their tradition. The ancient Jews expressed their belief that things would change, that an unjust situation or society would be made just. This was a moral attitude, based on a view of God as good and of man as the servant of God's intention to perfect society. Other ancient peoples did not develop any such attitude, and we do not know why the Hebrews should have done so. It is true that they never established a monolithic, bureaucratic monarchy, that there was always fragmentation and change, that no one dynasty ever got hold of all the resources of society in the style of the governments of the great Near Eastern river valleys. There was always a possibility of change in Hebrew society; it was (relatively) open and democratic, and perhaps this made possible the development of a reforming religion.

Just as important in the Hebrews' impact on medieval culture was their idea of the covenant. Covenant theology is central to Judaism, and scholars like Albright tell us that it was actually derived from the commercial contracts of the markets and oases of ancient Judea. However, the religious covenant was not (like a commercial contract) freely entered by both participants. The Hebrew convenant was imposed by God; the Hebrews did not ask for it and indeed they often rebelled against it (and such rebellion was sin). God chose the Jews for His own purposes to be His witnesses in the world, to be agents of history and of divine Providence, to proclaim His word and advance history to its end. The covenant imposed religious, moral, social, and political obligations upon the Jews, many of whom resented them—but God kept issuing commands, recalling His people and punishing them for breaking the covenant or turning away from Him. This concept had a significant impact on Christianity; medieval Christians thought of themselves as the new chosen people, the true spiritual brotherhood, the new Israel. The medieval Church assumed the obligation to be God's agent for the advancement of human history—this partly accounts for both the restlessness and arrogance of medieval churchmen.

Among the Jews, God's particular spokesmen were the prophets. Modern scholars emphasize the continuous tradition of prophecy in Judaism (a tradition that goes back at least to Moses, Joshua, and Samuel, if not to the patriarchs), but it makes more historical sense to use the term to refer to the particular group who appeared in the marketplaces of Judah and Israel in the sixth and fifth centuries B.C. Amos, the first Isaiah, Jeremiah, Ezekiel, and others took it on themselves to announce that God spoke through them: no priesthood or congregation appointed them as prophets. What they said was often annoying and disturbing, particularly to the royal court and the temple priests—there is a tradition that Jeremiah was stoned to death for his warnings and criticisms of the ruling class. The prophets certainly were not of royal blood, nor did they belong to the priestly elite. It is impossible to establish that they belonged to any specific social class or group, although Amos (and probably the first Isaiah) evidently spoke with the voice of the country against the city, expressing the discontent of the peasantry. But this is not true of all the prophets, by any means. Several of them appeared fairly late in the development of Judaism: the second Isaiah obviously wrote in exile. Jeremiah's later writings, also, may have originated in exile, and some scholars believe that they reveal the influence of Persian and Hellenistic ideas. But there is no easy political or social explanation for the appearance of the prophets, and no social category that suits them all.

No matter why the prophets appeared: their very existence, and the acceptance of their writings as canonical books of the Bible, was exceedingly important to medieval Christianity and to western civilization. By accepting their works, Judaism gave sacred status and moral sanction to a group of critics or rebels against authority. Rare in any society, this was singular in the ancient Near East, with its congealed monarchies and elites in which all authority came from above. The Jewish prophets spoke from below, with the voice of the people, and they criticized the elite for their violations of the covenant and their failure to live up to their moral obligations as God's witnesses. The prophets had a strong sense of history, and they perceived the doom about to overtake Judea and Israel. (This was not much of a feat: it must have been obvious that the great empires—Babylonia, Assyria, Egypt—that surrounded the Jewish principalities must eventually swallow them up.) Their works expressed powerful social consciousness along with eschatological dreams: the prophets perceived present evils as well as future triumphs. They denounced existing corruption and social injustice; they foretold national defeat and dispersion, but tempered their vision with promises:

> For out of Zion shall go forth the law,
> and the word of the Lord from Jerusalem.[1]

Jerusalem will be a great city again, said the prophets, and in the new Zion, God's covenant will be observed and the principles of justice fulfilled. The prophetic emphasis on individual conscience and social justice, and the promise of the achievement of God's kingdom in this world, became pervasive elements in medieval thought.

The Hebrew prophets had no official status: they spoke as individuals. Despite bitter opposition, they achieved enormous influence in their own day, and the acceptance of their writings as part of the Bible had significant consequences for the medieval Church. A churchman who opposed official doctrine might rebel against the established order and still feel that he remained in the Biblical tradition, and many rebels named themselves as God's witnesses, as part of a holy brotherhood, and spoke against the priestly hierarchy. The medieval Church (and the philosophical-religious tradition of the West) owes much of its rebellious, individualistic, anti-authoritarian elements to the prophets. Their successful insistence on the right to speak and to be heard gave

---

[1] Revised Standard Version. Isaiah 2:3.

theological base and moral sanction to radicals within and without the Church.

A very different and equally important strain in the medieval Church—authoritarianism—was also derived from the Hebraic tradition. Medieval churchmen consciously modelled themselves on the teachings of the Hebrew Bible, which they accepted as the word of God. Believing themselves to be the new Israel, God's emissaries in the world, they assumed immense power over human souls and believed they had the right—even the duty—to use force against those who resisted the truth. The authoritarian, hierarchic structure of the Church institution was inherited largely from the Roman Empire (the pope replaced the emperor, and the Church, the Empire), but its justificatory theory came partly from the Old Testament. Churchmen took over the Biblical view of history and its tradition of positive leadership, in which religious leaders were charged by God with the duty to advance human history toward its final triumph. Their duty included the use of force against unbelievers, heretics—even Jews. The Church was God's holy brotherhood, and just as ancient Israelites who resented the obligations of the covenant were forced by God to do their part, so a medieval pope was expected to force the enemies of God to join in the advance of Christianity.

Medieval Christians believed that history would arrive at its appointed end when the Church became truly universal, when all men were Christians. They had little idea, at least before the thirteenth century, of the size of the world or the number of non-Christians in the East; they believed that the triumph of Christianity was close at hand and that the use of force to complete the task was God's will—that it was justified by the immensity of the accomplishment. Their philosophy, oddly enough, was taken over by the aggressively secular Marxists, whose view of history is to some extent a secularization of the Christian philosophy (which may help to explain its appeal). When the whole world is Communist, say the Marxists, the dictatorship of the proletariat with its necessary force and suffering will be at an end, and the happy time—the time of triumph, the classless society—will arrive.

Thus the hierarchy of the Church, the priesthood and the papacy, based its theory and authority on the Hebrew doctrine of the covenant and of divine Providence while religious dissenters took their inspiration and justification from the Hebrew prophets. Medieval heretics, subversives, and dissenters (and there were already many of these in the fourth century) based their right of dissent on the prophets, who spoke outside the temple, who spoke because God spoke in them. It is not true that these men upheld the right of conscience as we understand it, or that they defended every man's right to believe as he chose. On the contrary, they believed that they had God's voice, that they spoke the truth, that anyone who disagreed with them was wrong. They were dissenters, not libertarians; they did not tolerate contrary opinion, they damned it. The prophets (and the medieval heretics after them) were inclined to be just as authoritarian as the priestly hierarchy; they were religious radicals, not liberals. Their courage in resisting the elite provided those medieval Christians who opposed the power or doctrine of the pope with a Biblical precedent and allowed them to see themselves as the true Israel. Medieval heretics generally regarded themselves as especially holy, as a community of saints working for the ultimate triumph of God's will in the world. Both the medieval Christian Establishment and its opposition, then, derived sanction from the Hebrew Bible.

Chapter Two

THE FOUNDATIONS OF
MEDIEVAL CHRISTIANITY

I. The Transition from Judaism to Christianity

CHRISTIANITY AND POST-EXILIC JUDAISM

There are obvious continuities between Judaism and medieval Christianity, but scholars differ very much over how the teachings of Jesus fit into the story. Clearly there was much in medieval Christianity that was *not* derived from the Hebraic tradition, and it is necessary to define the essence of Christian theology in order to find out how its various elements fit together.

The essential difference between Judaism and Christianity, of course, is the concept of the Incarnation. Christians believe that the Holy Spirit assumed human form, that spirit became flesh, that Jesus Christ was both a human being and the Way to salvation—the Saviour. Man is too weak, too rebellious against God (too sinful) to reach salvation by his own efforts. This is not implausible if one assumes that righteousness consists in living a pure, puritanical life free of selfishness, aggression, materialism, and anger. Men could not get through one day without these sins; it is in man's nature to rebel against God, to fail to live as He wants us to live. (We may question the assumption that God wants man to live this way, but that is another problem.) Because man cannot live as God wants him to, he is a sinner—there is a fundamental corruption in human nature. The story of the fall of Adam is a paradigm or model of man's rebellion against the purity of mind and holiness of temperament that God demands.

Since it is impossible for man to be pure and saintly, how can God forgive him? In an apparently hopeless situation, man cannot escape from his own nature and must be eternally damned. The Christian solution is that God loves man so much, is so generous, that He gave some of Himself to redeem man. The divine spirit assumed human form and suffered, was punished for man—became man's scapegoat. God can forgive man because the God-man sacrificed Himself for all men; He saved men by His love because they could not save themselves. Man cannot be saved by his own efforts, but at a certain moment, God's love comes from outside to liberate him from the degradation of human nature.

That is the central message of early medieval Christian theology. Obviously it was very different from the Judaism of Moses, and it was once assumed that the changes all took place with the teachings of Jesus. Scholars now realize, however, that important changes occurred within Judaism itself before Jesus ever appeared. Students of post-exilic Judaism (that is, of the religious ideas of the Jews after they returned from exile in Mesopotamia in the third century B.C.) believe that Judaism was evolving during this period into a saviour-religion, and that Jews were responsible for several important steps in the development of what eventually became medieval Christianity.

In the post-exilic period, which was a time of great unhappiness and repeated foreign conquest, the Jews could see that the triumph of Zion predicted by the prophets had not taken place. The failure of Israel to achieve the promised independence and leadership caused disillusion and dismay, and inevitably, religious beliefs changed in response to circumstance and emotion as Jews tried to discover how Zion might still throw off foreign oppression.

In another aspect Judaism was unsatisfactory to many Jews after their return. To those who had contact with other Mediterranean cultures through exile or commerce—mostly sophisticated, middle-class Jews—Judaism began to seem rather bleak and impersonal. Unlike various other Near Eastern cults, Judaism was silent on immortality and on the after-life (these concepts only become a Jewish dogma at the end of the twelfth century A.D.). During the turbulent centuries after the Exile, Judaism did not satisfy the longings of the devout any more than it fulfilled the national aspirations of the patriotic. That great reward of the faithful —personal immortality—was denied to pious Jews.

Judaism was founded on the concept of rewards and punishments, and this very system led educated Jews to a question which became almost a fixation in the post-exilic period: Why does the righteous man suffer? It was obvious that sinners often flourished in this world, that rewards were unequal and often unjust. The puzzlement and concern aroused by this question is best expressed in the Book of Job—one of the most beautiful and skillful books of the Bible, but hardly an advertisement for Judaism! (Scholars believe that its happy ending was added by a later writer who found the book too disturbing as it was written.) Job is a good man, a thoroughly righteous man visited with a terrible series of calamities—deaths in his family, ill health, loss of livelihood, and so on. His friends insist, at first, that Job cannot be the good man he seems, that God must be punishing him for some hidden sin. Perhaps his apparent philanthropy is nothing but an expression of pride, a cover for a stiff-necked, rebellious spirit. If that is not the explanation, then God must be testing Job to discover how righteous he is at heart. It is easy to be good when things are going well; the test comes with trouble, when only the genuinely good man can accept God's will. (This concept is based on the assumption that suffering is good for man, which became very important in later Judaism and Christianity.) At the end of all Job's discussions with his friends, God's voice comes out of the whirlwind and orders them to be still—and it is at this point that the later writer reported that Job was rewarded by God for his patience.

The story of Job reveals many of the concerns and ideas of the post-exilic period, including a growing belief in the value of suffering. Certain thinkers began to believe that suffering is redemptive, that it purifies its victims. At the same period there developed the concept of vicarious suffering, which marked a great step toward Christian theology. In the book of Isaiah, Chapters 53 and 54, there appears a Man of Sorrows who wears a crown of thorns and suffers for others. Isaiah's Man of Sorrows represents Israel (the Jewish people), and offers an answer to those who wondered why sinful Gentiles prospered and conquered the earth while pious Jews languished in captivity. (The so-called second Isaiah, the author of the latter parts of the book of Isaiah, was an anonymous writer who probably lived in exile in Mesopotamia. His work is thought to show the influence of Zoroastrianism.)

Christians later applied the description of Israel to their own Man of Sorrows, claiming that Isaiah foretold the coming of Christ. Christians localized and personalized Isaiah's Man of Sorrows in Jesus Christ even while they made him into a universal saviour, whose wounds on the Cross were the means of salvation for all men.

Further development towards resolving the problem of suffering emerged in the first century B.C. with the idea of a personal saviour—the Messiah. There were stories of a hero from the house of Jesse and David, the king who would claim his birthright as a ruler of Israel, throw off the yoke of the Romans, and bring about the long-awaited triumph of Zion. This saviour was a human, personal messiah, a political and social being rather than a metaphysical or sacramental figure. He was not the Christian Saviour, but he was sent by God, and the appearance of messianic ideals marked another step in the evolution of Judaism toward Christianity. The doctrines of the value of suffering, of vicarious suffering, and of redemption by a messiah all pointed toward Christianity, which evolved out of late Judaism, and was later mixed with Greek and Roman ideas.

THE NEW TESTAMENT

There has been continuous and vehement debate among scholars as to the place of Jesus himself, and of St. Paul, in the transition from post-exilic Judaism to early Christianity. The debate has involved many Protestant scholars and some Jews, but until recently it was ignored by most Roman Catholics, largely because the Church denied the evolutionary development of Christianity. Until this century, Catholic churchmen liked to imply that the medieval (and modern) Church sprang full-blown from the head of Jesus. In this century, however, liberal Catholics, using an Aristotelian term, say that the modern Church was *potential* in earliest Christianity, and Catholic scholars have joined in the arguments over origins. In this field as in many others, the intellectual emancipation of present-day Catholicism has powered a creative burst of intellectual activity among Catholics. The Church is no longer an anti-intellectual institution, and Biblical scholarship has shared in the benefits of the change.

There are three dominant schools of interpretation of the

historical significance of the New Testament, especially of the Gospels. These are not necessarily contradictory, but they emphasize different aspects of the problem. Scholars of the Higher Criticism (developed in Germany in the second half of the nineteenth century) decided that Matthew, Mark, and Luke tell roughly the same story—not entirely the same, but their accounts have much in common. These three Gospels must have been derived from a common source, an account of Jesus' life and teachings by a contemporary (or contemporaries), or near-contemporary. That source has disappeared, but the first three Gospels were based upon it by the later writers. The Gospel of St. John is quite different; it is a reinterpretation of Jesus and of the Christian message in terms of Platonic philosophy. The interpretation of Jesus in Matthew, Mark, and Luke is a development out of and beyond post-exilic Judaism, but John gives a full-fledged theology of the Incarnation, with Jesus as a divine Saviour. He begins "In the beginning was the Word"—the *logos,* the divine Idea of Plato. According to the Higher Criticism (and it was enormously influential), the first three Gospels were written between 40 and 70 A.D.; John between 100 and 120.

A second school, the "liberal" interpretation of the New Testament, appeared first in Germany and flourished (particularly in the United States) in the first forty years of the twentieth century. According to this view, Jesus was a saintly, holy man who taught a philosophy of social righteousness. He was a radical social leader who preached non-violence, pacifism, and generosity, and favored the poor and downtrodden over the rich and powerful.

The third school is headed by Rudolph Bultmann, a distinguished German Biblical scholar and philolologist who is a neo-Lutheran or neo-Augustinian. Bultmann believes that the New Testament is not a historical document but a collection of legends and "midrash," or commentary. The Gospels are a group of stories about a teacher of righteousness, stories of a kind commonly told in later Judaism about saintly men and important rabbis, and they offer very little biographical information or theological principle. However, Bultmann is convinced that Jesus was firmly rooted in the eschatological tradition of post-exilic Judaism, that he was out not to reform the world or its institutions but to preach its end, to warn men that their sinfulness and corruption could be overcome only by divine intervention.

The appearance in 1947 of the first of the Qumran or Dead Sea Scrolls aroused great excitement and curiosity among Biblical scholars, who had high hopes of new information and understanding of the life and teachings of Jesus. The Scrolls have given us some new insights into Jesus' world and his message, but nothing startlingly new. They do show, for instance, that John the Baptist was a historical figure, that baptism was a common rite in Jewish circles, that Jesus' lifetime was a period of great millennial, apocalyptic, messianic yearnings among Jews, and that groups were gathering around various kinds of hellfire-and-damnation preachers, of whom Jesus may have been one. The Scrolls tell of groups of Jews who withdrew to communities around the Dead Sea to lead a form of monastic life. These people did not withdraw entirely from the world; they were also a military group prepared to fight the Romans. (Scholars already knew most of this, but the Scrolls have deepened their understanding of such phenomena.) There was one such group, called the Essenes, which was much involved in apocalyptic and millennial speculations and preached a stern morality, and John the Baptist (or Jesus himself) may have been an Essene, or influenced by the Essenes.

After centuries of argument and speculation about the life and teachings of Jesus, what is really known about him can be stated in a few simple paragraphs. Jesus came from the north of Judea and appeared in Jerusalem with a small group of followers who were poor men, mostly fishermen. The Jews of that time were extremely bitter and disturbed under Roman rule, and Jesus responded to their anguish, as did many preachers and teachers then at work in the streets and temples. Jesus proclaimed that the kingdom of God was within and advised men to worry about their own souls instead of social revolution or national redemption. The only good thing in the world is love—love of man for man and of man for God—and a man must find love and goodness within himself, must turn his mind from aggression and anger to peace and joy. The world was approaching its end, and this was the last moment to save oneself, to become humble and poor in spirit, and to love God and condemn the world. The only revolution that mattered was the revolution of the human heart.

That was the essence of Jesus' message, and he kept repeating it although people wanted him to say much more. When officials tried to trap him into denying that taxes should be paid to Rome, he held up a coin and showed them the likeness of Caesar, saying "Render therefore to Caesar the things that are Caesar's, and to God the things that are God's."[2] Again, he called himself the "Son of Man" (a phrase used by Jews to refer to the Messiah), but if he thought of himself as a messiah at all, it was in the old sense of a preacher of righteousness or helper of men rather than a national saviour against the Romans or the Saviour-God of later Christianity. His was a simple teaching, and not new. Jesus talked about those elements of Judaism that emphasized love, justice, non-violence, joy, and brotherhood.

Jesus' teaching was simple and his influence small, but he preached at a time when the Jewish community was profoundly disturbed and its leaders fearful of sedition and rebellion. There were active underground organizations whose members stored arms and planned assassinations, and Jesus became a victim of Jewish resistance and Roman fears. Anyone who gathered a crowd in Jerusalem was likely to get into trouble, and finally Jesus was arrested. The Roman governor, Pontius Pilate, was an unintelligent and insecure official who believed that the execution of a supposed leader of the undergound would please his superiors. He offered the crowd a choice between Jesus and Barabbas (who is described in the Bible as a robber but may have been a genuine leader of the Jewish underground), and the crowd preferred to save Barabbas. Jesus was crucified (a common Roman method of execution), and his disciples ran away.

The disciples saw visions of Jesus a few days after his death; they believed that he had risen from the dead, and certainly he stayed alive in their memories. They returned to Jerusalem after the excitement died down and began to meet regularly to share a meal and talk about Jesus. He was crucified during Passover, and at the *seder* on the evening before the execution, Jesus (knowing that he was to die) may have asked his disciples to remember him when they gathered to eat the unleavened bread and drink the wine of Passover.

After his death the disciples met frequently to re-enact this last supper, and even in their poverty and obscurity, their evident contentment began to attract some attention. People wondered why such poor, simple men should seem so happy: they annoyed

[2] R.S.V. Matthew 22:21.

the synagogue authorities and fascinated other poor men who hoped to share in their secret. The disciples told others about Jesus when they were questioned, and the story began to spread, but their answers did not add up to anything resembling a new religion. Nothing tremendous had happened: in the years immediately following the Crucifixion, the Christians were a tiny group of poor men who met to remember a man who preached ancient, simple aspects of Judaism—devotion to God and purity of heart.

THE CONVERSION AND TEACHING OF ST. PAUL

The next stage in the development of Christianity came with the appearance of Saul of Tarsus—Paul—the creator of Christianity as it developed into a new religion. Saul was very unlike the disciples of Jesus. He was a wealthy, prominent Jew from Asia Minor, a learned man who spoke several languages and had studied classical philosophy. Saul went to investigate reports of sectarian troubles in the Jewish community of Jerusalem and discovered (and harassed) a group of Christians, whose ideas were beginning to spread to other Jewish communities in the eastern Mediterranean world. Then, as for several centuries, there were many more Jews in the Diaspora than in Judea. Hearing of a Christian sect in Damascus, Saul set out to warn the Jewish community there against admitting Christians to their synagogue. On the road to Damascus Jesus appeared to him in a vision, asking "Saul, Saul, why do you persecute me?"[3]

From that day on, Saul was the most dedicated and devoted of the followers of Christ. He had never met Jesus, but had heard of him and before the vision hated him. (There is some evidence that Saul was an epileptic, and there is speculation that his vision occurred during a seizure.) In any case, Saul (in Greek, Paul) returned to Jerusalem, where he presented himself to the Christian community. From the beginning there was tension between Paul and the disciples—between the wealthy, middle-class scholar and the illiterate fishermen—and Paul soon departed to preach the Gospel to the Jews of the Diaspora. He was a brilliant, forceful speaker who spoke several languages, looked respectable, and was accepted in synagogues throughout the Mediterranean

[3] R.S.V. Acts 9:4.

world. Paul angered and upset a great many people, but he also persuaded large numbers of converts. His eloquence, power, and charisma won wide acceptance for his interpretation of the life and work of Jesus.

The response to Paul came from Gentiles as well as Jews. The slums of the cities of the eastern Mediterranean teemed with unhappy, frightened people who lived in a world of political instability, desperate poverty, and natural disasters, and these people found the message of the Gospel ("the Good News") very attractive. Jesus said that what is in a man's heart is more important than his group or background, and Paul stretched that concept to include the Gentiles in his mission. Not all of his converts lived in slums, however: many were wealthy, respectable men who wished to accept Christianity without becoming Jews. The great stumbling-block was circumcision—a major operation for an adult (especially in those days) and a source of shame and humiliation to a Roman citizen in the public baths. However, the original disciples, including Simon Peter and James (the brother of Jesus), argued that the followers of Jesus must accept and live by the law of Moses. There was a major controversy between Paul and the disciples, some of which is reflected in New Testament writings, but in the end Paul won his point. He had to win: he had wealth and followers while the disciples had nothing, and he would have gone ahead with his new Christianity even if they had not agreed with him.

By this time, Paul had elaborated the simple teaching of Jesus —part of ancient Judaism—into a new and universal religion. Christianity, according to Paul, was a new dispensation, a new witness (testament), a new chapter in history—a new religion for all people. He preached (at least in the beginning) that his was an inward religion of love, that the depths of the human heart were more important than the law. To Paul, the Torah was a snare because its negative approach ("Thou shalt not") promoted rebellion. Genuine goodness was spontaneous; it arose from within and was not encouraged by interdictions. It was Paul, not Jesus, who believed that the new dispensation made the Torah obsolete. As far as anyone knows, Paul remained an observant Jew until his death, but he believed that the law of Moses was not necessary to Christians.

Paul also preached the corruption of man, that man is too

wicked to save himself by his own efforts. The prophets were wrong to demand that man reform and save himself; man cannot be holy unless God saves him. God decides who shall be saved, which men shall have faith and righteousness and which shall fall back on their own resources and be doomed. It is likely (but not certain) that Paul also taught that Jesus was the divine Son of God—God in human form, by whose sufferings men are saved. It is not clear from the surviving writings of Paul whether he believed that Jesus was simply a teacher of righteousness—the Messiah (Teacher) of the new dispensation—or a divine Messiah who came from God to save mankind; whether Jesus showed the way or *was* the Way. Belief in the divinity of Christ may have become part of Christianity after Paul, but Paul certainly moved in that direction. He taught that Judaism is not enough, that obedience to the Torah cannot save men, that salvation takes place within the human heart but comes as a gift ("grace") from God.

After many years of travel and preaching all over the Mediterranean world, Paul began to fear that his message of love might lead to anarchy. In many ways he was a paradoxical figure: a stern, conservative, disciplined man whose religion was one of love and freedom from the strictures of the law. Later in his career, Paul began to stress the necessity of leadership and authority even in Christian communities where salvation was accepted as an inward grace. God loves everyone, but that does not give men the freedom to indulge all their desires. Men need leaders, and Christian leaders must be obeyed because they know more than other men and are closer to God. Christians were a community, a flock, and each flock had its shepherd, or bishop, whose authority must be recognized by the faithful. Thus St. Paul became the founder of the hierarchy of the Christian Church as well as much of its theology.

II. The Church and the Empire

THE FIRST CHRISTIAN CENTURIES

The development of the Church between the death of St. Paul (in about the middle of the first century A.D.) and the conversion of the Emperor Constantine (in 312 A.D.) was much affected by its status as an illegal organization. The Church expanded steadily in size and influence throughout this period, particularly in the eastern, Greek-speaking part of the Empire which had most of the population. After the year 200, about 10 per cent of the people in the eastern part of the Empire were Christians, and by the end of the third century there may have been 20 million Christians in the Roman Empire—out of a population of about 70 million. Probably the Church was a secret, hermetic organization until at least the late second century, but that was a common characteristic of the mystery religions that flourished in the late Empire. By the late third century, then, the Church was still in a legal sense underground—but it was also a vast and wealthy international organization whose membership included 20 to 25 per cent of the people of the Roman Empire.

Obviously, the inner development of Christianity was in part dependent on growth and the passage of time; inevitably, it was affected by its social and physical environment and cultural milieu. As new members joined the Church, they introduced their own backgrounds and concerns. Also, the Church accommodated itself, to some extent, to existing circumstances—that is, to the institutions of the Empire. Its own organization developed along the territorial and institutional lines of the Empire, and cultural and philosophical strains appeared within Christianity that were neither Hebraic nor apostolic. From one point of view, then, the Church was thus corrupted from pure, apostolic Christianity. On the other hand, it may be claimed that only thus could the Church progress, adapting itself to a changing world, to new people and new ideas.

By and large, the Church of the Roman Empire adopted conservative social attitudes. Some institutions or attitudes of Rome were clearly contrary to the standards of Christian morality, but little protest was heard from Christian bishops. Romans idolized their emperors, even worshipped them as gods; one-quarter of the population of the Empire was enslaved; scenes of unspeakable cruelty and horror took place in the Roman circus, where public executions and public torture were the major diversions of the Roman populace; perhaps 20 per cent of the female urban population of the Empire were licensed prostitutes. None of these things accorded with Christian morality, yet (for the most part) the

Church was silent. Certainly Christians did not approve of the state religious cults, and they avoided participation in these when they could. Bishops expressed disapproval of public executions, prostitution, and mistreatment of women, but disapproval did not imply outspoken protest or rebellion. Churchmen were almost entirely silent on the subject of slavery, and even when they complained of the moral atmosphere of the Empire, they apparently had no thought of forcing any changes.

One explanation for the accommodation of Church and Empire might be that Christianity was not primarily or only a religion of slaves and of the downtrodden. Many (or most) of the Christians of the Empire came from the middle classes, and a few from the ranks of the aristocracy. The men who rose to be leaders of the Church were particularly apt to be of substantial family, to be well educated, to be unlikely to attack the prevailing social order. Also, of course, they were afraid: the Church was an illegal institution which was tolerated just as long as it did not cause serious trouble. Most of the emperors (except for a maniac like Nero, who persecuted everyone) left the Christians alone, and indeed Trajan established indifference as official imperial policy in the first century A.D. By keeping quiet, by making it possible for the Empire to tolerate it, the Church became increasingly conservative in the first three centuries.

During these same centuries, Christian doctrine was profoundly affected by classical thought, particularly by Platonism. The dualism of the body and soul entered Christian theology, and this Platonic idea became a central, persistent strain in Christian teaching. Dualism can easily be used to justify social conservatism, because if the body perishes while the soul is immortal, then the life of the body is not very important. The material world, and how people live in it—whether slaves are emancipated and hungry people fed is relatively trivial; cruelty and slavery can be tolerated if men can look forward to heaven. This world is not good (Christians always noticed the evils around them), but heaven must be a wonderful place where God makes up to His people for their sufferings on earth. The Church accepted slavery on the strengths of such arguments until the Protestants took up the cause of emancipation in the nineteenth century; in sixteenth-century Spain, Christians were still arguing over whether black slaves had souls or were animal creations of the Lord.

The Church developed a strict, organized hierarchy during its first three centuries. This included a distinct priesthood, with priests separated from lay Christians; Christian priests became officeholders on the Roman model. Just as Roman governors exercised the power of the state quite apart (and regardless of) their personal qualities, so Christian priests carried the power of the Holy Spirit. Of course priests *should* lead a moral life, but their power and effectiveness was not derived from personal qualities or puritanical lives. Like the Empire, the Church worked out a strict system of hierarchy based on levels reminiscent of the Platonic concept of the Chain of Being, the continuous hierarchy between pure matter and pure Idea. In the Christian Church, obedience was due from priest up to bishop, from bishop to archbishop, and from archbishop up to the pope father in the West and the patriarchs in the East. Borrowing Platonic philosophy and the Roman system of government, the Church developed the Christian priesthood, with its priests set apart from ordinary men. Jesus never made that distinction, although modern Roman Catholics argue that the distinction was implicit—or potential—in apostolic Christianity.

Under the Empire, Christianity developed a distinct and complex culture. It was heavily classical, with elements of Greek philosophy, Roman law, and classical rhetoric. Christians did not develop their own language, philosophy, law, or even organization—they adapted what they found. Tertullian, the North African priest of the late second century who disapproved of the classics, thundered "What has Athens to do with Jerusalem?" Even Tertullian, however, used an oratorical style based on classical rhetoric. Some of the Christians denounced elements of classical culture, but almost all of them made use of it: they absorbed classicism in speech and thought.

Churchmen did censor classical literature for their own students; rejecting much of the eroticism of Roman prose and poetry, they simply obliterated certain passages and ignored certain books. Certainly they did not believe in freedom of thought, and they felt entirely justified in censoring what they did not approve. They set up their own schools based on Roman models and the study of grammar and rhetoric. Obviously these were good schools, because the men who ran the Church in the first three centuries were able and well educated. They made an underground religion into a successful, universal institution—an achievement requiring astute, tough, and determined leadership. One may question how well these early priests and bishops served Christianity by making the Church a viable imperial institution—did they betray the ideals of Jesus when they created a conservative social organization?— but it is impossible to question their effectiveness.

Philosophically, too, the Christians of the Empire made a great many changes in apostolic Christianity. The Hebrew Bible, with its stories of violence and savagery among primitive tribal peoples, was not very attractive to Romans, partly because Jews were very unpopular in the later Empire. Roman Christians solved this problem by allegorizing the Bible, by agreeing with Paul that the spirit and not the letter of the law (and the Bible) is important. The struggles of these obscure Jews depicted in the Old Testament were allegorical representations of spiritual truth, not historical facts, and if the Bible were symbolic of mystical truth, then its deeper meanings could be interpreted in accordance with Platonic philosophy.

The allegorization of the Bible was attempted first by a Jew, not a Christian classicist. Philo Judaeus, a prominent member of the Jewish community in Alexandria in the first century A.D., approached the Hebrew Bible as the allegorical expression of a deeper philosophy which could be synthesized with Platonism. Philo's writings had little influence on Judaism, because the Alexandrian community had almost disappeared (through assimilation and persecution) by the fourth century, while the Mesopotamian Jewish community and its orthodox legalistic Talmud survived to become the dominant influence on the development of medieval Judaism. There was, however, an active Christian community in first-century Alexandria, and Greek-speaking Christian scholars took up Philo's ideas and applied them to the New Testament as well as the Old.

Christian scholars searched the Bible for "deeper" meanings compatible with Platonic philosophy, and they discovered such concepts as the dualism and separation of body and soul, personal immortality, the Trinity, and the Incarnation. It is doubtful that any of these theological bases of later Christianity were expressed in the Gospels (at least in the first three Gospels), but Christians of the later Empire sought and found them. Christianity was once again transformed into a new religion—a mystical, sacramental, hierarchic, Platonized religion acceptable to Roman citizens. The simple message of love and humility was not well suited to classically-educated gentlemen, so they adapted it to meet their needs. Constant growth, transformation, and adaptation is a continuing theme in the history of ancient and medieval Christianity.

THE FALL OF ROME

The causes and consequences of the fall of the Roman Empire have been inexhaustible subjects for speculation and argument. Historians have even questioned whether there was such a phenomenon as a fall—perhaps the Empire just gradually disappeared. However, it is quite obvious that in the political-military context at least, something happened in the fifth century. For the first time, the Romans were unable to drive German invaders out of the western part of the Empire. As early as 406 A.D., large areas of Gaul, Spain, and North Africa were out of the emperor's control, and by 430, the western emperor ruled in name only. There was a semblance of imperial government until 476, but the real turning point was 430: after that date, the old Roman Empire no longer functioned. However, the eastern, Greek-speaking part of the Empire (with 60–70 per cent of the imperial population) survived for centuries. This "Byzantine" Empire did not fall finally until the Turks took Constantinople in 1453, although it was temporarily in the hands of Crusaders from the West in the thirteenth century.

In the fifth century, then, the western Roman Empire could no longer defend itself against invaders. For strategic and military reasons including a breakdown in communications, lack of resources, and bad generalship, Rome was beaten in battle and the old Empire collapsed as a political entity. German rulers replaced the emperor, and the Empire was divided into several German kingdoms. Despite revolutionary political change, however, it is fairly clear that the social and political institutions and the culture of the late Empire did not vanish, but were replaced only gradually (and never completely) over the next two centuries. Modern historians, by and large, regard the fall of Rome not as a single military disaster but the consequence of long-range internal processes. Most historians believe that the collapse was not a German triumph but merely the final chapter of the decline of Rome, that the late Empire was a "hollow husk" vulnerable to anyone—even to primitive Germans.

This interpretation was first propounded by Edward Gibbon in *The Decline and Fall of the Roman Empire,* an early and still influential book on the subject. Like all eighteenth-century historians, Gibbon concentrated on narrative rather than analysis, but he did halt his narrative to append to Chapter 38 a discussion of the reasons for the fall of Rome. He offered two explanations, of which the first has been widely accepted. The Empire, said Gibbon, collapsed under its own weight. It grew too vast to be supported by its institutions, communications, education, resources, and legal structure. Managing the Roman Empire was an enormous, exhausting task which demanded constant attention and hard work, and the balancing act finally toppled. The twentieth-century French historian Ferdinand Lot elaborates this thesis in *The End of the Ancient World,* in which he described various aspects of the imperial structure (government, economy, morale, and so on) and showed that each had grave functional problems. These problems expanded like snowballs until the entire structure collapsed.

Gibbon's other explanation for the decline of Rome was the success of Christianity. (He did not say that Christianity alone caused the decline, but it was one factor.) With its other-worldly ethic, Christianity distracted the Roman elite from the problems of the Empire, which could be solved only by intense and continuous application. The Church was a distraction—and indeed, Christianity was indifferent if not hostile to secular pursuits. Also, the Church deprived the Empire of its natural leaders, as able and educated men chose to become bishops and abbots rather than imperial governors. One might answer that this was not entirely the fault of the Church, that these men must have been alienated from the state to begin with. By the late Empire, government must have seemed a difficult and dangerous (if not a hopeless) job, and many men looked for alternative careers.

There is no doubt that the Empire had very serious economic problems, and many historians have blamed these difficulties for its collapse. But these economic problems were not new. The Empire was not a strong economic entity at any time, and although its weaknesses became more apparent after the second century A.D. (when the Romans stopped plundering newly-conquered people), it is questionable whether they became sufficiently serious to cause the fall of Rome. There is evidence of economic deterioration (for example, of a decline of trade after the year 200), but the evidence does not include the kind of reliable statistical information that would permit quantitative conclusions. Societies always undergo economic change of one kind or another, but change does not always signify disaster.

We do know that the population of the Empire declined markedly, perhaps by 20 per cent between 250 and 400 A.D. This happened primarily because of a great outbreak of bubonic plague in the fourth century. The decline in population shrank the markets, reduced the volume of trade, diminished international exchange, and thus weakened the relationship of various parts of the Empire. Separate regions grew more localized, turned in on themselves, and thus may have weakened the political unity of the whole. Commerce declined for other reasons, too—notably because of the Romans' failure to develop any industrial technology. Without a factory production system there was no specialization, and handicrafted goods could be produced anywhere: there was no need to import pottery from Greece when it could be produced in Gaul. Between 200 and 400 A.D., partly through population decline and partly through failure to industrialize, the volume of trade may have declined by 50 to 80 per cent.

Did economic crisis contribute to political disunity and disaster? After all, citizens in various parts of the Empire might have looked to Rome for solutions to their economic problems, thus strengthening the central government. (This happened in the United States in the 1930s.) Perhaps they did turn to Rome, but if so, the imperial government provoked greater alienation and disloyalty by its inability or unwillingness to help. Taxation was extremely heavy by the late Empire, and merchants and wealthy townspeople undoubtedly resented paying large taxes when they got little or nothing in return. Undoubtedly, the combination of economic difficulties and government ineffectiveness caused widespread hostility to the state.

Another factor in the decline of Rome was slavery: the Empire rose and fell as a slave society. It is argued that Rome's failure to develop an industrial technology caused economic disintegration, and that this failure was a direct result of slavery. For the first two centuries A.D. Romans could rely on slave power for all their needs, and this inhibited technological change. After 200, with the end of the wars of conquest, there was a severe shortage of man-power, but by the time this became critical (in the fourth century) it was too late to industrialize. Historians speculate that it was too late because the institution of slavery had left its ineradicable mark upon the attitudes and life style of the Roman elite. It was beneath the dignity and outside the competence of the upper classes to involve themselves in production. The upper classes lived off inherited land and slaves, contributing nothing to the economy and concentrating on a purely literary form of education that prepared their sons only for government. Because the economic base had seemed perfectly secure, aristocrats were not trained to apply themselves to economic problems. When production, economy, and slave power declined, the Roman forms of life and education were too deeply entrenched to adjust to changed circumstances.

This seems a rather deterministic interpretation, but there is an interesting parallel in Chinese history. China had a vigorous industrial technology at the end of the first millennium A.D., a more refined system than anything in Europe even in the fifteenth century—travellers from the West (like Marco Polo) were much impressed with what they found. However, the Chinese ruling class gradually retired from involvement in economic matters, and by the sixteenth and seventeenth centuries the education and interests of the mandarins were purely literary and intellectual. They lost interest in and even knowledge of science that could be applied in technological development. By the middle of the eighteenth century, when the Chinese economy was in desperate need of revitalization (and of the application of scientific knowledge) in order to compete with western industrial powers—and indeed to resist western invasion—the mandarin class was so traditional, so congealed in its genteel style, that it was unable to recover what it once had had. Even in the face of military threat and economic disaster, it was too unprogressive to adjust to changed circumstances.

Like the mandarins, the Roman aristocrats could not or would not recognize the changes around them, and this is obvious from contemporary letters and writings. It is true that they had adjusted to Christianity, but that was a scribal religion based on a written text, and they could accept a new religion more easily than they could jettison their literary culture in favor of practical endeavors.

The problems of Rome were severe, but by no means insurmountable. All societies have problems, and very often they are resolved, but the Romans suffered a failure of leadership that made it impossible to solve problems because they were not even recognized. They let difficulties get too complex without attacking them, and the Germans took advantage of their mistakes. The Empire never reached a point of total disintegration, but it was rapidly moving toward it when the Germans took over.

The disproportion between German and Roman arms has often been exaggerated by historians who imply that Rome must have been a "hollow husk" if with its enormous resources of men and arms it could not drive out the barbarian tribes. Certainly the Germans were outnumbered and inferior in arms, but the disproportion was not so great as it seems because the Romans, for a variety of reasons, were unable to bring their full power to bear. First of all, they were greatly hampered by their traditions of recruitment and military service. According to Livy, Rome was once a nation in arms; in the early days of the Republic, every Roman male would drop his plow or pen to rush to the defense of the state or to conquest. This may or may not be an accurate description of the republican attitude, but it certainly was never true of the Empire. Even by the first century A.D. it seemed perfectly natural to the Romans that their legions were manned by mercenaries. Middle-class citizens—city people—did not want to fight, and aristocrats were not often allowed to join the army. Senators and emperors had bitter experience with aristocratic generals who built up large private followings and then marched on Rome (Julius Caesar was only one of such officers), and those whose loyalty was certain were needed as governors and officials. With the middle and upper classes excluded, the army had to fill its ranks with freedmen, dispossessed peasants, city rabble (notoriously bad soldiers, partly because they were undernourished)—and Germans. After about 100 A.D., hundreds of Germans waited along the Rhine-Danube frontier for an opportunity to move into the Empire. Conquest would have seemed inconceivable then; these tribes wanted only to settle down. The Romans made treaties with certain German chieftains, allowing them to cross the river and become mercenary allies (called *federates* later in the fourth century) who fought to defend Rome against their own kinsmen. This was not an ideal arrangement, but it worked fairly well for two or three hundred years. The Romans never had as many soldiers as they needed, and as the population declined they relied more and more on German mercenaries. In 200 A.D. the proportion of Germans in the army may have been 5 to 10 per cent; in 400 A.D. it was perhaps somewhere between 30 and 50 per cent.

There was a serious shortage of officers, too, and in the later Empire they often were promoted from the ranks. (Constantine's father, for example, was a Balkan peasant who worked all the way up to assistant emperor.) These officers were able men, by and large, but they were Balkan peasants or Germans who had spent their entire lives in the army. They lacked education or training in the Roman traditions, and their loyalty was more likely to be directed toward the army itself than the Roman state. They served in the army to advance themselves, and if they were not successful they were apt to become dangerous. Certainly Vergil, or Cicero, or Livy meant little or nothing to these officers; they had no training in citizenship or devotion to the state. When it came to a crisis, the men on whom Rome depended (because of its system of recruitment) knew and cared nothing of Roman history, law, or tradition.

Like most empires, the Roman Empire required vast quantities of men and money simply for defense. It had an incredibly long frontier with few natural defenses (the Rhine-Danube system was a natural defense, but not a very good one—it could be crossed). The Empire stretched from Scotland to Central Asia, and from Austria into the Sahara—a fantastic extent. The Roman frontier was so long and open that three to five million men would have been necessary for a secure defense—and there were only fifty million citizens of the Empire. It might have been possible, in a society like the Republic as described by Livy, to mount such a defense, but the Romans of the Empire were not interested in joining the army. The old Roman aristocracy enjoyed fighting, but their descendants—and the other classes in society—did not.

The Roman army was chronically understaffed, and its leaders continually faced the problem of where their men might be most

effective. The so-called military reforms of Constantine and Diocletian (early fourth century) were in a sense confessions of failure,
for many legions were withdraw from the frontier and stationed
in central places from which they could move into trouble spots as
these appeared. The Romans abandoned the stationary defense
(which they could not manage) for a more mobile policy. It was a
good idea, but communications and transportation were not fast
enough to move men to a battle before it was well under way if
not over. At the Battle of Adrianople in 378 A.D., the first defeat
of Rome by Germans, the emperor waited for reinforcements until
he became impatient enough to go ahead without them and was
killed and defeated. That battle was critical even though it settled
nothing politically, because it showed the Germans that Romans
were not invincible. Any German tribe, or *volk*, was tiny in comparison to Rome (perhaps 20,000 men at most), but even 20,000
men was more than Rome could usually put into the field at any
one place or time. The Empire was not necessarily a hollow husk,
but it was fatally unable to adjust its military system (in recruitment, tactics, and organization) to meet new challenges and changed
circumstances.

There is one factor in the fall of Rome which is often over-
looked or misunderstood, and that is the extent to which the Empire was ever a genuine unity. In the beginning, certainly, imperial
unity was artificial, and in many ways this remained true to the
end. The Romans were vicious, aggressive conquerors, but as rulers
they were fairly beneficent—of necessity: they had neither the men
nor the materials to run an oppressive regime. In the first two
centuries A.D. the Roman rulers demanded very little of the conquered people. Taxes were extremely low (almost negligible); there
was no real economic control or interference; the cities had self-
government; people were allowed to speak their own languages
and worship their own gods as long as they worshipped the emperor too (and here the Jews got into trouble). With only a few
thousand aristocrats to govern its Empire, Rome could not establish the kind of stern, oppressive system that could enforce heavy
demands. Individual aristocrats made large private fortunes out
of the business of government, but they did so in an Empire which
was not much more than a superficial political unity imposed upon
the old Mediterranean variety of cultures, societies, and economies.
After 200 A.D., when the Empire began to get into economic

and military trouble, the Romans began to demand much more. Heavy taxes were levied, and the emperor decided to put an end to local autonomy, partly in order to get more money out of the cities. Economic controls, such as Diocletian's edict on prices, were very unpopular. A tough, centralized administration was attempted, and although this was never very successful (due to a primitive communications system), it was totalitarian in spirit if not in practice. Finally, when fanatic Christian bishops convinced the emperors in the late fourth century that there was only one true religion and all others must be proscribed, the Empire began to try to control thought. In the end, Roman Catholicism alone could be practiced in the West and Greek Orthodoxy in the East, and there was an end to freedom of religion and culture.

The new controls made people extremely restless and unhappy; they began to wonder what they were getting in return for their money and their loyalty (if any). The Empire was no longer providing protection in return for negligible taxes and a token allegiance; it was making severe demands on the populace. Furthermore, people had forgotten the horrors of war and foreign invasion during the long peace. The Germans did not look too frightening, and it was believed that taxes would be lower under their regime—as indeed they were! It is often said that the Romans of the late Empire lost their public spirit, but this is not to say that they had become corrupt. Indeed, in private morality they were much more puritanical under Christian rule than under the license and permissiveness of the first century A.D. However, the Empire had become a burden, and when great demands were made on its constituents the essential artificiality of the imperial structure was revealed. Many people had never been genuinely committed to Rome or involved with the Empire, and they were not very much distressed at the prospect of its defeat.

III. Patristic Thought

FOURTH-CENTURY CHRISTIANITY

The ideas and opinions of a few great thinkers of the fourth and early fifth centuries molded the outlook of the medieval western (Latin) Church. The term is old fashioned, but St. Jerome, St. Ambrose, and St. Augustine were in a real sense "Fathers" of the Roman Catholic Church of the Middle Ages. In the same period Eusebius, bishop of Caesarea, friend and advisor to the Emperor Constantine, and one of the Fathers of the Greek Church, also exercised a strong influence on the development of western Christianity.

Medieval Christians did not always follow the teachings of the fourth-century Fathers (although most of them claimed that they did), but the authority of these men remained second only to that of the Bible. Among thirteenth-century scholars, for example, a reference to St. Augustine was almost as unimpeachable as a quotation from Scripture, although (like Biblical quotations) it might be answered by reference from the same source that proved the opposite. The Church Fathers were men of great sophistication, and their writings wove various strands of thought into the Christian synthesis. Their ideas were not always consistent: they could be arranged along a spectrum more easily than a closed circle, but they shared a great many important assumptions.

Any society has groups that can be identified with prevailing social patterns and institutions and others which oppose or defy the Establishment. The Roman Empire of the third century had its critics and enemies, including Jews, nationalistic groups from the eastern Mediterranean, and certain Romans of ancient aristocratic families who had never accepted the rule of the Caesars. The largest and most important group in opposition to the Empire (or at least unconvinced that it was the best of all possible worlds and the end of history) was that of the Christians, who had serious reservations about Roman morality and political philosophy.

The differences between Christianity and imperial Rome were implicit from the beginning of the Christian era, but churchmen tended to avoid direct confrontation with the imperial authorities —partly because they lacked the wherewithal to defy the Empire, and partly because they believed sincerely that the end of the world was at hand. Christ said "Render unto Caesar the things that are Caesar's," and the early Christians avoided challenging Roman ethics, believing that Caesar would not be able to enjoy his worldly possessions very long. St. Paul was concerned that Christians should have the opportunity to proselytize, to gain converts, under the Empire; he did not want to risk the destruction of his infant

Church by a direct challenge to Caesar. "The powers that be are ordained by God, and be ye in subjection to the higher powers."[4]

By the end of the second century A.D., however, Christians were no longer convinced that the end of the world was necessarily imminent and that pagan culture could be ignored. Tertullian (a North African bishop) uttered statements of serious dissent from Roman power and classical culture. Confrontations increased, and in the third century there were great persecutions of Christians throughout the Empire.

Very suddenly, with the conversion of the Emperor Constantine early in the fourth century, the once-persecuted became the victors and the religious, social, and intellectual atmosphere of the Empire underwent rapid and profound transformation. Constantine became the great benefactor of the Christian Church—now a prosperous, fashionable institution with flocks of new adherents. Church membership was dangerous to an ambitious man in 300; by 315 (in the West at least), it was advantageous. Significant intellectual adjustment was required, as churchmen moved into positions of influence where they were supported and protected by the emperor and the imperial family. Understandably, certain clerics saw the emperor as a man of destiny who came from the North to conquer Rome and redeem the Church from persecution. These men regarded the conversion of Constantine as the most wonderful event since the Resurrection, and they were not likely to criticize the Christian Empire. Their attitude was one of accommodation: they believed in the identification of Church and Empire. Christians had always preached that the individual soul was all-important, that the kingdom of God was within—and their cooperation with the state was in one sense a betrayal of their highest ideals. In the light of the events of the fourth century, however, it is understandable.

Eusebius, advisor to Constantine and chief spokesman for the newly-established Church, explained that Christ's birth in the reign of Augustus proved that Church and Empire were partners. Born at the same time, the two institutions would coexist in triumph until the Second Coming. Eusebius and his colleagues sanctified the Empire, and they were as lavish in support of the state as

---

[4] *Letter to the Romans*, Chap. 13.

the Christian emperor had been generous to the Church. These fourth-century churchmen gave moral and religious sanction to imperial rule; priests and bishops preached the divine appointment of the emperor and his representatives to rule Christians. The emperor was regarded as the image of God in this world, as close to God as anyone on earth can be, and this made it difficult for a Christian to criticize the emperor or his lieutenants. All the conservative implications in the political teachings of St. Paul were revived and stressed in the doctrine that opposition to the established authorities is religious error as well as treason: to resist the ruler is to resist God. This became the predominant belief of fourth-century churchmen, and it still is expressed by churchmen who appear at public functions to sanctify and bless the power and prestige of the state. From this turning-point in the fourth century grew sixteen centuries of tradition, so that it is still the norm of priestly conduct (and also of ministerial and rabbinical conduct) to support, serve, and sanctify authority.

Churchmen such as Eusebius, who actually lived through the period of persecution before Constantine, showed real fervor in the sanctification of the Christian state. Opposition or indifference to the state would have required a view of public authority as immoral or amoral machinery, but the men who committed the Church to identification with the state believed that the Christian Empire was ordained by God. They certainly did not have the point of view (or the necessary fanaticism) to refuse the imperial favor until they could be sure that the emperor ruled according to the precepts of Christianity. Constantine did, in fact, establish a degree of peace and order, but he was also a violent and angry man who had his own wife and son put to death during a fit of anger. Churchmen asked God to forgive the emperor, but they did not renounce his gifts or step forward in public dissent. The Church was joined to the state without regard to the personal character of the emperor or his public policy, and even when churchmen like St. Ambrose quarrelled publicly with the emperor later in the fourth century, they did so when the ruler hurt the Church and not when he hurt ordinary people.

Very rapidly, then, the Christian Church became an authoritarian, compromising public institution. Fourth-century churchmen became magnates of the Establishment, and most of their successors have followed in that tradition. The great exceptions, such as Martin Luther and Martin Luther King, shine brighter by contrast.

However, despite its rapid and decisive transformation from a spiritual brotherhood into an authoritarian organization, the Church never abandoned its doctrines of love, faith, inner spirituality, and self-sacrifice. Ambiguities appeared within Christianity and were perpetuated, as Christian ethics and theology came (at least potentially) into conflict with its public policy. Remnants or vestiges of the early, anti-Establishment attitudes of the underground Church survived within the institutional Church, and that conflict has made the history of Christianity noble, agonizing, and complex. Most of the vast, prolific writings of the Church Fathers reflect the adjustment of the Church to the state, but there are fragments of dissent and rebellion which became very important later on. The rebellions of the later Middle Ages took their primary inspiration from the New Testament, but they also exploited strains of anti-authoritarianism within the patristic writings.

It is complexity—or ambiguity—that gives the western Church (and western civilization) its special character. Jerome, Ambrose, Augustine, and others were great men whose lives and thoughts were not simple or polarized. Their doctrines, like those of their contemporaries, tend to be conservative, to encourage compromise with the world, but the minor strain of dissent—of liberation from the prevailing order—became very important in western Europe.

Dissent existed only in the Latin Church; in Greek Orthodoxy, the emperor was the head of the Church and the Church served the state. Byzantium and its Orthodox religion became a congealed oriental system. Temple and palace were one and the same, as they had been in Near Eastern monarchies since the third millennium B.C. In the East, the only available form of dissent was mysticism, which was of no particular benefit to society. Mysticism, like drugs, offers personal escape from intolerable circumstances. It was a very strong movement within the Byzantine Church, but it was never translated into religious reform, revolution, or social change. The Greek Church remained nearly immobile for centuries, mostly because the Church opposed the state only when the emperor directly attacked the Church (as in the iconoclastic controversy of the eighth and ninth centuries).

Only in the Latin Church (and only in European civilization) was there any attempt to apply morality to society, to create a new moral order and a better world—the kingdom of God in society as well as in men's souls. This may be an unattainable or even foolish ideal, but it is at the heart of western history and of western civilization.

St. Jerome

Unlike other important Christians of the fourth century, St. Jerome held no great office in the Church. He was not a public man or a bishop but a schoolteacher, and not an impressive figure but a pious, rather effeminate (and probably latently homosexual), timid man. Jerome came from a wealthy Roman family, and although he was born across the Adriatic from Italy, he spent most of the first part of his life in Rome and received an excellent education. Later he ran a school in Jerusalem, and throughout his life he loved to engage in pietistic, moral dialogues with various wealthy matrons about the condition of their souls.

Jerome, then, was a private man who might have been a poet or a dramatist in another era. His life revolved around two poles: the Christian Church and the love of language. Jerome had one of the great literary minds of all time, with enormous sensitivity to the meaning and esthetic of words. To such a man, all beauty is literary beauty and all meaning, literary meaning. To some extent this kind of literary sensibility must imply a liberation ethic—or some kind of resistance to authority—if only because authoritarian institutions such as governments and churches do not use language but jargon, repetitive phrases which are not supposed to have meaning but merely enforce obedience. Language has its own internalizing ethic; it is individualistic, and thus threatening to any monolithic system which demands a chorus or litany. Extreme sensitivity to the meanings of words was a burden to a devout, pious Christian and throughout his early life Jerome struggled to find Christian justification for the literary approach—a struggle reflected in his famous Dream. Jerome dreamed (so he said) that he was accused before the Judgment Seat of God of being a Ciceronian (not a Christian), and claimed that he was so upset by the dream that he went to live for five years as a hermit in the Egyptian desert. This may not be strictly true, but it is certain that he had great difficulty integrating his literary genius with the litanistic approach of the Church.

Eventually Jerome found a successful compromise. He used his linguistic sensitivity and his knowledge of Latin, Greek, and Hebrew to translate the Bible into Latin—a task worthy of his literary ambitions and yet suitable for a good servant of the Church. The job was colossal, because he had to transform as well as translate, to communicate the Holy Book of alien Near Eastern people to the Roman world, and to ordinary people as well as scholars. Jerome wrote in something between the Ciceronian Latin of intellectuals and the vulgar language of the streets (the language which eventually became vernacular French, Spanish, and Italian). His Vulgate was entirely correct and grammatical, in no way offensive to scholars, and yet it could be read and understood by the masses as long as the masses were literate at all. (It was not Jerome's fault that the schools of the Empire failed in the fifth century and that there were no literate masses to profit from his work until the eleventh or twelfth century.) This was a monumental achievement: to phrase alien concepts and words within the concepts and words of Latin, and to do so in a style acceptable to scholars and accessible to the masses. Jerome's compromise between his own inclinations and his Christian piety was of inestimable benefit to the Church and to western civilization.

St. Ambrose

Unlike Jerome, St. Ambrose was the very model of a public man. He came from an old Roman aristocratic family of the military and official class; in the fourth century, they saw which way the wind was blowing and became Christians. Ambrose was given an excellent classical education, worked his way up in government, and eventually became the governor of Milan. In the fourth century (as in the nineteenth and twentieth), Milan was a center of radicalism and upheaval. It was the second city of Italy (and remained so until the rise of Florence in the thirteenth century), but the Christian community as well as the rest of the citizens were constantly in turmoil. In the fourth century bishops were still elected at public meetings of all the worshippers, and there was a fierce dispute over the election of a bishop for Milan while Ambrose was its governor. Expecting a riot, he appeared at the meeting with his guard; the crowd shouted "Elect Ambrose!" and he became Bishop of Milan—or so goes the story.

Ambrose became the dominant force within the Christian Church in the crucial decades of the 370s and 380s (he died in 393). Naturally, he brought the attitudes of a Roman official to the Church and to society. With his bureaucratic cast of mind, he played a large role in moving the Church toward a legalistic style of ecclesiastical life and toward the establishment of canon law as a system based on punishment, duty, office, and obligation. He was deeply concerned with obedience, believing that the role of the bishop was like that of a Roman governor. Bishops had already begun to depart from their early role as pious wise men—the spontaneous leaders of the Christian flock—and Ambrose crystallized the new concept that bishops were authoritarian figures quite separate from ordinary laymen. A bishop dictates, decrees, and pronounces edicts, and the ordinary Christian is more apt to fear than love him. Ambrose himself (not Jesus) became the model and prototype for the average medieval churchman; most medieval bishops were aristocratic, efficient, legalistic administrators who concentrated on obedience and tax collection.

Ambrose also had a great influence on the attitude of the Christian Church toward love and sexuality. This was an important, difficult question, and the early Church waited a long time to take a stand on it. The earliest Christians were often accused of holding "love feasts" (although that may have been a slander), and certainly Jesus himself was unusually free and open with women, particularly with "fallen women." He treated prostitutes as his equals—most uncommon in the Roman world!—and some of his most devoted disciples were women of the streets. A censorious attitude towards women entered the Christian thought-world with St. Paul, who favored celibacy despite his admission that it is better to marry than to burn. Was sexual love a Christian experience, the fulfillment of the human personality and an expression of divine love, or an instrument of the devil? The Church did not really make up its mind until the fourth century, when Ambrose (and Augustine) threw their weight on the side of Paul.

Ambrose believed that virginity was the ideal state (especially for women), even better than celibacy. This can be regarded as a somewhat progressive attitude because it is true that women were terribly abused in the Roman world. They were regarded as machines for the gratification of men, and probably it was a step forward for a woman to regard herself as a vessel for Christ, to keep herself for God. Ambrose did thus raise the position of women somewhat above utter degradation; his ideas allowed them to be more than tools of men. However, the consequences of his stand were extremely serious in the long run.

The negative view of sexuality established in the fourth century made the Christian attitude toward love and marriage conservative, fearful, and unsatisfactory. Paul's neurotic opinions were elevated into a general code in which virginity was the "best" state for a Christian, celibacy the next best, and love within matrimony (and within the necessity for constant procreation) a fair third. This code is still entrenched in Rome, to the chagrin of modern Catholics who want the Church to adopt a more positive, humane, and sensible attitude. Certain theologians want the Church to admit that sexual love is good in itself, but the acceptance of contraception is a necessary aspect of that reform. Ambrose made contraception almost the equivalent of mass murder, with devastating long-term results. He may have had good reasons for his disapproval in the late Empire (contraception was associated with masculine aggression and irresponsibility), but the modern consequences may bring about the total destruction of the Catholic Church. Even in the Middle Ages, the Christian attitude toward sex produced obsessions and neuroses. Medieval monks indulged in flagellation and excessive fasting; and masochism, anxieties, and eccentricities reflected sexual deprivation. Under Ambrose the Church committed itself to oppose sexual pleasure, and it has never thrown off that ancient and unfortunate attitude.

St. Ambrose is most often remembered for his attitude toward the relation of Church and state; he was frequently pictured in medieval art as the stern bishop who drove the great emperor Theodosius out of the Church. Ambrose did temporarily deprive Theodosius of the sacraments (excommunication in the form particularly used for rich or powerful people). This was a radical act in that it ended the deference shown by churchmen to the state since the conversion of Constantine. Ambrose stood up to the temporal power, told the emperor to stay out of Church business, and announced that the palace belonged to the emperor and the church to the bishop. Theodosius' crime seems rather insignificant today: he ordered Ambrose to rebuild a synagogue burnt down by a zealous Christian mob—the emperor was no lover of Jews, but he did believe in law and order. Ambrose expressed the displeasure of the Church, declaring that this was not a civil matter, and he refused to allow Theodosius into the church to receive the sacraments. The emperor humbled himself, begged pardon of the bishop, and was received back into the fold.

Probably neither Ambrose nor Theodosius invested this episode with much significance, but later medieval thinkers took it very seriously. The incident was used to demonstrate that there *is* a line between Church and state, that neither institution absorbs the other, and that morals and religion are outside the jurisdiction of the emperor. So interpreted, the stand of Ambrose against Theodosius became the very beginning of a new political theory of Latin Christianity in which the Church claimed independence from the state (the Greek Church made no such distinction). Departing somewhat from Eusebian subservience, Ambrose rescued the autonomy of the Latin Church.

The Church, of course, was just as authoritarian as the Empire. Ambrose was no liberal, and neither institution expressed any concern for the rights of individual conscience. Independence was reserved for the leaders of the Church, not for individuals within the institution; it was agreed that the bishop—not the emperor— had the right to interfere in matters of morals and religion. This belief was expressed in Ambrose's famous debate with Symmachus, a wealthy and learned Roman aristocrat who was one of the few remaining pagans in the Roman upper class. Ambrose had the ancient Altar of Victory removed from the Senate house, dissociating the Christian Empire from the pagan tradition. Symmachus made a passionate, intelligent plea for freedom of conscience, asserting that there was one God but many ways to worship Him. Ambrose replied that the Church must not tolerate error, that tolerance of falsehood and evil was sinful, and that error must be rooted out. The Christians had the truth, and God gave His bishops the right and duty to persuade the world of it.

Ambrose and his colleagues made the Christian Church an

institutional, public, political organization; they gave it structure, a legal system, and an efficient bureaucracy. All these things were badly needed in order to survive the chaos of the early Middle Ages.

An authoritarian Church was bound to demand a certain autonomy as a functioning political institution, and that requirement held the seeds of various anti-Establishment movements. Certainly these churchmen were not libertarians. They believed that just as the emperor had the responsibility to maintain order, so the bishop had the responsibility to maintain theology and morals—by force, if necessary. However, their political Church did become a second authority in the world, and its very existence introduced a certain tension into western society. When the Church is totally absorbed by the state (or vice versa) there is no pressure and no possibility of opposition. When the two are separate—or at least distinct institutions—there exists at least the possibility of departure from monolithic totalitarianism like that of the fourth century—not toward liberalism, but away from the inclusiveness and absolutism of Eusebius and the Christian Empire. One of the most progressive factors in the Middle Ages was the continuing struggle between Church and state. Both institutions were authoritarian, both wanted to control the minds of men, but because there was tension between them, there was the possibility of emancipation. Later, rebellious men could play off pope against emperor, Church against state, and thus make room for intellectual freedom.

St. Augustine

Of all the Fathers of the Church, St. Augustine was the most admired and the most influential during the Middle Ages. He was well suited by background and experience to conduct a fundamental examination of the relationship of the Christian experience to classical culture. Augustine was an outsider—a native North African whose family was not Roman but Berber (a Semitic people). They were townsmen, once fairly wealthy but newly-poor under the burden of taxation in the late Empire. Augustine was forced to make his own way and to depend on others—on his parents, who struggled to educate him, and on various friends, school authorities, and officials. Not born to the imperial power elite, he could disassociate himself from the Empire and its destiny.

Augustine was enormously learned. He was a genius—an intellectual giant—and he received a very thorough classical education. He was not much of a linguist (his Greek was poor and he never learned Hebrew) but was a master of Latin rhetoric; certain passages in *The City of God* equal the writings of Cicero in complexity and eloquence. Augustine was educated to be a classical scholar. He abandoned the scholarly profession (and the avenue to political office it opened up) to become a priest, but when he entered the priesthood he was sufficiently learned to confront the question of the relevance of classical culture to the needs of the Church. Having spent almost every waking hour between the ages of fifteen and thirty-five on the study of philosophy and literature, Augustine was in an excellent position to decide what part—if any —of the classical tradition might be jettisoned in the Christian era.

Despite his scholarly achievements, Augustine was no armchair theologian. As a priest and as bishop of Hippo (a fairly poor, undistinguished, and remote town in North Africa) he was deeply involved with the lives and problems of his flock. What Augustine said about man and God came not only from his multicultural background but from his profound commitment to the needs and troubles of people. This is a rare combination at any time, and particularly within the Church, whose scholars have usually been cloistered from the life of the community.

It has been said that Augustine said nothing strikingly original—perhaps this judgment is true, yet when all he said is put together, something new does emerge. He presented a whole theory of man and society which drew upon classical culture even while it self-consciously opposed that tradition. Thus Augustine's philosophy epitomizes medieval culture, which drew heavily upon ancient civilization and yet fought its influence. In that sense, Augustine was the first medieval thinker, and he may also have been the last: no one ever quite reached his level of insight and integration.

Augustine died in 430 A.D., and his last twenty or thirty years were spent amid the disintegration of the Roman Empire. That was a very different world from the world of Eusebius, which was a time of triumph for Church and Empire alike. Augustine lived in an era of dismay, pessimism, confusion, at a time when it was necessary to evolve a philosophy which would allow the Church to survive the Empire—to maintain its mission and identity separate from the dissolving Roman world and from classical culture.

Perhaps the most important basis of Augustine's philosophy was his view of human nature. He believed that the Platonic concept of morality and ethics was wrong, based as it was on the classical view of man. Greek and Roman philosophers believed man could be trained to be capable of rational decision-making, that ignorance was the cause of evil and that properly educated men would exercise their rational faculties and do good. (That view of man was revived in the Enlightenment of the eighteenth century and became the moral basis of modern liberalism. Liberals assume that men will be good if their environment and education are good, that improving men's circumstances will improve their behavior.) Augustine denied this classical concept. Men may know what is right, he said, but something prevents them from acting rightly; human nature is disfunctional.

Evil, immorality, wretchedness, and violence are defects of the will, not of the intellect. The will is the mind (or soul, as described by Augustine, or personality) directed toward an end outside itself: it is action, or active conduct, directed to a goal. Men know that hatred and selfishness are wrong but they cannot escape from their "carnal will," or love of self. Love is will joined to the object of its desire; a man can love himself and exclude all the rest (carnal will), or love God, and through Him, humanity (excluding himself). These are the polarities of human nature.

Christian theology enters Augustinian philosophy at the point where he claims that evil exists because men are inescapably selfish and bad; they cannot love outside themselves, and thus they produce all the misery of the world. Spiritual will never triumphs over carnal will unless God helps—only when God chooses men to love Him (which they cannot do on their own) can they escape their nature. God's choice is grace: and it is a free gift that cannot be bought at any price or effort.

Augustine's understanding of humanity improved on the classical view by its recognition of the violent, hateful, and corrupt aspects of human nature. It appeals to modern theologians and thinkers because it accounts for otherwise inexplicable phenomena such as Auschwitz and Hiroshima. Augustine realized that wealth and learning did not necessarily improve human nature, that reading the classics did not dilute the savagery of men. "Even their virtues are only splendid vices," he said of contemporary aristocrats. The Roman gentleman, as much as the peasant, had his dark side—his instinctive drive to dominate and exploit. Augustine was no democrat, but in this understanding he did achieve a kind of social or moral egalitarianism that amounted to a revolution in thought. When the accoutrements and defenses learned by the wealthy and educated man are stripped away, the brute is revealed, exposed as identical in depravity with his peasant cousin. Augustine was the supreme pessimist among Christian thinkers; he was (and is) influential because he came very close to the inner reality of human life.

As well as a new and persuasive view of human nature, Augustine possessed a special social and historical vision that became extremely influential in the development of medieval thought and of the entire course of western civilization. Impressed, no doubt, by the circumstances of his own time, Augustine told the Christian Church that it could and must survive the Roman Empire. He said the Empire had never been a moral institution, that although it had established earthly peace it had never made men good (or even better)—no political institution could do that. The best a government could do was to provide enough peace and security so that the pilgrimage to the Heavenly City could continue: everything really important happened in the human heart, and in the way men acted toward each other in their daily lives. One great empire had crashed, and others would rise and fall. Romans were no better than Germans, and political forms could not of themselves raise the level of goodness in human society. A government that established peace had done all it could; beyond the basic need, social and political institutions made no real difference.

Augustine has been called a conservative, but that is an ambiguous term: a conservative can also be a radical. Insofar as he believed that salvation did not arrive through political or social change, he was a conservative. However, it was radical to deny the state's claim to salvation—the claim that citizenship in a particular system gave a man a virtuous or evil character. Augustine said that such distinctions between systems were futile and false, that Christian doctrine did not accept the absolute character or inner moral integrity of any political system. (Churches forgot this in the centuries after Augustine, and churchmen are only now beginning to return to the Augustinian view.)

In another aspect of his social philosophy, Augustine attacked the cyclical view of history fashionable in the ancient world. Greek and Roman historians believed that history kept repeating the same cycle of growth and decay, that circumstances recurred, that men stepped into the same river over and over again. In Christian theology, however, Jesus came to earth only once. The Incarnation was a unique historical event, and so are all historical events unique. Augustine's affirmation of the Judaic concept (as against the Greek) had enormous social impact. Belief in an inevitable, repetitive cycle must produce indifference to contemporary circumstances, but belief in uniqueness—the confidence that history is advancing to the singular triumph of the kingdom of God— produces quite a different attitude. Not only are men inspired to collect and record as many unique events as possible (writing more, and ultimately better history), but they are bound to adopt a meliorative philosophy. The primordial western cast of mind sees men marching toward a glorious future through the dregs of the present; belief in progress is the very heart of western thought.

To Augustine, the future triumph was religious; he perpetuated the Judaic, messianic, apocalyptic idea. He saw the Second Coming of Christ as the ineffable end of history, when men would be judged and the world that we know would dissolve in glory. Since the eighteenth century, westerners have secularized the progressive tradition of Judaism and of Augustine. They have invested social and political institutions with quasi-religious sanctions, believing that social change, political programs, and revolution will bring about the final triumph: the Communists, for example, see the achievement of a classless society as the end of history. Augustine might have deplored the secularization of his historical view, but one cannot deny its influence. Belief in progress inspired the restlessness and struggle for perfection that brought about the western hegemony over the rest of the world in the nineteenth century; for good or evil, belief in progress and continual change has given the West its distinctive character.

A great contemporary dispute about the nature of the Church forced Augustine to make a decision of enormous consequence to the medieval world. The North African Donatists of the fifth century believed in a church of the saints, a minority church whose members received God's grace before they could join the holy brotherhood. Augustine believed that everything important happened within the human heart, and he might have been expected to agree with the Donatists. However, he denied their views, insisting that the Church was catholic, universal, and heterogeneous. Sinners and saints would be separated at the end of history, not by the institutional Church. The brotherhood of saints was real but it was internal: its collective group was not the Christian Church but the City of God.

Augustine's Church was the instrument of the Holy Spirit, and its mission was to act in this world. In Platonic terms (which Augustine often used), the Church was the earthly embodiment of the Holy Spirit. Its function was to absorb, to educate, to reform the world, and it could not do this if it was against the world or retired from the world. Augustine believed that churchmen had to work in the world to slowly, painfully transform it.

Thanks largely to Augustine, the Christian Church of the fifth century made the difficult decision to be a universal institution. Had it decided otherwise, it might not have survived the next five hundred years. The Church had to absorb the great lump of German barbarism into Christendom, and after five centuries of struggle it did succeed in converting most of Europe to Latin Christianity. This was accomplished only because churchmen went into the world and lived and struggled with violent people. Many monks did not retire to the cloister; they carried Christianity to the frontier. Augustine did this himself, believing that the Church (like Jesus) had to suffer with the world in order to save it. Those who love God love humanity also, and Christians were willing to encounter men on their own ground. This willingness has been the glory of Roman Catholicism, and Augustine was largely responsible for its tradition of service. He recognized that the Empire was gone, that the barbarian world was real, and pressing, and that churchmen must live with violence and misery to convert and educate and transform society—the great mission of the medieval Church.

There are obvious ambiguities and contrary directions within Augustine's thought. This may be partly because he was a busy man who did not have time to work everything out; at the end of his life, in fact, he published a small book which rejected some of his earlier ideas. More important, though, the contradictions in

Augustine's thought reflect deep ambiguities within Christianity itself (and within Judaism). Christian doctrine never resolved all of its tensions, and this may have saved it from becoming a congealed, monolithic system like that of Confucius. The conflicts themselves eventually became productive impulses toward conflict and change.

Augustine was both a radical experientialist and an authoritarian institutionalist, and both of these tendencies were strong in medieval Christianity. Augustine claimed that the all-important fact was the relationship of the individual to God, that the Heavenly City was a mystical, internal, secret, spiritual brotherhood whose membership would be revealed (and whose reign begin) only at the end of history. The institutional Church was very different, but it was essential to the fulfillment of God's purpose. It was absolutely necessary for everyone to belong to the Church, to obey its leaders and to take the sacraments. The instrument of the state could and should be used to force people into the Church, which must have absolute authority in this world. Augustine's ideas were used to justify the Inquisition, the persecution of Jews, and the destruction of heretics and of heresy. Membership in the Heavenly City was won only when a man's will was directed entirely toward God—and membership in the earthly Church was implied as a prerequisite, although Augustine was sufficiently liberal to hint that certain good men (the Hebrew patriarchs) who had not had the privilege of Church membership might still belong to the Heavenly City.

Obviously, two very different kinds of Christianity were involved in Augustine's thought. One was the mystical, internal Christianity of individual religious experience; the other was Roman, legalistic, and institutional. The two concepts or doctrines can be combined (although ultimately they do not entirely mesh) in a theory never fully stated by Augustine but worked out by later thinkers. These men, inspired by Augustine, saw the domination of the Church in the world as a necessary, temporary condition. The Church was a historical institution, and at the end it would disappear like other institutions. Only the Two Cities would survive the end—one for eternal blessing and one for eternal damnation. Until that day the Church must exist to communicate God's will and love to men. It is God's chosen instrument. He acts on the world through the Church. In this theory the Church was not absolute in an ultimate sense but only in a relative historical sense, and the triumph of God's will and of the Heavenly City was an end that justified the Church's control over the individual conscience.

As a radical individualist (who must have half-consciously sympathized with the Donatists), Augustine said that all that mattered ultimately was the Christian experience, not institutional membership. The Church was a temporary institution—this Augustinian doctrine paradoxically allowed the medieval Church to excuse its own failings. The Church was not the Holy Spirit but only the vehicle of the Spirit, in which incompetence and corruption could be expected. The Church was not the City of God but only a way-station to the City, and it could afford to be less than rigorous in its demands on its leaders. This was a useful doctrine in a violent, chaotic, underdeveloped society. The Church was bound to be absorbed and corrupted by society to some extent, but a Puritan, Donatist church would have been destroyed completely in resistance to its violent environment. Augustine's interpretation of the Church allowed it to face its own failings, to accommodate, to socialize; it also allowed the Church to be somewhat corrupted by participation in the Germanic world. But if the Church had remained aloof from the primitive world, it would have betrayed Jesus' directions to preach the good news everywhere and in the face of all obstacles. Augustine's doctrine was socially realistic and well suited to the circumstances of early medieval life.

It is difficult to categorize Augustine as a conservative or a radical. Much of what he says sounds conservative in modern terms, but in an ultimate sense, if radicalism is defined as the refusal to accept conventional solutions, as insistence on confronting issues and getting to the roots of problems, as determination to attain the salvation of humanity and not to accommodate to power and society, then Augustine was a great radical.

Hellenisation and Romanisation

It is now possible to look back over the development of Christianity in its first four centuries and perceive some broad patterns. Christianity emerged out of a radical Jewish sect whose doctrines were fundamentally reinterpreted in the light of Greek, particularly Platonic philosophy. The development of Christian doctrine was also marked by the propensity to adapt the savior-god idea prevalent in Mediterranean Hellenistic culture. It is true, as recently emphasized by J. Pelikan and other scholars, that the Church from the second through the fourth century resisted full Hellenisation of its doctrines—the attempt of some Christian groups and teachers to divest Christ of all humanity and make him purely divine; to introduce Graeco-Roman polytheism into Christian doctrine by making definite hierarchic distinctions in the Godhead (God the Son distinct from God the Father); and other Hellenic ideas such as the cyclic view of history. Proponents of full-scale Hellenisation of Christian doctrine, from the early Gnostics to the fourth-century Arians, lost out after bitter controversy and were condemned by the Church as "heretics" (adherents of doctrinal error). The development of Church doctrine in the first four Christian centuries can, therefore, be categorized as partial but not full Hellenisation.

At the same time, the Church rather easily accepted Romanisation. God became the Emperor of the Universe; and the Roman emperor the adjutant of this divine Emperor. The bishops assumed the status of Roman governors, and the Church applied to the priesthood the Roman distinction between the powers of office and the personality of the officeholder; obedience to sacerdotal authority was demanded irrespective of the charismatic or even moral quality of individual priests. The Church, and particularly the Roman Church, by the fifth century had fully absorbed Roman authoritarian traditions.

Yet in perpetuating the Hebrew Bible with its prophetic anti-authoritarian traditions and the millennial view of history, in absorbing the Stoic doctrine of separating private morality from social and political institutions, in disseminating the moralistic rhetoric of the classical tradition, and in looking with favor upon Neoplatonic mysticism, ecclesiastical culture also provided ingredients for the formulation of a radical, anti-authoritarian philosophy. For many centuries these radical possibilities in Christian thought would remain largely ignored and inert, but fortunately for western civilization they would become very active and socially important in the eleventh and twelfth centuries.

Chapter Three

THE EARLY MEDIEVAL WORLD

I. Understanding the Early Middle Ages

THEMES AND PROBLEMS

The centuries between 500 and 1000 A.D. in Europe—the early Middle Ages—form a period which is difficult to study and superficially unrewarding. It is not an attractive period; early medieval society was, beyond a shadow of a doubt, disordered, violent, and underdeveloped. No great thinkers and no original thought lightened the darkness of the West, and except for one or two Italian cities dominated by Byzantine influence, no art or architecture of esthetic value survives from this era. It was a period of disintegration and confusion, but it poses some important historical questions, of which the first—the traditional question—is how, in spite of violence and disorder, western people managed to preserve and perpetuate the great ideas and cultural forms of the ancient world.

The second major question of early medieval historiography is equally important but less often expressed. How did this primitive society actually function? How were the chaotic conditions of the year 500 transformed into the viable society of the year 1000? The social groupings and political and judicial forms developed during the early Middle Ages were the very forms and institutions on which were built the national bureaucratic states of the High Middle Ages. These forms were later altered and embellished, but they constituted the outline of the European social structure right down to the Industrial Revolution.

The disorganized, backward society of the early medieval era produced the skeleton of European society; indeed, as we examine the period closely we see that it was very creative in social (including political, legal, and economic) organization. When the Germans invaded the Roman Empire, the center of civilization was on the Mediterranean. Western Europe was a thinly populated, economically underdeveloped province with enormous forests and swamps over about half of its available land. By the year 1000, however, there was a self-contained and self-conscious western European society, the work of internal colonization was well under way, the population was growing, and urbanization had begun. Western Europe, once a backwater of Mediterranean civilization, had entered on an independent and thriving existence.

The extreme shortage of sources for the history of the early medieval period makes it very difficult to study. The late sixth and seventh centuries are less well documented than any period since the third century B.C. The sources simply did not survive, or perhaps they were not ever written, and historians have had to piece together a story of complex social development from very limited material. Most of the records that do exist are ecclesiastical; they were written by churchmen and concentrate on clerical concerns. There are many accounts of miracles performed by early medieval saints, but almost nothing on what it was like to be a farmer in the seventh century. To make matters worse, much of the modern literature on the period is so overlaid with prejudice, ideology, and political commitment that it is nearly useless. The idea that European government and law were born in the early Middle Ages is not new. It was a dogma of nineteenth-century historians, who were wedded to the organic interpretation of history, the belief that the early form of an organism predetermined its adult form. Historians were eager to present views of early medieval society that would hint at its ultimate state: they looked for early evidences of German power, British freedom, French nationalism, and so forth. Some of these historians were intelligent and resourceful, but their work was governed by preconceptions that are alien or distasteful to our assumptions and world-view.

Historiography

The first historian to give an extensive account of the Germanic invasions was Gibbon, in *The Decline and Fall of the Roman Empire*. As a great admirer of the Roman world, Gibbon assumed that the German invaders were barbarians; he gave an account of disorder and violence and let the matter rest there. The first thinker to theorize on the subject was the French *philosophe* Montesquieu, who assumed that Europe fell into a cultural decline after the cataclysm of the fifth and sixth centuries, emerging only in the Renaissance. Voltaire and other *philosophes* of the Enlightenment made similar observations, and it is quite apparent that their view of what happened was governed by their dislike of the Church. The Roman Catholic Church and its culture and institutions (particularly the papacy) were fully established during the early medieval period, and these historians liked to paint the period as dark as possible in order to discredit the Church by revealing its birth in barbarism and obscurantism. This they accomplished—the *philosophes'* attitude persuaded a great many people. It is ironic that modern radical Catholics take a similar position as they attempt to persuade their Church to throw off the vestiges of medievalism, to modernize, to expel superstition and barbarism. The newly-fashionable radical Catholic view perpetuates the view held by the first radical secularists of the eighteenth century, who aimed to discredit the Church by identifying it with the evils of its formative period.

The *philosophes* were followed by the Romantic writers of early nineteenth century, who took a quite different view of Germanic society and emphasized its liberation from the rigidity of Roman life. The Romantics believed these to be centuries of emancipation, of ardor, of sacrifice—of "terrible beauty," when the freshness of youth triumphed over the decrepit rigidity of the ancient Empire.

A new school appeared in France in the 1860s and 1870s with the emergence of a group of scholars who chose to emphasize not conflict and cataclysm but the transition, blending, and continuity of classical culture and Roman institutions. This can be seen as a manifestation of French nationalism, because these scholars were looking for the origins of their own nation. They did not like to think that France emerged from *Germania;* they saw the French as civilized, rational people quite unlike German barbarians. They argued for the continuity of Roman institutions, described the German invasions as momentary disturbances, and claimed that the invaders were rapidly and thoroughly absorbed into the continuing framework of Rome. These Romanists stressed, for instance, the development of feudalism (which earlier historians believed to be a manifestation of German violence) from the Roman aristocratic patronate system in which lords had large estates, peasants, and bodyguards of soldiers. These scholars also emphasized the preservation of classical forms of thought within the Church.

The leading exponent of the thesis of continuity was the brilliant historian Fustel de Coulanges, who taught at the Sorbonne in the 1870s. The thesis won belated support in the 1920s and 1930s from two non-French historians. The Austrian Alfons Dopsch was a great admirer of the Germans (in fact he became an enthusiastic Nazi); he saw the German invaders of Rome not as fresh adolescents but sober citizens. Dopsch wrote an enormous book claiming that the Germans absorbed all that was valuable from Rome during the years when they occupied the Rhine-Danube frontier, and that the invasions represented a blending of two civilizations at similar levels of culture, not a disastrous upset of a higher culture by primitives.

The most prominent twentieth-century supporter of the thesis of continuity was Henri Pirenne, a Belgian who was the most celebrated medieval historian in the period between the two world wars. Pirenne was a very clever and articulate man, and a notable public figure. He made dramatic statements, and his dialectical approach attracted wide attention. Pirenne did not accept the Germanic invasions as a great upheaval; he found evidence for continuity in commerce, in way of life, in government, education, and law. *Romania* could have disappeared only in a major cataclysm (and he found none in the fifth century); Europe in the sixth and seventh centuries was still basically Roman.

Pirenne believed that the great change came not in the fifth century but in the late seventh and eighth, with the Muslim conquest of the southern, eastern, and western shores of the Mediterranean. The Mediterranean became a "Muslim lake" (one of Pirenne's fine phrases), and western Europe was forced back on its own resources. The center of European life moved north when Mediterranean commerce was blocked, and Europeans founded new centers and new institutions. Charlemagne was not an emperor in the Roman tradition but a new man—a European. Mohammed made Charlemagne possible. Pirenne's book *Mohammed and Charlemagne* was extremely influential, and the old argument between those who believed in the continuity of Rome and those who emphasized the cataclysm of the fifth century and the dominance of Germans in the post-Roman period shifted to a discussion of *when* Roman culture and society disappeared—in the fifth century, or in the eighth. Pirenne substituted a Muslim for a German cataclysm.

Pirenne was one of the first historians to adopt a functional approach to early medieval society. He recognized that tradition cannot account for everything, that institutions develop in response to needs created by a particular environment or situation and people draw on tradition to create the institutions they need. Thus Pirenne departed from the old organic interpretation; he posited the cataclysm and described medieval institutions as varying responses to it. Unfortunately, however, his sweeping, metaphorical explanations did not well serve the cause of functional history, which requires careful detail and close analysis. Pirenne presented a facile paradigm, and he tended to underrate the importance of the German invasions in order to make his point. Certainly there was great upheaval and dislocation in the fifth and sixth centuries, and this cannot be ignored. Even more important, historians of Islam are not convinced that Europe actually was cut off from the Mediterranean by the Arab conquests. Apparently there was no systematic policy of excluding Christians from Mediterranean trade, and there are evidences of European trade in the eighth and ninth centuries. Pirenne's explanation was simplistic and his thesis largely vitiated by errors and omissions of data.

After World War II many French scholars returned to the old theory of a fifth-century cataclysm. They found that the archaeological evidence, as well as analysis of the literary texts, corroborated the old idea of the trauma of the German invasions. These men (writing for the most part in the late 1940s and early 1950s) admitted that their own experience under German invasion and occupation gave them insight into what European life might have been like in the sixth century. Robert Latouche and Pierre Courçelle are fine representatives of this school, but most of their work is restricted to the period of the invasions and does not go on to the development of medieval institutions.

There is no grand, sweeping interpretation of early medieval society, but there are suggestions of a successful approach in the work of some of the functional historians. As we have seen, the founder of the functional school was F. W. Maitland of Cambridge, who died in 1906. His *History of English Law* indicated that medieval legal structure developed in response to need, but Maitland did little with the early period, and unfortunately his work was not noticed or emulated for many years. Pirenne showed some understanding of the functional approach, but Marc Bloch (who was much influenced by the development of French sociology) was the first real functional historian of the Middle Ages. Bloch's great work *Feudal Society* does not begin with the invasions and the making of feudal society: it describes its functioning after about 800. However, in the essay "The Rise of Seignorial Institutions," published in Volume I of the *Cambridge Economic History* in 1940, Bloch did discuss the formation of medieval institutions. This article is particularly good on the nature and meaning of lordship, but unhappily, Bloch never had an opportunity to round out the discussion in further work.

The Austrian scholar Heinrich Fichtenau wrote a history of the Carolingian Empire in which he offered a functional explanation of Charlemagne and his world. However, Fichtenau could not escape entirely from the typical German ideological and intellectualized approach. He did make an effort to explain who Charlemagne really was and how his rule worked; Fichtenau was not content to dismiss Charlemagne as either a "glorious" Roman emperor or a "violent" Germanic chieftain. How did Charlemagne live, what did he do; was he intelligent, was he literate? These are the real questions about Charlemagne and the eighth century, and although Fichtenau is not entirely clear and definitive, his work does represent an advance over previous histories. Historians need a sociology of the early Middle Ages, but the sources are fragmentary and are written in difficult, obscure languages. We still do not know precisely how the world of the year 1000 developed from the world of the late Roman Empire.

II. Social Institutions: A Functional Model of the Early Medieval European World

The Family

Essentially, early medieval society was based on five social institutions, and everything happened within the relationships of

these five forms. The first institution was the family—kinship or
the blood tie; the second was the community—*communitas* in the
Latin term, and *volk* in the German (these have slightly different
meanings, but can both be included in our word *community*). The
third institution was lordship, which might be described as manor-
ialism and feudalism. The last two institutions were special (but
important) varieties of the other forms: the Church—a special kind
of community set apart from others—and kingship, or monarchy—
a special kind of lordship. These five forms included all the relationships within medieval society.

The basic unit of society in the medieval world was the family, just as the basic unit of society in the Roman Empire (at least
outside the cities) had been the patrimonial household. Despite
the highly organized legal and political system of Rome, with its
public law and taxation, the family was essential in the functioning
of society. In rural society, the patrimonial household held large
estates, controlled the land, and perpetuated its control through
successive generations. The family exercised jurisdiction over the
peasants on its land and offered them protection; in a sense, the
Roman family included its peasants. In the cities, of course,
the family was not as essential. Public government and finance
operated in urban areas, and public services were provided by imperial or municipal government.

Even in the cities, however, the family was important, because
the government itself consisted of a group of families (aristocratic
or bourgeois) who inherited their status and power. Members of
certain families traditionally were senators or consuls for the imperial government, and the *curiales* (town councillors) of the cities
came from hereditary groups of governing families. The system
broke down only when these families could not agree on how to
share their offices, or when one family became too ambitious. According to Sir Ronald Syme in *The Roman Revolution*, this kind of
situation was responsible for the Roman disorders of the first century B.C. Trouble was likely when new families from outside the traditional group aspired to power, and it may be that the great upheavals in the third century A.D. arose from the rejection of such
"new men." The result was civil war, which came to an end in
the fourth century when the new families were integrated into the
old aristocracy.

The medieval world inherited the tradition of family domina-

tion of political and social life, but the tradition was ignored by
the liberal historians of the late nineteenth century, whose middle-
class outlook led them to overlook or despise such domination.
They called it nepotism and dismissed it as corruption and a sign
of disorder, projecting into the past their ignorance of the facts of
politics. Family domination is almost a constant of history, but it
was not until the 1930s that historians began to understand political realities: Syme for the ancient world, Marc Bloch for the
Middle Ages, and Sir Lewis Namier for the eighteenth century.

Rural society in the Roman Empire was completely dominated
by the patrimonial household, but this could not be the exclusive
rule in the cities, where several families competed for or shared
power. It may be that one weakness of urban society was the
inability of its aristocracy to absorb the proletariat in the way that
rural lords absorbed the peasantry into their own families. Beginning in the second century A.D., and in pronounced numbers by
the fourth century, aristocrats began to leave the cities for the
countryside, abandoning the urban proletariat and producing problems of public welfare as well as ready material for political agi-
tators and demagogues. The aristocratic, patrimonial style does not
fit well with city life in any society because most city people are of
no possible use to the aristocrats, who can use only a limited
number of servants. On the land, as long as land is available, any
number of peasants can be taken into service and included within
the familial government.

For its blood kin, the Roman family provided sustenance and
education. Aristocratic families controlled the schools which young
people attended after about the age of twelve (up to that age they
were educated at home by tutors). Small groups of wealthy parents
hired and paid the teachers and dominated the schools, which
trained their children to take over the leadership of the family and
of society. The Roman family was a caring, paternal institution,
but extremely demanding, and the Roman father was apt to be aggressive and dictatorial in a masculine society.

The Roman family can be studied in the context of the government of the state, but the German family *was* the government—all
the government that existed. Roman aristocratic families controlled
the *res publica*, but at least they had a concept of a state distinct
from the ruling families; in Germany there was no such theory or

practice. At the time of the invasions the German *volk* was not a state; it was regarded as a family, descended from a common ancestor who was descended in turn from a god. The *volk* was an extremely large unit, and although there remained a consciousness that all the Visigoths or all the Franks were members, in each case, of one family, in practice a *volk* comprised several families. Even these were large social units—everyone within at least seven degrees of consanguinity. Germans married their cousins, although this became complicated after they were converted to Christianity. By the ninth century the Church forbade marriage within the seventh degree of consanguinity; in the twelfth century, within the third degree. (These rules strengthened the Church by giving it the opportunity to grant exceptions or to permit divorces between married people who "discovered" that their relationship fell within the forbidden degree.)

The Germanic family provided nearly all the government or education that was available, and although other institutions gradually came into operation, the family was all the peace, protection, and government that existed on a day-to-day basis at the time of the invasions. There were interruptions in familial jurisdiction (more interruptions as time went on), but at the beginning of western medieval history, the family bond was the only loyalty and commitment.

The German family was a political, social, and educational institution, and its most important function was peacekeeping. In a society without public law, it provided at least some elementary protection against violence. The institution of the vengeful bloodfeud allowed the family to function as the first and most important peace unit of the early Middle Ages, at least insofar as it discouraged the slaughter of members of important families. Revenge was very important to the Germans; it was the prime means of instilling peace and social order.

The family provided food and booty, of course, and it brought up its children as well as it could under conditions estimated at not less than 50 per cent infant mortality. Children had no education except in arms; unlike the Romans, the early Germans were unconcerned with literacy and learning—it brought no advantage. After the invaders settled down in Rome, the family became responsible for the provision of land for male offspring and dowries for girls.

The Germans tended to share their land equally among their sons until about 1000, but by the twelfth century, primogeniture had become the normal arrangement in western Europe. The Church (and Church-trained lawyers) favored primogeniture; besides, by the year 1000 the population had grown to such an extent that not all the sons could be satisfied by a division. Too much division, after all, weakened the status of the entire family by depriving it of an important, wealthy landowner at its head.

In the beginning, the German family was not a patrimonial institution. Its members were blood relations, not peasants or servants (although there were some slaves). Originally the Germans had been pastoral people, not agricultural; they worked hard themselves and could not afford to keep many servants. Later, they learned the patrimonial arrangement from the Romans; they took over Roman estates with the peasants included, gave them protection and sustenance, and took them into the extended family— usually in some sort of sharecropping arrangement.

It would be difficult to identify the functioning of the sixth-century family as Roman or German. Elements of both systems were used to develop a system responsive to the needs of the time. It was a period without effective central government but with plenty of available land that needed work in order to provide enough food to keep people alive, and the family dedicated itself to fighting and land use.

Gradually, important families came to look upon the Church holdings (the bishopric or abbey) within their domains as part of their own estates, and to educate one son to take over as bishop or abbot. With its leaders usually related to the local lord, the Church served the family which controlled its property. Churchmen provided spiritual service by singing Masses continually for the souls of departed family members, and this spiritual service was extremely important, as it was believed to assure the entry of aristocratic souls into heaven. By the eighth century, the term *familia* was used to describe a group of ecclesiastics—monks under their abbot or priests under their bishop—who were economically self-sustaining and holding property in common. By the eighth or ninth century, not only the organization of the Church but its attitude resembled that of a family, concerned with preserving and enhancing its wealth and status.

The family was (by far) the most effective institution in western Europe in the eighth century, largely responsible for whatever justice, order, peace, or education existed at all. However, the family could not do everything, and other institutions gradually developed to compensate for these inadequacies. There was even a certain amount of ideological opposition to family exploitation and absorption of political and religious life, and this increased with the passage of time. However, the family remained essential throughout the medieval period. Society consisted of groups of large families, and other institutions can be described as specific or specialized functions of the family. Disputes outside the family powers were handled by the community; lordship compensated for malfunction of the family as a security or peacekeeping unit; the Church served to square the family accounts with God; kingship might be regarded as a special accolade seized by one family to demonstrate its superiority.

Although it is true that many churchmen were servants or flunkeys of great families (in England this situation continued through the eighteenth or nineteenth centuries and is best displayed in the novels of Jane Austen), and although the Church itself existed in a familial structure of loyalty and commitment, it did have its own ideology and traditions which at times ran counter to the domination of the family. Christianity emphasized election over inheritance and universality over the vertical division of society. This conflict with the institution of the family became very important in the long run; nonetheless, it is likely that historians exaggerate the extent to which the Church of the early Middle Ages was ideologically opposed to the Germanic way of doing things. In actual practice it cooperated a great deal with the Germanic world. There was some opposition at all times and one can say at least that the medieval world was created by the interaction of the Church with Germanic institutions—or that the medieval world was a product of the familial organization of society, intermixed with the universal ideology of the Church.

COMMUNITY

In the nineteenth century, liberal English historians believed that the Germanic *volk* or communty was a strong, significant institution of the early medieval world. This was an old assumption: seventeenth-century English radicals liked to believe that before the Norman Conquest England was run by democratic communities of freemen who met and decided how to manage their affairs. They believed that the Normans (French despots), then the Scottish Stuart kings, had imposed Continental-style tyrannies on free people, and the democratic Levellers urged Englishmen to rise against these outsiders and re-establish the strong communities of medieval times. The belief became important again in the nineteenth century when liberals looked for a suitable historical background for contemporary politics. In his monumental *History of the Norman Conquest*, written about 1860, E. A. Freeman assumes that a democratic Anglo-Saxon community operated in early medieval England and that the nineteenth-century Parliament was a revival of this early institution.

In nineteenth-century Germany, a belief in the strong medieval community was tied in with German nationalism. Historians thought that the German *volk* existed before the invasions and that Germans marched into the Empire in a cohesive group. In the 1870s and 1880s, German historians tended to believe that the *volk* operated on liberal, democratic lines. Their evidence was taken largely from the Roman historian Tacitus, whose *Germania* appeared in 98 A.D. Tacitus said that a German chieftain had to obtain consent from his warriors before taking action—but Tacitus himself was one of that small aristocratic minority in Rome who disapproved of the Empire and hoped to re-establish the Republic, and his evidence is ambiguous at the very least. Tacitus was anti-Caesarian and his work is extremely subtle; it may be that he wrote of a system unlike that of Rome in order to criticize contemporary Rome, in which the Senate had become a formality and the emperorship a dictatorship. In *Beowulf*, one of the few contemporary German sources, there is no real evidence of democratic community: affairs evidently were run by the king, with the companionship (not necessarily the consent) of a few great lords and drinking companions.

The fullest documentary record of Germanic life is in the *Dooms*, the Anglo-Saxon laws which were written down after 590. These refer to the *Witan* (literally "wise men"), which was believed in the nineteenth century to be the ancestor of the English

Parliament but in reality was probably a gathering of the hunting and drinking companions of the king. The king issued laws with the "advice of the *Witan*," but was this necessary, or was it simply a formality? The Germans may have had a community political structure that lapsed during the period of the invasions, but it probably did not involve more than the king, his family, and his chosen friends.

There is little evidence, either, of anything that can be identified with any assurance as national consciousness, or the idea of a nation, or a national community. Kings referred to themselves in documents as "King of the Franks" or "King of the West Saxons," which seems to indicate that they felt some such identity, but they almost never *acted* as kings of a people. It may be that their documents were issued in that style because their advisors were churchmen, educated in the classics, who had seen Roman documents and chose to imitate the imperial style. It has been argued that the Germanic peoples were supposedly liable to military service to their kings—indicating a national consciousness—but the fact is that kings never did call up all their people. Germanic armies actually consisted of the king's retainers, his feudal vassals, and a few great lords who were threatened or bribed into service.

It seems, then, that the *volk* did not function as a national political or military unit. Probably there was a vague idea or sense of a nation, but no real functioning as such, and certainly there was no nation in the sense of judicial functioning. There was no national system of courts—courts were local, and the localities were small. The king's court was used occasionally for important trials, but only because local courts could not handle very important magnates; when a duke and a bishop collided they had to be tried by the king. On this matter (as on others), historians have argued from silence, which is bad history. They have blown up rare incidents into patterns, assuming that the incidents were ordinary but the evidence destroyed. Actually, these incidents were extraordinary—the missing evidence indicates that nothing happened, and documentary silence is evidence of nothing at all.

Assuming, then, that there was almost no significant national consciousness in the early Middle Ages (political, military, or judicial), what *was* the early medieval community? It was a local unit, an extra-familial peacekeeping institution. As such it was extremely significant, as it gave men their first experience in public life and public institutions. In the earliest days the community was no larger than the so-called hundred, or township; later on, an attempt was made to increase the real working community to the level of the county or shire. The community was small, first because its function was to intercede between families; more important, because of the notoriously bad transportation and communications of early medieval times. Transportation was by foot, oxcart, or horseback, and European horses were small and weak until the eleventh century, when contact wtih the Arab world allowed interbreeding.

The most important accomplishments of the early medieval community were legal and judicial. The community cooled the bloodfeud by providing an alternative, a system by which families could get justice without taking vengeance in the potentially-devastating feud (which might last for years and decimate families). Also, the judicial institution solved the problem of murder by stealth, of assigning guilt for crimes committed in private. At the *moot*, or assembly, the elders gathered to establish *wergeld* (man-money), a table of compensation for various degrees of crime. The murder of a slave cost the murderer something, the murder of a free man cost him more, and so on—all the way up to the murder of a king, which no one could afford. *Wergeld* was not always accepted by the bereaved in place of bloodfeud, but it was accepted often enough to be an established custom, and to be socially useful.

The Romans, of course, had a sophisticated and effective system of judicial procedure in which opposing attorneys presented written briefs to a panel of judges who interrogated (or tortured) witnesses in order to get at the truth. The early medieval Germans used no such system, but not (as liberal nineteenth-century historians believed) because they were too liberty-loving to accept Roman law. They did not use the Roman system because its written pleading required literacy, skilled lawyers, and an authoritarian state. The Germans had no legal profession, no state, and no literacy outside the Church. They were forced to take judicial decision out of the hands of judges and leave it to Wodin—later, to Christ.

The Germanic peoples, believing that God would give his opinion on moral matters such as murder and theft, developed trial by ordeal and by compurgation. The Church did not like trial by ordeal (brought into the Empire by the Germans), but they accepted it and cooperated in the system until 1215.

The ordeal was a grim business, heavily weighted against the defendant—but most defendants were of low social class (and therefore not important to society) or were ill-famed people widely believed to be guilty. In a trial by ordeal, a man was first accused in court, where the form of his ordeal was selected. Then he was taken to church, where a priest threatened him with hell for perjury, attempting to get him to admit his guilt (if he did so he was hanged immediately). If he did not admit guilt he was tried by cold water, by hot iron, or by hot water—a variety of miserable procedures. The defendant might be thrown in cold water, bound hand and foot, and left to sink or float. It was believed that water would not receive a guilty person, so the man who floated was hanged while he who sunk was pulled out (if possible) and set free. Another man might be made to walk three paces holding a red-hot iron; if his burns appeared to be healing within three days he was considered innocent. Another defendant might be set to retrieve a stone from the bottom of a pot of boiling water—again, if his burns healed, he was free.

In the year 800, courts were held about once a month in every tiny village. After each court, five or ten people might be sentenced to death—and hanged forthwith. It was a grim and sordid and violent world, but through their communities men were learning to develop public, extra-familial processes to preserve law and order. These beginnings are significant as beginnings rather than for any intrinsic justice.

The third institution of the medieval judicial community (aside from the establishment of *wergeld* and the trial by ordeal) was trial by compurgation, generally reserved for defendants of high social status. Ordeals were good enough for peasants and known criminals, but a high-born man was tried in a manner more suitable to his rank. He appeared in court, charged with a crime, and swore his innocence. He brought in a number of "oath-helpers" (compurgation means "swearing with" or "oath-helping") as character witnesses, to swear that his oath was "clean," and that he was an honest man. The defendant had to produce a number of witnesses to equal the *wergeld* of the victim; each man had his weight (or price) and the defendant's problem was to find enough oath-helpers to balance the price of the man who had been killed or assaulted. This might not be easy if the defendant were guilty, for medieval men took perjury extremely seriously. Their view of eternal damnation was entirely realistic and material, and no man wished to jeopardize his hope of heaven. Nevertheless, certainly a high-born or wealthy defendant had a better chance to escape the consequences of a crime than a low-born—but that has not changed in the twentieth century.

The *wergeld* and trial by ordeal and by compurgation seem extremely crude forms of judicial process, and indeed they were crude in comparison with Roman law or to modern systems of justice. Their major importance is as almost the only self-governing, extra-familial institution encountered by the average man in early medieval society. Nineteenth-century British constitutional historians regarded medieval community courts as essential origins of British justice and in one sense this is correct: these courts were autonomous, and the men of a neighborhood operated them on their own and thus obtained valuable experience in self-government. In England, this autonomous experience eventually was transported to the national scene. William Stubbs, the great nineteenth-century historian of the English constitution, believed that the origins of Parliament can be found in local medieval courts. It certainly is true that only in England, where medieval institutions were most purely Germanic, did the self-governing community survive the age of absolute monarchy that began in the fourteenth century and reached its peak in the sixteenth. The inter-familial judicial organization of each little village was far more important than any sense of nation which may have existed during the early Middle Ages.

LORDSHIP

The term "lordship" is often used as an equivalent to "feudalism," which in itself is not a medieval usage but a word invented by seventeenth-century lawyers. It was taken up by the French political theorists of the pre-Revolutionary era, who used it in a pejorative sense to describe a deplorable system of aristocratic privilege. Later it was picked up by Karl Marx, who identified the pre-capitalist stage of western economic development as "feudalism." "Feudalism" is used here to signify lordship, and not any ideological position.

Lordship may be defined as the extra-familial domination of one man over another—that is, domination apart from the accepted relationship of father and son. This was increasingly characteristic of medieval society: lordship was an important institution even in the sixth century, but by the tenth century it was central to social life, second only to the family and at times even in competition with the family.

Nineteenth-century historians, wedded to an organic view of historical development, sought the germ of lordship in the ancient world. Romanists found it in the *patrocinium*, or patronage, of the later Empire, when certain men (some free, some servile) placed themselves under the protection of great landowners or aristocrats. Germanists, on the other hand, pointed to *gefolge*, the "following" or "follow-ship" described by Tacitus as a military group led by a successful warrior, a generous Ring-Giver. Certainly lordship existed in various forms in the ancient world, but its continuance and increasing importance during the Middle Ages indicate that it must have answered some contemporary need. Marc Bloch presented lordship as a substitute for the father-son relationship, explaining that a man sought a lord when his own father was weak or crippled or dead, when his own family could not sustain him. This makes sense in the context of the early medieval world; both peasants and warriors were adopted into the lord's family as surrogate sons to work or fight for him. The medieval father was a stern, exploitive figure, and the lord operated in the same pattern: he was a surrogate father.

The lordship of one free man over another is described by historians as feudal lordship; over a serf, as manorial lordship. In feudal lordship, the surrogate-sons were generally known as vassals, from a Celtic word meaning *boy*. The vassals were "the boys" —appropriate enough, when they are seen as a group of toughs who lived in the household of the lord and did his fighting. By the eighth century, French vassals were called *chevaliers* (meaning horsemen); in England they were *cnihts*—from the same origin as the German *knecht*, or slave, which meant a servant. By the tenth century, however, *chevalier* and knight had the same meaning—an armored horseman. Beginning in the eighth century, lords put their best fighters on horses and equipped them with armor (a crude chain mail at this period). The tenth-century vassal was a free man, a professional warrior who served a lord in exchange for the booty the lord could supply. By the year 900 a ceremony of vassalage had appeared in which the vassal knelt in front of his lord, his hands between those of the lord, and swore his homage and fealty in a general promise to love what the lord loved and shun what he shunned. The lord swore in turn to protect and sustain his vassal, to render him the dignity shown by a father to his son.

Despite popular misconceptions, early medieval lordship was a simple father-son substitution, and land was not involved in the relationship—not in the beginning. After the eighth century, with warriors in armor and on horseback, it became expensive and inconvenient to maintain a fighting force in a lord's own household. Lords (beginning with the head of the Carolingian family in France) began to give land to their vassals, to "enfief" them with a piece of land and the income from it. Very often they gave away Church lands and thus did not impoverish themselves; the Church frequently had more land than it could use, or churchmen were promised "protection" in return. By the tenth century, however, lords very often had to give away their own property—but it was never given away absolutely. It was not the property but the possession of the vassal; he had tenure, he had the use of the income, but the land remained (theoretically) the property of the lord. By the middle of the tenth century, with the emergence of the feudal contract, a vassal gave homage and promised to fight for a lord in return for possession of a certain property, and by the eleventh century—in practice if not in theory—a fief was likely to be hereditary. When a vassal died, his son swore homage and came into the possession of the family fief.

By the tenth century, then, feudal lordship had become the nexus for the relationship of landed families. Whereas in 600 the relationship involved two individuals in father-son relationship, by 1000 it involved whole families; lordship had become a vehicle by which a great family established satellite families bound in alliance by the feudal contract.

Under manorial lordship, the medieval system of peasant serfdom, a peasant family was bound in perpetuity to its land or to its village. Once a family had "bowed its neck" to serfdom it was extremely difficult for them to escape servile status. The best way out was through the Church, but after about 800 Church offices were ordinarily kept for noblemen, and peasants had few opportunities to escape the land. Peasant families were bound to serve the lord's family. They were given strips of land to work, a share of the crop, and protection, but they owed dues and services to the lord—forever. Serfs constituted a hereditary labor force which existed in perpetuity on a specific estate.

The medieval serf was similar in some respects to the Roman slave, but he did have certain personal rights. He could not be sold, nor could he be moved from the land. As a slave of the land— as opposed to a personal slave—a serf could not be taken from his family, and this was extremely important in a family-oriented society. Peasant families remained intact and perpetuated themselves; manorial lordship (like feudal lordship) as an institution was closely related to the institution of the family. Lordship of both kinds provided satellite fighting (knightly) families or laboring (serf) families to ally with or work for great landed (lord) families. In theory, feudal lordship was based on the competing principle of contract and not on inheritance, but in practice lordship became a function of family-centered social life.

THE CHURCH

In any discussion of the early medieval Church there is a strong temptation toward anachronism, toward exaggeration of the degree of centralization—of papal control and influence—that actually existed. It is true that elaborate claims were made by the papacy, but pretensions must not be accepted as facts. The modern Roman Catholic Church is a product of the High Middle Ages, and of the sixteenth century, far more than of the early medieval period, when Rome had little centralized power and the institutions of the Church were very different from those of the modern world.

The medieval Church had four main institutional bases. The first of these (and the least influential) was the secular clergy— churchmen who lived and worked in the world, including parish and cathedral clergy. Next in influence was the episcopate—the bishops who presided in the various cathedrals; and these were headed by the pope, whose special position made the papacy a separate ecclesiastical institution. Last, and most varied and influential, was the regular clergy—the monks and nuns who lived under the Rule of poverty, chastity, and obedience.

The parish clergy had the least influence and power; in fact they did not exist at all until about 800. Before that time there were bishoprics in major cities and monasteries scattered around the countryside, but no clergyman served the average village. Priests rode out from the cathedrals (or from the nearest monastery) once or twice a year, visiting villages to conduct the Mass, to baptize and to marry and to preach to the villagers. For the rest of the year the peasants were neglected by their Church—not willfully, but there was no institutional service or sufficient trained personnel for their needs.

In the eighth century the great Anglo-Saxon missionary St. Boniface led the Church in its first attempt to work out a parish system, and this was fairly well developed by the tenth century. As parishes were established they became a very definite part of the manorial world of the Middle Ages; the local lord built a village church and hired its priest much as he might build a mill and pay a miller. The village church was a proprietary church and the priest was the dependent of his lord—part of his entourage. In the thirteenth century successful attempts were made to bring the local churches under episcopal jurisdiction, but the principle of the proprietary church stayed active in many parts of Europe—notably in England, where it is still a part of the organization of the Church of England. The subjection of local church to local lord may seem theoretically improper, but in the family-dominated, local society of the early Middle Ages it was probably inevitable.

The other branch of the secular clergy—the cathedral clergy —had a privileged position. Cathedral clergymen were led by a bishop who headed a diocese. (The territorial divisions of the Church were adopted in the fourth century from the territorial divisions of the Roman Empire, with its dioceses and provinces. These divisions are retained today: the leader of a diocese is a bishop; of a province, an archbishop.) In each diocese there was a cathedral, usually in the largest city—by the seventh century, this was often the only city, existing because of and through its cathedral. Every cathedral had its priests whose major function was the conduct of religious services. The liturgy grew increasingly elaborate during the Middle Ages, and cathedral priests had to be competent musicians (although they often had children's choirs to sing for them). The medieval songs are known as Gregorian chants after Pope Gregory the Great, who may have organized the liturgy late in the sixth century. It is evident that music and phrasing were borrowed from Jewish services during the second and third centuries, but the origins of much of the liturgy are obscure. We do not know how the services sounded in the early Middle Ages: our knowledge is of the Gregorian chants of the twelfth and thirteenth centuries.

When the cathedral clergy were not singing or conducting religious services they had to manage the affairs of the diocese, to control its large properties and to advance the interests of the Church. They were literate men, of necessity, and an overwhelming preponderance of them were of good family. The chances are that many were the illegitimate sons of noblemen (or bishops); their world was the world of the great aristocratic families. The cathedral clergyman had one of the easiest and most attractive jobs of the medieval world.

At the head of the cathedral clergy, of course, were the bishops themselves, and their backgrounds were similar to those of their priests and clerks. Bishops were princes of the Church, deeply involved in the political life of the neighborhood: their social status was similar to that of a count or duke. Bishops presided in the local courts and exerted great power in local affairs—civil as well as ecclesiastical. Most of them were thoroughly committed to the interests of their noble families. It was the family, usually, that secured the bishopric for its sons, and the family continued to exert great pressure on behalf of its properties and status after the bishop took office.

Bishops might also be under pressure from the king, from reforming or aggressive popes, or from the Church in general. Most of them were fairly well educated, and a few were genuine theologians or canon lawyers. In the ninth century a group of French bishops, hoping to deprive the pope of real power, proposed a collegiate structure to replace the hierarchic structure of the Church. This worked out in practice for about two hundred years, but it worked because the popes were weak and not because the concept really won support. Most medieval theologians, trained in Roman law and Roman political concepts, tended to support the central power of the papacy.

Medieval bishops had burdensome and important day-to-day jobs, and most of them were competent and materialistic business-men. A few served as missionaries on the frontier of Christendom, notably St. Boniface, who converted a large part of western Germany in the eighth century and became the first bishop of Mainz and archbishop of Germany. However, Boniface was a very special and zealous kind of churchman. Most of his colleagues, lacking reforming passion, pursued their private interests even through periods of reform. They were lords of the Church, not scholars or missionaries.

The papacy is probably the most written-about institution of the medieval Church: in recent centuries it has been regarded as the central base of medieval Christianity. Actually it was not an important institution at all until the fifth century, when it grew to fill the space left by the disintegration of the Roman Empire. The idea of the special relationship of the Bishop of Rome to Christ cannot be traced back before the second century, except for the fairly ambiguous statement in the Gospel of St. Matthew 16:22: "And I tell you, you are Peter, and on this rock I will build my church, and the powers of death shall not prevail against it. I will give you the keys of the kingdom of heaven, and whatever you bind on earth shall be bound in heaven, and whatever you loose on earth shall be loosed in heaven."

This statement can be interpreted in various ways: in the first place, there is the play on the name "Peter," which is the Greek *petros,* or rock. Jesus may have meant to praise Simon Peter as a steadfast, rocklike disciple, or Simon may have represented all of Jesus' faithful disciples. Protestant theologians have claimed that Jesus meant he would build his church on the devotion of faithful Christians. Early in the second century, however, the Roman Church began to give this statement a special interpretation which is known as the Petrine doctrine. It was not fully or dog-matically stated until it was explicated by Pope Leo I in the mid-fifth century, but most bishops of Rome after about 130 were inclined to believe that Jesus handed over his own powers to Peter and therefore that the bishop of Rome spoke with the authority of Jesus himself. This doctrine implies the belief (nowhere clearly stated in the Bible) that Jesus was the divine Saviour, the sacramental Son of God, who had special powers to bind and loose the souls of men. It also assumes that St. Peter was in fact the bishop of Rome, and it is generally accepted that this was so, and that Peter died a martyr in the persecution of Christians by Nero around 70 A.D. Pope Pius XII ordered excavations in the Vatican in 1939, and bones dating from the first century were discovered. These are believed by many faithful Roman Catholics to be the relics of St. Peter.

In the early years of Christianity the bishops of Rome won celebrity and special status by their position as leaders of the largest and most important city of the Latin world; they had no special status in the East. Even in the third century, papal claims were sufficient to cause a group of North African bishops to express dissent from the Petrine doctrine—to deny the special authority of the bishop of Rome. In the fourth century, bishops of Rome played very minor roles in Church affairs, largely because they were personally nonentities. In the late fourth century, the bishop of Milan (St. Ambrose—a powerful and vigorous man) was the real leader of the Latin Church. In the fifth century, however, the imperial authority disappeared and the bishopric of Rome grew much more important. Roman aristocrats—well-educated, competent men—converted to Christianity and began to manage the Holy See as they had managed the Empire. The Chair of Peter was filled by a series of capable and powerful popes, one of whom was Leo the Great, who became a genuine moral leader of society (at least in northern Italy).

There is little evidence that even strong and successful popes had any influence outside of Italy in the sixth or seventh centuries. In the French Church (and France was the largest, wealthiest Christian country outside of Italy), bishops were either independent or allied to the ruling Merovingian dynasty; they were totally free of Roman influence. The pontificate of Gregory I the Great at the end of the sixth century is traditionally considered a turning point for the papacy, but it was so only in a limited sense. Gregory was a Roman aristocrat, a sound theologian and a pious missionary —an excellent pope who deserved his appellation. He recognized the need for the papacy to break out of its Italian limitations and to become involved with the Germanic countries, where the Church was subservient to the great families. He tried to promote an alliance with the Merovingian kings of France, who were not much interested in the prospect, and when he failed to win much influence over Germanic Christians, he turned to pagans. Gregory sent missionaries to England and elsewhere to convert new Christians who would presumably be led by Rome. The policy of involvement with the Germanic world bore fruit in the eighth century when the aristocratic Carolingian family formed an alliance with the papacy, exchanging protection and some ecclesiastical reform for the Church's sanction for their takeover of power in France.

The Petrine doctrine was not fully realized in the eighth century or later: the papacy had very little real authority in the early Middle Ages. However, it did have an ideology, which was stated fully in the eighth-century *Donation of Constantine*, a blatant forgery which purported to describe Constantine's surrender of his authority over the Latin-speaking world to the bishop of Rome. In actual practice, the pope could be dominated by any strong king such as Charlemagne, and this remained true (outside of Italy) in the ninth and tenth centuries. The papacy's greatest asset was its elaborate ideology, which offered a view of a theocratic society under the leadership of a priest—quite contrary to stark reality. In reality, the papacy of 950 existed on the same level of dependence on the Roman aristocracy as it had in 450; in medieval society, power, wealth, and social organization were determined by family groupings. The family-dominated society had no supportive ideology but it had substantial reality, whereas the papal claims had an elaborate doctrinal basis but little foundation in fact until the eleventh century. Claims had their importance, however; they provided ambitious popes with a drive to move forward, to make vigorous if usually futile efforts to reach the goals so clearly outlined in the Petrine doctrine.

The regular (monastic) clergy was in many ways the most influential and interesting institution of the Church in the early Middle Ages. The monastic ideal became popular in Alexandria early in the second century, and it thrived in North Africa because of the influence of Neoplatonic philosophy. Neoplatonist Christians pushed the mystical potential of Platonism as far as it could go (and further, probably, than the philosopher would have approved), and they developed a whole scheme of salvation and style of life. Holding God to be pure Spirit, they believed that man—to be godlike—must be as purely spiritual as possible. Man must lose consciousness of his body—must experience catharsis—in order to purify his soul and enter into spiritual union with God.

The original impetus to monastic life came from this desire to escape the physical, material world in order to contemplate the mind of God. Pious men began to leave the world in order to live as hermits in the desert, and these desert "saints" were respected and influential. They were true idealists, believing in the separation of mind and body and the highest possible degree of physical abstinence, and their ideas were not challenged, (in theory) until late in the twelfth century. Men abandoned the world of the power elite, of everyday life, and of material objects to seek internal happiness in their own souls.

The "eremitic" monasticism of the desert saints was only one form of the monastic movement. In "cenobitic" monasticism holy men lived a communal life for mutual aid and sustenance. Spontaneously, they formed loose communities in which abbots ("fathers") had little control over their monks. This style of monasticism was perpetuated in the Byzantine Empire and became the dominant style in Ireland in the seventh century (when there was substantial trade between Ireland and Byzantium). Irish monks received their training and education in large communities, but almost all of them served as missionaries out in the world at one time or another. Irish monasticism was distinctly missionary in tone, and extremely influential for that reason.

The Benedictine Rule was accepted by monks all over western Europe between the sixth and ninth centuries. St. Benedict was a Roman aristocrat who disapproved of severe mortification of the flesh, and he substituted rigorous discipline and hard work for flagellation and unreasonable fasting. During the next three centuries, western monks—despite the vows of poverty, obedience, and chastity, and despite the cloister—became increasingly a part of the outside world. The best-educated and ablest monks left the monastery to serve kings and nobles. As the only literate civil servants available, they provided most of the work of government. Certain monks always separated themselves from the world, but western monasticism was too complex an institution to be symbolized by the cloister.

Monasteries provided not only civil servants to the outside world but also whatever culture existed amid the chaos of the violent early medieval centuries. Monasteries compiled libraries, operated schools, retained artist-monks to illuminate manuscripts; their exclusive hold on contemporary culture gave them enormous influence on the European cultural outlook. Monasteries were founded for religious reasons, but as time went on, monks took on more and more tasks and performed them well. There were always a few genuinely saintly men who took the vows in order to avoid the world's temptations and grow close to God, but not more than 10 or 15 per cent of the Bendictine monks conformed to this ideal. Another 25 to 30 per cent were oblates—gifts to God, sacrificed in early childhood by a grateful parent (in the case of peasant children, by a hopeful or grateful noble lord). A third significant group of monks and nuns was composed of misfits for whom the monastery was a refuge. These might be old people, cripples, or weaklings rejected by aristocratic families. Many nuns took the veil because they had failed to find a husband by the customary age and had been dumped in the convent by fathers or brothers unwilling to support superfluous women. A fourth monastic group was made up of drones—people who realized that monastery life was easier than life outside. They took vows for materialistic reasons such as food and protection, and as time went on their number grew. By the ninth century it was very difficult for a peasant to get into a monastery at all, except in a menial position. Nunneries, in particular, were filled with high-born ladies whose relatives had bought them a place.

Tenth-century monasteries were varied and bustling social institutions rather than simple communes for religious mystics. Many monks were engaged in agricultural work on their enormous properties—and they were good at it, being the most progressive farmers and the most skillful managers anywhere. Another group (and an important one) was fully absorbed in the duty and privilege of singing the Mass. The liturgists who sang Masses night and day (in some monasteries they virtually sang around the clock) were prized, talented people whose work earned large endowments for their monasteries. Noble families, believing that monks were close to God and that their prayers would reach Him, paid the monks to pray for the souls of their dead relatives. Probably 20 per cent of all monks were engaged exclusively in liturgical service and some monasteries specialized in elaborate Masses for the dead and became rich and powerful because they performed a valuable function for the power elite.

A somewhat less popular but very important service was performed by monks who won noble patronage as scholars or artists. There always were a few monks who found, transcribed, and illuminated manuscripts; our earliest copies of all the Latin authors were made in medieval monasteries. The work of these monks is now priceless, and fortunately it was fairly valuable to medieval noblemen.

The elite group of monks, of course, went into the world to serve secular lords by keeping records, writing letters and speeches, and contributing their learning and sophistication to political life. Several of Charlemagne's officials and advisors were monks, and other monks became courtiers or ministers of state and exerted enormous influence on the political scene. As students of Roman history, monks tended to favor centralized authority, and their concepts and phrases dignified Germanic kingship. In an illiterate society, an educated man might be regarded as a wizard—Arthur's Merlin was one of these—and the learning of the educated monk was apt to be quite awesome to his contemporaries.

At all times there were a few true idealists among the monks, who devoted themselves as missionaries to the conversion of Europe. In the seventh and eighth centuries there were several of these heroic men (often martyrs); their numbers declined with the decline in the number of remaining pagans. Perhaps only 10 to 20 per cent of the Benedictine monks in the early centuries (5 or 10 per cent later on) were true Augustinians who attempted to establish the City of God, but their influence always was out of proportion to their number.

In summary, then, the regular clergy and the institution of monasticism were thoroughly integrated into the structure of early medieval society. Monasticism was associated with the great families, with lordship, and with the other social institutions of the period. By the tenth century all the important monasteries were patronized by some aristocratic family, and the monks provided significant services for the great families (primarily that of salvation) and drew their income from such service. Abbots were part of the feudal elite; they were vassals as well as landlords, and they performed the military obligations of a vassal through their own vassals if not in their persons.

Although the monks were very much a part of family-dominated western society, they also represented something very different. Because the monasteries were intellectual, ideological centers they came into contact with the universalist thinking of the patristic Fathers. Theirs was the only non-familial thinking of the early medieval period, and monks alone could conceive of society as something more than an assemblage of families. The radical universalist implications of patristic thought were rarely translated into political or social action. Its influence was confined to a few monastic royal ministers, but these did give their masters a sense of office apart from that of the head of a family or a feudal lord. Not until the eleventh century did the radical, universal side of Christian thought—the ideal of a just society established according to Christian principles—become important in European life.

KINGSHIP

Traditionally, historians have regarded early medieval kingship as a very important institution, and medieval kings have been seen as foci of political life, or as aggressive reformers who made genuine attempts to reform the chaos of contemporary social life. This historiographical approach was developed out of the contemporary sources, which include programmatic pronouncements by early medieval monarchs. Historians tended to take statements of intention seriously, to make policy equivalent to practice—a serious mistake. Most of the work on medieval history between about 1890 and 1950 (and even today, to some extent) was done by German scholars who emphasized the history of ideas and tended to assume that ideas, once expressed, must have come into practical existence. Actually it is extremely difficult to find out what really happened. The records are fragmentary and confusing, requiring difficult research and balanced judgment for their interpretation. German historians have assumed that an organized national community existed in the early Middle Ages, and that national consciousness allowed the king to rule with the consent and cooperation of the community. There may have been some degree of national consciousness, but it is very difficult to establish its extent or importance.

The traditions of medieval kingship were those of Rome, of Christianity, and of Germany. The Roman Empire, of course, had a well-formulated ideology and institutions of monarchy, and by the late Empire this was an absolute monarchy. Emperors could not always do just what they wanted to do, of course, but the system operated as though the imperial will was all-powerful; no constitutional mechanism existed to frustrate or modify it. In any absolute monarchy (even that of Louis XIV), effective limitations were set by primitive communications networks and by the small size of the civil service, which frequently made it impossible to implement the royal will even when it was accepted as law. The ideology of absolute monarchy was developed out of Roman law based on the Hellenistic and oriental tradition that the people surrendered their natural powers to the monarch and could never revoke the surrender. With Constantine, the emperor became the earthly reflection or image of God, as close to God as a human could possibly be. To question or resist the Christian emperor was a sin as well as a crime.

The great contribution of Rome to political thought was the concept of office. Romans believed in obedience to the office without regard to the person of the officeholder, and that the emperor held the sovereignty of the state whether he was a good or a bad man (or an effective or an incompetent leader). The essence of modern political theory is still the public authority of the state; departure from this concept involves moral rather than political questions.

The Christian tradition of kingship was ambiguous. It tended to favor the power and authority of kings, but statements or concepts could be found in the Scriptures which would deny or limit the royal power. The royalist tradition was based on sacred history, particularly on the Old Testament stories of Saul and David. The anointment of Saul by the prophet Samuel became an extremely influential image, and anointment was a key constitutional ceremony after about 750 A.D. David refused to resist Saul when the king behaved badly—on the ground that Saul was the anointed of the Lord—and his refusal was a powerful example to medieval men. The sacred authority of kings was a self-evident proposition, like the force of gravity, and resistance to kings was unnatural.

In the New Testament Peter said "Obey God rather than men," and this text was used to justify resistance to a king who went against God. An atheistic king had to be resisted, of course —but an atheistic medieval king would be hard to discover! A king who abused the Church or clergy might be resisted, however, and indeed there was very little opposition to medieval kings that was not sanctioned by some churchman. (Even in 1215 the barons who forced King John to accept the Magna Carta had the support of the Archbishop of Canterbury.) After Christian ideas were widely accepted, medieval kings, like priests, were never assassinated. An exception was William Rufus of England, who was killed in a staged "hunting accident" in 1100. But William Rufus abused the Church and the clergy and made friends with Jews, and evidently that was enough to justify his murder.

Christian kingship retained the legacy of St. Paul, with his belief that "the powers that be are ordained by God." It is unlikely that this was intended as a general political statement, although it has been interpreted as such: Paul was warning the Christians in Rome not to attract persecution by becoming conspicuous. In general, Christian teaching sanctified kingship unless a king flagrantly violated God's will. A king who was a violent person or a war leader was not likely to be treated as a sinner unless his violence was directed against the Church itself.

It is questionable whether there was any real tradition of Germanic kingship. A German king was the equivalent of a chief, a war leader, the best fighter of a group. *Beowulf* gives the fullest picture of a Germanic king, and Beowulf was a strong fighter who parcelled out the booty after a battle. He was the Ring-Giver, or Booty-Giver, for the tribe.

The Roman, Christian, and Gemanic traditions were amalgamated in the medieval system of choosing kings. In Rome, the king supposedly was elected by the Senate and people, but in practice the throne was inherited after about 300 unless it was taken by force. It has been said that late Roman and Byzantine monarchies were despotisms tempered by assassination, and a successful assassin could claim that his success proved that God was on his side. After a man took the throne by force he was confirmed by election, and his relatives inherited the throne until a new family began the process over again. It was a hereditary tradition in which dynasties were changed by force.

In Christian kingship the ruler was designated by the Church, which anointed the monarch. Among the Germanic peoples, kingship was loosely elective. There was no formal election, but the leader had to win the approval of the fighters and to be a suitable fighter himself. No children or women or old men or weaklings could hope to rule. German kings ruled people, not territories, and the people were loyal to their leader as long he was "throneworthy," or effective. Kingship was personal, not a public office; there was no concept of the state. By 600 it had become customary for kings to inherit within a family, but there was no primogeniture —kingship passed to the best war leader in a family, not necessarily to the eldest son.

Medieval people achieved a synthesis of these three traditions of kingship suitable to their needs and to their understanding. They never got away from the idea that kingship was personal and the king the best fighter among the people: military skill remained the most important attribute of an effective or respected king. Even the famous Charlemagne, who ruled from 774 to 814, won wide loyalty primarily because he was a great warrior who could give his followers much booty. When he grew older (and less terrifying), his hold over his people began to slip.

After the mid-eighth century, medieval kings followed the Christian tradition of anointment. Society was then being Christianized, and Christian ideas were taken very seriously. Anointment gave stability to the reigning monarch, who was regarded as a priest and thus fairly safe from assassination. Kings tried hard to impress the sacred, priestly qualities of their office upon their people. The Christian tradition was useful, too, in the transference of kingship from one dynasty to another. When a satellite family of great nobles grew in wealth and influence to become the equal or superior of the royal family, it could get moral sanction for taking over the kingship through the ceremony of anointment. This was used first in 751, when the Carolingians replaced the Merovingian kings whose chief ministers they had been. It was a natural change—the Carolingians had produced a series of excellent fighters and strong personalities who acquired more property and power than the kings—but in the pristine German tradition there was no possibility of a peaceful transfer of power. With the cooperation of the Church, Pepin III, the head of the Carolingian family, became the first anointed king of medieval Europe. Naturally the Church approved of anointment, which gave churchmen some power over the selection of a monarch and made the Church indispensable to royalty. On the opposite side, however —it was almost impossible to oppose a king, once anointed. The Church exerted its maximum control when a king died or lost the support of the nobility and it could threaten to transfer its allegiance to a new family, forcing the king to obey its will.

The Roman tradition of kingship had little influence until the eleventh century, largely because Roman government had depended on a system of law and a strong bureaucracy which early medieval kings did not have. Also, early medieval men simply could not conceive of public authority—of a state apart from personal leadership. To the Romans, the will of the emperor had the force of law because the power of the state was behind it, but this was not intelligible in the early Middle Ages.

The Roman tradition did operate in the meliorative attitudes of a few great early medieval kings. Partly because they took Christian doctrine seriously, four or five rulers did make an effort to be something more than mere fighters. Charlemagne, Alfred, Canute of Britain, Otto of Germany, and one or two others did try to establish peace and law in society and the right ordering of the Church. No medieval king, not even these, conceived social welfare to be among his responsibilities, and none of them tried to compensate for poverty or misery or famine except in the alms-giving that was expected of any Christian nobleman. The maintenance of law and order and the right ordering of the Church were all the social duties of a Christian ruler—but implementation of even this short list of royal obligations was extremely difficult.

In so far as the Roman tradition was perpetuated in medieval kingship, it was perpetuated through the monks who guided their royal masters. Being educated in classical history and rhetoric, monks knew that Roman emperors had aimed at grander ventures than mere conquest. They revealed to their kings the image of Constantine or Theodosius, who were more than war leaders. Given the conceptual level of the period and the conditions of social life, that was all of the Roman tradition that could be perpetuated in the early Middle Ages.

Medieval Society

Early medieval society rested, then, on the five institutional bases of family, community, lordship, the Church, and kingship. By far the most important of these was family, which can be regarded as the basis for all the other institutions. The early medieval European world was entirely agrarian, with almost no urban centers of any importance. Communications were terrible—almost non-existent at some seasons and in some areas; even horses were rare and expensive until the eighth or ninth century. Family was an essential institution in the Roman Empire, and it was still central in the thirteenth century, but it was never as important as in the period beween 600 and 1000 A.D. In the Roman Empire there were important cities and good roads; the same is true of the thirteenth century. In the seventh century, however, a man could not enter into close communication with extra-familial groups; he could not get away from his family or work outside his family except in rare instances. In the Empire or in the High Middle Ages men were involved in collective groups in cities or in quasi-centralized national states, and these institutions tended to diminish the absolute power of the family.

The domination of the family was special and exclusive in the early Middle Ages, and it tended to absorb all other institutions. The community, after all, was really a group of families joined together in small judicial groups. Lordship was (in origin at least) a substitute for a familial relationship; the Church was controlled by the great landed families; kingship (in the German tradition) was an accolade won by the greatest family in the area. Ideology was less significant during the period of exclusive family domination because ideology and family interests are always at odds; under the Roman Empire, and again in the eleventh century, men were moved by ideas and called to action by moral commitment. This ideological commitment was true of only a small group of monks in the eighth century, when most men were called to action only by family interests.

Until quite recently, historians did not sufficiently recognize that the family was the most important social institution in western society right down in to this century. Traditionally, family ties have always claimed the most loyalty and had the most effect on social life in the West. In periods of relatively good communications and transportation, with strong cities or national institutions, the domination of the family has been less evident; in other periods— notably in the early Middle Ages—the family has gobbled up everything, with little competition from ideology or bureaucratic and urban institutions. Few of the liberal historians of the nine- teenth century were able to appreciate the importance of family, largely because their own universalist bias made a family-centered society repugnant. The social reforms the liberals wanted usually required the expelling of aristocratic family interests from politi- cal life. Especially in England, liberal historians were part of a movement which opposed the domination of society by aristocratic families, and they liked to present history as a series of collective, ideologically based movements—which, used as an historical norm, is fundamentally a false premise. The importance of the family was rediscovered by conservative historians such as L. B. Namier, who interpreted the political history of the eighteenth century in Eng- land in the light of the struggle among a few great families. Some left-wing skeptics have also understood that the domination of the family has been the basic social situation of western Europe down to our own century.

III. Byzantium and Islam

BASIC ASSUMPTIONS

Any approach to the history of the Byzantine Empire—or that of Islam—is necessarily grounded in the historian's own back- ground and commitment; the attitudes expressed here are those of a confirmed westerner. Admiration for western civilization is un- fashionable today; yet it would be wrong to forget the achievements of the West in our belated recognition of its failures. Also, the ideas and opinions here were developed in the light of a teleological in- terpretation of Byzantine and Islamic history. It is quite clear that an impartial observer in the year 1050 would have pronounced

Constantinople or the cities of Muslim Spain vastly superior to the urban centers of western Europe. In wealth, intellect, sophistication, and resources, these cities far outshone Paris, London, or even Rome. We should, however, not forget that the West progressed enormously from its eleventh-century level of civilization while Byzantium and Islam had gone as far as they would ever go. The Byzantine Empire survived until 1453, but its last four centuries were years of agonizing decline. It is true that two of the greatest Islamic thinkers lived after 1050 (Averroes in the twelfth century and Ibn Khaldun in the fourteenth), but it is also true that the power, prosperity, and technological development of Islam made no significant advance after about the beginning of the twelfth century.

The Commerce, Society, and Government of Byzantium

Byzantium is an old Greek name for a colony founded by Greeks in the fifth century B.C. In the fourth century A.D., the Emperor Constantine selected and named the city of Constantinople (on the site of the old Greek colony) as his eastern capital; Roman emperors had begun to make use of eastern headquarters in the third century when it became obvious that the frontiers of the Empire were too long to be defended from Rome. Constantinople (now Istanbul) is a superb natural fortress, virtually impregnable. The Arabs, and then the Turks, besieged the city for more than seven hundred years before it fell in 1453, and the British attempt to take Constantinople in 1915 produced the disasters of their Gallipoli campaign.

Byzantium made an excellent eastern capital, and it survived the fall of the western Empire in the fifth century. By 600, Constantinople was one of the largest cities in the world; by 1000, it probably had more than a million inhabitants. As a natural stopping-place for goods moving overland in an east-west direction, Byzantium was always extremely prosperous. Byzantine merchants made large profits when they received goods from Asia and re-exported them to the west, and travellers to the east usually stopped over in Byzantium. One such group of travellers was the Latin Crusaders, who visited Constantinople on the way to the

Holy Land—much to the dismay of the emperor, who feared they would remain, as eventually they did in 1204, when they seized the city, and held it for six decades.

As a thriving commercial center, medieval Byzantium had a prosperous and successful merchant class. By western standards, however, it was a strangely inert class: the Byzantine merchants played little or no part in the political life of the city or the Empire; and the economic life of the Empire had no direct relationship to its political or cultural life. Byzantine history offers an excellent example of a functional dichotomy of the economic base of a society and its power setup, or intellectual life. This presents an obvious contradiction of the Marxist theory that the means of production determines all the characteristics of a society.

The Byzantine merchants controlled the economic life of the Empire, but they never achieved political power or even political or social self-consciousness. As far as we know, they did not even aspire to political power, but we do not know very much about aspirations: although they were wealthy and literate, the merchants left no written record of their hopes or their intellectual condition. The emperor protected the city from invasion and the merchants from competition or interruption of trade, and the merchants were able to organize the commerce of the city in their own interest. They operated a system of guilds, and although they paid a fairly high customs tax, that was the main tax they had to pay. It was not nearly as high as the taxes of the late Roman Empire which had ruined the bourgeoisie. The fifth-century eastern emperors modified the Draconic tax system of Rome and also inaugurated the tradition of protecting their merchants against foreign competition. No non-Greek could engage in commerce in Byzantium without a special (and rarely-granted) license from the emperor. The early prosperity of the Venetians—the first Italians to grow rich through commercial expansion during the medieval period—can be ascribed to their position as nominal subjects of the Byzantine emperor. The Venetian merchants were the only Italians allowed to trade in Constantinople in the tenth century, with the result that they were far ahead of their colleagues in less-favored western cities.

For centuries, Byzantine merchants continued to make money in commerce just the way their ancestors made money before them. They made no technological advances—no significant improvements in shipping, no development of industrial machinery. Like other eastern merchant classes, they became a static, self-sustaining group perpetuated by inheritance, neither open to new-comers nor mobile in itself. (This situation tended to favor Jewish merchants, who flourished in protected, non-political societies, and indeed, Byzantine Jews did very well compared to Jews in west-ern Europe.) The Arab and Indian merchant classes were much like the Byzantines, and probably Chinese merchants had similar atti-tudes. In accordance with the thesis of the German sociologist Max Weber, who believed that the rise of the bourgeoisie was the central, determining factor in modern western civilization, Byzantium should be characterized as an oriental society. The western bourgeoisie after 1050 A.D. worked actively for political and social mobility, developing an ethos and world-view of their own; by the eighteenth century (or before), the European bourgeoisie—descendants of the medieval merchant class—was attempting to transform all of so-ciety along middle-class lines. In Weber's view, it is this funda-mental development of western history that sets it apart from the history of China—or of Byzantium.

The Byzantine Empire was governed by the imperial family, the bureaucracy, and (sometimes, particularly after the tenth cen-tury) the landed aristocrats. Dynasties gathered their supporters into bureaucracies, and bureaucratic posts often became hereditary. However, these hereditary bureaucracies were broken up when (as often happened) new families forced their way into the govern-ment, killed the emperor, and took over the civil service. Frequently —almost routinely—aristocratic families usurped the throne and the treasury and started the cycle over again, forming identical governments under different names. Byzantine political history is like that of China: a rough, dramatic story that does not describe the development of any real political community. There was no re-lationship between the central government and society, no repre-sentative institutions, no possibility of democracy. There was one dynasty after another, surrounded by bureaucracies which changed their personnel with each new leader but retained their ancient characteristics. For hundreds of years, Byzantium produced bureau-crats who were able and literate, skilled in law, tax collection, and record-keeping. (We assume the last from fragmentary evidence; few records survived the devastation wrought by Latin Crusaders in 1204 and by Turks in 1453.) In the eleventh century, the imperial bureaucracy began to lose control over the landed aristocracy and this weakened the military power of the state and Constantinople's ability to withstand new Turkish invaders.

BYZANTINE CULTURE

The intellectual and cultural life of Byzantium was almost entirely ecclesiastical: that is, its artists and thinkers were churchmen, or were patronized by churchmen, and most of them were monks. Until the eighth century at least, Byzantine monks were popular secular leaders as well as devout religious men, and many of them left the monastery to preach and teach in the world. Byzantine monks had enormous influence with the masses, who were fanatically pious and superstitious. Huge processions used to form behind monks carrying icons—pictures of Christ or his Mother or the saints—and people would march and sing in the streets, witnessing their faith and devotion. Eighth-century Byzantine emperors began to find such phenomena threatening, and indeed, there may have been a real possibility of a communal, anti-despotic movement led by monks. In the early eighth century the emperor denounced icon-worship as superstition and ordered the destruction of the images.

In the "iconoclastic controversy" much of early Byzantine art was destroyed. The details of the conflict are obscure, but it must have begun as a reactionary movement (an imperial reaction against contemporary phenomena) and evolved into a kind of revolution. It seems likely that the controversy became a struggle for social leadership between the imperial family (with some of the aristocracy) and the monks. Although the icons were restored in the ninth century, the emporor was generally successful in breaking monastic power, but the details are not clear because the entire affair was played down or suppressed in Byzantine historiography: the authorities wanted no historical model to inspire other movements. In the end, imperial domination of the Church was established even more firmly in such matters as the appointment of abbots and the supervision of monks—but the monks remained in control of the cultural life of the Empire.

In monastic hands, Byzantine culture became rigid, static,

and traditional. Concerned chiefly to preserve their hold on education, art, and literature, the monks grew afraid of anything new. As conservative guardians of the intellectual life of Byzantium, they permitted only the repetition of traditional forms. No secular movement, no scientific movement, no radical movement livened Byzantine intellectual history, which barely progressed over more than nine hundred years. No Byzantine book survives that an educated person would want to read in the twentieth century except as academic research. The sixth-century Justinian Code is an exception, but the Code—although a great intellectual achievement —was created before the iconoclastic controversy and was built on Roman ideas. Even the work of supposedly important Byzantine scholars such as Photius (a tenth-century monk) is derivative, fragmentary, and of no particular interest or value today.

Byzantium did achieve excellence in art and architecture, although the important achievements in the latter field were largely confined to the sixth century, when the great Cathedral of Santa Sophia was built under the patronage of Justinian. In their two artistic specialties—mosaics and manuscript illumination—Byzantine artists have never been surpassed. Their subject matter remained traditional, but their exciting use of color and their semi-nonrepresentational style remained a unique contribution until the development of abstract expressionism in the twentieth century.

The spectrum of artistic style extends from representational art, in which the artist attempts to show the world exactly as it appears, to nonrepresentational abstract art, in which he tries to portray through his art the impact of the world upon his senses. Most artistic expression, of course, falls somewhere between these poles. It was the ancient Greeks who first developed representational (or naturalistic) art and carried it to its finest achievements, and in fact such art was described as "classical" until about 1500. Even the Greeks, however, were not completely naturalistic in their approach to the human body (their main subject); they idealized the human face and form instead of portraying individuals with all their flaws and special characteristics. To a Platonist, an ideal form is more real and more significant than any individual, and the attempt to portray ideal beauty gave Greek art an impressionistic or idealistic aspect.

The Greeks—the first humanists—believed that a perfect human body or face was the most beautiful imaginable, and they depicted their gods in the image of beautiful people. At the opposite extreme were the Jews, who believed that the beauty of God was so far from the beauty of humanity that physical depiction of the Deity was worse than impossible and regarded attempts to portray God as rebellious and sinful slanders on His majesty. Romans followed the Greek tradition, although (as often occurs in the later stages of a classical, naturalistic period in art) Roman art became increasingly particular, forceful, and individualistic. The Romans began to neglect ideal beauty to portray the majesty of an emperor or the valor of a soldier, and by the second century A.D., their painted and sculptured figures had considerable individuality. In more general terms, however, the Roman artists stayed within the Greek tradition of "classic" naturalism, of representational art.

A major and fundamental change took place in the fourth century, when artistic change coincided with (or reflected) other important historical developments. In the fourth century the West was moving toward despotism, toward centralization, and toward Christianity—with its new theological concerns and its providential view of history. The contemporary changes in artistic style involved more than simple failures in technique, although it is quite obvious that western art of the fourth century (and later) was vastly inferior to classical art in execution. It was awkward, grotesque, cumbersome; the artists evidently could not effectively handle miniaturization, for they liked to make enormous and hideous statues—of which the prime example is the monstrous head of Constantine as Colossus.

Besides technical problems, however, there was a real change in the concept of art and the motivation of the artist. Fourth-century artists were not primarily interested in the portrayal of ideal beauty, and their style departed from classic naturalism to move toward nonrepresentational expression. Their works were designed to impress some principle upon the viewer—usually a principle of majesty or authority or hierarchy—and to arouse the respect and loyalty of illiterate masses toward a ruler of Church or state. Perhaps in reaction to the increasing disintegration and disloyalty within the Empire, art became an agency of communication—often crudely propagandistic.

Everything Byzantine began (and much of it ended) with the culture and institutions of the fourth-century Roman Empire: Byzantine technology, for example, never did develop much beyond the level of 350 A.D. Because of the iconoclastic controversy, few examples of early Byzantine art are available for study, although some early mosaics survive in Ravenna and in Santa Sophia. From these it is obvious that the early Byzantine artists perpetuated the quasi-nonrepresentational style and the didacticism of the late Roman Empire, with an important difference—an enormous improvement in technique. The mosaics of Ravenna and Constantinople are artistic masterpieces first and propagandistic devices second.

After about 300, artists looked around for new media and new forms in which to express a new view of the world. Sculpture, wall painting, and relief—the traditional ancient forms—were no longer satisfactory: wall painting became rare after 200 and almost disappeared after about 400, and Byzantine sculpture was never anything but crude. However, Byzantine artists developed new forms of mosaic and manuscript illumination, and these were borrowed by western artists from the Carolingian period on. The artist in mosaic used small colored stones to create patterns with a glaze of color; the illuminator applied a thick color overlay to the pages of a manuscript. After the end of the great age of cathedral building in the fifth and sixth centuries, Byzantine artists did their finest work in these special and demanding media, both of which gave full play to their characteristic command of color.

The Byzantine style was impressionistic, reminiscent to us of late nineteenth-century French painting. The artists did not attempt to portray the human body realistically, but figures were recognizable and their work was not completely abstract. All their imaginative expression, their elegant use of color, was designed to make an immediate didactic impression of some principle such as obedience to divine or imperial majesty. More than 95 per cent of Byzantine art was devoted to the service of Church or state; apart from an occasional historical scene, the art works of Byzantium proclaimed the universal hierarchy dominated by emperor and bishop. In the magnificent mosaics of the Church of San Vitale in Ravenna, Justinian and his empress, Theodora, are surrounded by soldiers and churchmen and symbols suggestive of their position as God's earthly representatives.

Few depictions of Christ survive from the early period, and most of those that do exist are found far from the main centers of Byzantine civilization, indicating that only their distance allowed them to escape destruction during the iconoclastic controversy. Later works, however, portray Jesus as Christ Pantocrator—the ruler of the universe—and they emphasize the stern majesty of the Son of God rather than the humility of the Son of Man. Jesus is not shown as a babe in arms or a suffering martyr; in the mosaics of San Apollinare in Classe (Ravenna), for instance, he is a monumental figure surrounded by apostles and by sheep, symbolizing his role as shepherd of the Christian flock.

Obviously the great Byzantine artists felt very deeply about their themes, but their emotion was totally contained within the institutional framework of Byzantine culture: one looks in vain for evidence of individual feeling. Unlike the western artist, who eventually won the freedom to express individual ideas and attitudes in non-traditional forms (although perhaps not completely until the nineteenth century), the Byzantine artist never did escape the confines of the social and religious ideals of his world. However, the artists of Byzantium have never been surpassed in technique, and despite their inability to express a personal vision, an original theory, or a new view of the world, their creative achievement was enormous.

Byzantium supported its artists with a substantial part of the extensive resources at its command. Both mosaics and illuminated manuscripts are extremely expensive in materials and time-consuming in labor, and the artists were heavily subsidized by Church and state. The Byzantine Church, with its mosaics and its choir and its incense, made full use of these media to establish its impact upon the congregation. Overcome by the grandeur and mystery received through his senses in the cathedral, the worshipper must have been quite ready to accept the hierarchic, God-centered universe described by the authorities. The Byzantine artists, who broke away from classicism and achieved masterpieces of didactic art (a paradoxical and rare achievement!), played an essential part in the creation of the static—yet beautiful—world of Byzantium.

THE ISLAMIC WORLD

The Islamic Empire, an immense and complex phenomenon, at its height included countries from northern India all the way to Spain. Our knowledge of medieval Islam is still fragmentary, and while we probably have all the information about Byzantium that we will ever have (there may be new interpretations but it is unlikely that new sources will be discovered), our knowledge of Islam could—and probably will—substantially increase. There are large gaps even in straightforward information about what happened, perhaps because Islamic studies are very difficult for western scholars—several languages are necessary for advanced work, as well as arduous research in museums and archives. The Arab countries themselves have produced few historians, although the Lebanese Christian scholar P.K. Hitti is one exception. Most of the existing work in Arabic studies has been done by Germans and Englishmen, mainly because Kaiser Wilhelm II, hoping to reach agreement with the Turkish and Arab countries, fostered Arabic studies in the highly politicized German universities of the years before the first world war, and because of British imperial involvement in the Middle East. By all accounts, the most important contemporary historian of medieval Islam is Gustav von Grünebaum, whose presence at UCLA has made that university the most important center of medieval Islamic studies in the world.

The Islamic Empire consisted of several ancient Mediterranean cultures held together mainly by religion and language. They were united politically for about a hundred years, but after the middle of the eighth century the various parts of the Empire broke apart into independent states. No historian has been able fully to explain the Arabs' dramatic conquest of their vast empire, their rapid and unhindered success. After trying to break out of the Arabian peninsula for many centuries, they finally succeeded in the seventh century A.D., creating an immense empire within half a century. Historians have pointed out that the Arab tribes were never united until they accepted the Islamic faith, and this may have been a critical factor in their success. Furthermore, the Byzantine Empire had just defeated the Persian kingdom in a long and exhausting war and neither state was in a condition to resist the Arab advance.

Probably the best explanation for the Arab success can be found in the great contemporary conflict within the Byzantine Empire over the Monophysite heresy. Certain subjects of Byzantium, notably a large group of Egyptian and Syrian Christians, had been severely persecuted for accepting a doctrinal variation of Christianity rejected by the Byzantine Church. These people were willing to accept the Arab conquerors in preference to persecution from Constantinople, and in fact many Christians (in and out of the Byzantine Empire) accepted Islam. The Arabs did not enforce conversion, but Christians within their empire were second-class citizens who had to pay a special tax and had no political power. In general the Arabs did not persecute Christians for religious reasons, but most Christians chose to become Muslims after the Arab conquest of the Mediterranean.

Like the fall of Rome, the rise of the Islamic Empire represented the conquest of old civilizations by barbarian invaders. However, the Arabs were much more advanced than the German barbarians; they had a higher rate of literacy and were quick to accept urban life and to appreciate Greek science and philosophy and Roman techniques of government. The Arabs were a small minority in the countries of their empire (less than 5 per cent of the population outside of Syria), but Arabic very rapidly became the international language of literature and culture as well as government. At the beginning of the period of conquest, most of the literate conquered people knew Greek and very few knew Arabic, but Greek soon became a fairly esoteric study. This was quite unlike the linguistic history of Europe, where the German language became dominant only where Germans outnumbered the original, Latin-speaking population. The Arab conquerors took over the Mediterranean bureaucratic administrative systems, while the German kings (for the most part) did not; in order to gain positions in government and law the conquered peoples had to learn Arabic.

In most of the old Roman world, Latin remained dominant after the invasions and eventually was transformed into the modern Romance languages. Most of the subjects of the Islamic Empire accepted not only the religion of their conquerors, but their language as well. This is particularly extraordinary in view of the vocabulary of seventh-century Arabic, with its many words for "camel" and its paucity of words to express philosophic or scientific concepts. However, Arabic (like other Semitic languages) is very flexible, and its vocabulary grew very fast as the language was adapted for use in a great civilization.

RELIGION

Conversion to Islam was not very difficult for ordinary Christians, perhaps because Islam is a monotheistic religion which seems natural and acceptable to ordinary men. It was very different from the difficult, esoteric Christianity of Paul or Augustine, but not much at variance with the faith of the average believer. Early medieval Christian teachers tended to play down the Augustinian aspects of their religion as too stern and special to be widely acceptable; they ignored concepts of grace and election and preached a reward-and-punishment doctrine that was intelligible to their Germanic congregations. Islam, too, is essentially a religion of merit, and one which includes aspects of Judaism as well as Christianity.

Judaism is intensely moral, but the Jews have never made up their minds about the rewards of morality. The concept of personal immortality did creep into Judaism from Persia in the first century B.C. (it became a Jewish doctrine in the twelfth century), but even today not very much is taught in the synagogues about an afterlife. Jews are still troubled by a "Job complex," by uncertainty about why they must be good, why they suffer, why rewards and punishments are meted out in this world as well as the next. Muhammed overcame the Jewish *angst* by being extremely specific about how and why his followers must be good. Very strict rules of conduct lead a pious Muslim to specific rewards in a well-defined paradise—death is a triumphant release for a good man. Free of the Jewish uncertainty about rewards and the Christian doubt about how to achieve heaven (whether man must first love God or God must first love man and elect him to grace), Islam was a simple and appealing faith.

We know very little about the founder of Islam, although a great many stories and legends surround his name. Muhammed wrote the Koran (or took dictation from the Angel Gabriel); obviously he was a master of the Arabic language. He belonged to a poor but important family of Mecca, and he saw visions—like St. Paul, he may have been an epileptic. Muhammed certainly was a shrewd politician, and one of his first successes depended on his convincing the Jews of Medina that he was sympathetic to Judaism, and taking advantage of their money and support. He was something of a brigand, and he won early celebrity by Robin Hood–like activities among the desert caravans.

Islam is too simple a faith to encourage extensive theological analysis or speculation, and that may be one reason why Muslim intellectuals have tended to ignore religious questions. In the Christian world, where intellectuals were leaders of the Church, intellectual attitudes affected the development of theology, and abstract theoretical disputes became involved with significant power struggles within the elite. Islam is not a sacramental religion, and its leaders were not priests but teachers and preachers and jurists trained in moral and religious law instead of theology. Like rabbis, they acted as community leaders who gave advice on moral matters and exhorted the faithful to observe the law.

There were vibrant religious disputes within medieval Islam, leading to schisms, and these schisms have been perpetuated to the present day. But these disputes and schisms were productive of no significant intellectual advances. Orthodox Muslims (called Sunnites) believed not only in the authority of the Koran but also in a massive body of religious and moral law developed by orthodox religious teachers (closely paralleling the Jewish Talmud). The non-orthodox groups were the Sufite mystics, who believe in the authority of personal religious experience; and the Fatimites (named after Muhammed's daughter) who gave their loyalty to charismatic religious leaders who in one way or another claimed to have assumed the authority of Muhammed's prophetic utterances. Social and political factors contributed to the emergence of the Sufite and Fatimite dissenting groups—the Sufites seem to have gained adherence particularly among the discontented petite bourgeoisie and the doctrine of neo-prophecy was obviously convenient to ambitious political leaders. But, in comparison with the West, religious dissent in Islam was not productive of new world-views and social theories.

In the Islamic Empire, as in other oriental states, distinct social groups did not impinge upon each other as they did in the West. The government was run by the caliph (or emir or sultan), his family, his court, and his bureaucracy—religious leaders and intellectuals did not interfere. Merchants conducted their own business, as did farmers, and both of these stayed quite apart from city working people and large landowners. The intellectuals were in a small group by themselves; they were not community leaders but singular people who were fortunate enough to have enough money and leisure to study science or philosophy. Many of them made a living as physicians or government officials, or they lived on allowances from rich merchant fathers. They took no part in religion or government or commerce, and there was little connection between intellectual attitudes and other aspects of Islamic culture; the intellectual life of Islam was the private, personal pursuit of a few favored individuals.

Islamic scholars read the works of Plato and of Aristotle (in translations made with the help of Greek monks), and they tried to go beyond the Greek philosophers in knowledge of the nature and order of the universe and the nature of knowledge itself. By the tenth century, Islamic intellectuals fully realized that the universe was not exactly as the Koran described it. This did not bother them: like modern men, they accepted the bifurcation of reason and faith. However, their questions did bother the religious leaders, who denounced scholarship as a threat to Islam and asked the government to put an end to the teaching of science and philosophy. Particularly in twelfth-century Spain the government intervened at the request of the orthodox religious leaders, and it was at that time—in about 1200—that the intellectual life of Islam started to decline. The vibrancy and wealth of the Empire ceased its expansion at about the same time, but it would be hard to ascribe that decline to the suppression of the schools. After all, the intellectuals never had concerned themselves with the political, social, or economic affairs of the community, and their virtual disappearance could not have affected other aspects of the civilization.

ACHIEVEMENTS

A major accomplishment of medieval Islam was the preservation of the technology and commerce of the Mediterranean world. Islam was wealthy and its cities were large and bustling, probably healthy and pleasant places to live. The Muslim world provided at least a measure of effective government and political stability between the seventh and the twelfth centuries. The cultural and intellectual achievements of Islam are harder to measure: in art, at least, they were insignificant. The Muslims, like the Jews, were opposed to religious images, and this apparently discouraged artistic creativity.

The most important intellectual achievement of Islam was the transmission of knowledge from Greece and India to the West. Greek philosophy and science moved west through Islam to Europe, where it contributed to the intellectual revolution of the twelfth century. The Muslims also introduced Indian mathematics to Europe—indeed, they made original advances in mathematics, taking an important part in the invention of algebra. Islamic scholars also extended the Platonic and Aristotelian traditions and made important emendations to the classical intellectual heritage.

When all is said, however, it must be recognized that the Islamic Empire was less creative than Byzantium. Although the medieval Muslims left behind a wide variety of achievements, there was no single field in which they made a real and lasting advance (such as that achieved in art in Byzantium). Islamic mathematicians and physicians and physicists of 1100 knew more than the ancients, but their work did not constitute a revolution in thought. The scientific revolution came in the West between the fourteenth and seventeenth centuries, and although the revolutionaries made good use of Arabic work, one cannot give Islam the credit for their creativity.

Certain scholars believe that the medieval West derived its romantic tradition—based on the recognition of the importance of emotion and of individual personality—from the Islamic world, and the poetry of twelfth-century Muslim Spain is often cited as the connecting link between Arab and European romanticism. The connection is tenuous, however, because although some Arab literature was certainly erotic it was more fanciful than expressive of a new sensibility. The Arabs wrote love poetry, but their conceptualizations of love were often based on homosexual passion and the relationship between their poems and western works seems quite remote. Western romanticism really grew out of the monastic movement, and the connection between the ideal of the wandering saint and that of the knight-errant probably was more significant than any Islamic derivation.

We really know very little as yet about the institutions of the Islamic world, and our ignorance makes it difficult or impossible to add up the Islamic achievement. When more is discovered about the actual functioning of Islamic society, about the institutions of government and the working of the economy in various parts of the medieval Muslim world, we will be better able to bring the Islamic contribution into historical perspective.

Chapter Four

THE AGE OF REFORM

I. Europe in 1000

UNDERSTANDING THE HIGH MIDDLE AGES

The culture and society of the High Middle Ages in Europe has been very thoroughly explored during nearly a hundred years of extensive research and scholarship. We know a great deal about what happened between about 1000 and 1400 A.D.; the problems that remain are those of interpretation—not what happened, but why did it happen, and what does it mean to us?

The source materials for the period after 1150 are profusely available. Unlike the ancient world or the early medieval world, high medieval civilization is thoroughly documented, and the documents survive—institutional records as well as philosophy and literature. We have the day-to-day accounts of the business of the English monarchy after about 1150, extensive records of the French monarchy after 1200, and in the thirteenth and fourteenth centuries, an enormous volume of legal and economic documents. Monks kept elaborate records of almost everything that occurred in the monastic properties, from bee-keeping to requiem Masses. We can, especially for the period after 1170, know not only the acts of medieval government but the decision-making behind governmental action. This kind of documentation is extremely rare or nonexistent for any earlier period. Although medieval studies require a thorough knowledge of Latin and some knowledge of various other languages, and although the material is difficult and often tedious to work with, nevertheless the sources do exist and have been irresistible to historians.

THE ENVIRONMENT

By the year 1000, European society was relatively stable and successful—at least in comparison to the chaos and disintegration of 500. Europe was growing, economically and intellectually; technological resources increasingly were integrated with the social structure and the elite class was self-confident and reasonably efficient. The population was still thin, but it had started to increase rapidly for the first time since about 200 A.D. No one has fully explained why the population had been static for eight hundred years, but historians blame the plague, the endemic malaria of the Mediterranean region, the meagre food supply, and/or the chronic violence of European society. There always is an unknown factor in demography, but it is generally true that populations grow in times of economic prosperity. The population of western Europe in 1000 is conservatively estimated at eight to ten million people.

The environment was still primitive and underdeveloped, and perhaps half of western Europe was useless for agriculture. Large parts of Germany, northern France, and central England were covered with huge, uninhabited forests, while the areas around the North Sea in the Low Countries, northern Germany, and eastern England were unusable marshlands. These coastal lands have been fruitful since the seventeenth century, but at the end of the tenth century nobody in Europe (outside of Belgium) knew anything about drainage, and the shoreline was much farther inland in 1000 than it is today. Between the fourth and the eighteenth centuries, no one in Europe knew how to build good roads, and apart from a few Roman survivals there were no real roads in eleventh-century Europe. Europe was fortunate, however, in its extensive river system, especially in the Rhine, which made long-distance travel and commerce possible. The Danube was too far east for all except Vikings and Slavs and a few intrepid merchants, but there was heavy traffic on the Rhine, the Rhone, the Seine, and the estuary of the Thames. Centers of population grew up near rivers, and the noticeable emptiness of most of central France can be ascribed to the absence of useful rivers.

Western Europe remained technologically backward through the Middle Ages, but its situation was much improved around 800 by the coming into general use of a heavy, wheeled plow. Farmers began at last to get a fairly good yield from their hard soil which required a deep furrow. The light plows of the Romans which scratched the thin surface of the Mediterranean soil, were not effective in northern Europe, and this partly explains why the Romans did not settle far from a few centers of civilization in the north. It took several centuries for northern Europeans to develop their own equipment and techniques, but with the increasing stability of life after 900, the food supply began to grow—an essential factor in the progress of society and civilization. Until quite recently, after all, Europe was an intensely rural society; most people lived on the land until the Industrial Revolution, and most of their wealth came from the land. With the production of varied and abundant crops, including grapes as well as grains and high-protein foods like beans, European civilization began to move forward after 900.

Despite its emperors and popes and kings, tenth-century Europe had a patrimonial, nucleated society based on the domination by great aristocratic families over everything (even the Church) within their own territorial domains. Bastard sons and younger brothers of the local lord became bishops or abbots of local churches and monasteries. Religion, as well as government and economy and law, was dominated by the great families. Everything belonged to the lords, who became more and more greedy and aggressive—particularly on their own estates—as the years went by. By 1000, they were depriving their peasants even of the right to keep pigs or hunt in the forest—which, like everything else, belonged to the lord. As far as we know, however, there was no peasant dissent, and no rebellion. Either because they were too content or too effectively repressed, tenth-century peasants did not protest; the lower classes of rural society were (and remained for a long time) politically inert.

Change came to the stable society of 1000, of course, but it did not originate at the bottom of the social pyramid—rather, at the top, among the great aristocracy. The main characteristic of European social history is its constancy; the aristocratic, familial domination of society continued even past the Industrial Revolution. It was an effective system, and thus its persistence is not surprising. The aristocratic elite produced not only warlords but scholars, poets, musicians, religious leaders (most of the medieval popes came from high aristocratic Italian families, as have many modern popes) and patrons of arts and letters. Twelfth-century literature was courtly literature, the work of the aristocratic and royal courts. The aristocracy was entrenched because it was successful, and because its entrenchment represented continuity, order, and security in a world recently recovered from the agony of disorder and random violence. Protest was not likely to come from below, where the castle on the hill was accepted as the source of order and protection, but from within—from the ranks of the aristocracy itself.

Monarchy

The potential for change in the aristocratic, nucleated social system of tenth-century Europe came from the elite class itself, and particularly from certain great noblemen who wore crowns. Toward the beginning of the eleventh century, kingship began to become an important distinction between members of the aristocratic class, even between certain great aristocrats and their cousins or brothers. In 1000, kingship involved not much beyond ceremonial vestiges of the Roman style, but kings and emperors soon became more ambitious. Inspired by their clerical advisors' tales of Roman majesty, they discovered that ancient rulers led large armies, collected taxes, and lived more grandly than ordinary men. Emperors of Byzantium still lived in palaces and expected obeisance from their subjects. Very little had happened in Europe to make meaningful the concept of majesty, yet ambitious ideas and pretentious claims began to appear in advance of actual accomplishment.

The most pretentious of the European monarchs—the ruler with the fanciest title—was the "Roman Emperor" of Germany, who claimed that his title succeeded from the ancient emperors of Rome. In the year 1000 the German emperor happened to be a young man whose Byzantine mother had brought him up to her own ideas of what *imperium* should mean, and he was not content merely to enjoy better food and wine and clothes than his aristocratic neighbors. *Imperium* demanded something more substantial, and the Ottonian imperial family in the late tenth century made a serious effort to raise a large army staffed by men from outside his own household guard. The German emperor gathered some two thousand knights—an enormous number for that period, and extremely significant for the future. The tenth-century German Ottonian emperors and their kinsmen and successors, the Salian dynasty in the eleventh century, were the first medieval monarchs to create a quasi-political organization that extended beyond their family domains and were based on concepts outside of the aristocratic world.

The German imperial army posed problems of feeding and quartering, and thus its size indirectly produced further changes. The emperor needed money to support his soldiers, and eventually he began to develop vague ideas of taxing the community at large. He invented new dues and services to collect from noblemen (not simply from peasants), but he did not get far in the face of their opposition. Without state traditions and machinery, the emperor had no sanction for tax-collection, but that did not make his attempts any less significant. Aristocratic society was based on the legal equality of all the great families (one might be more powerful than another, but legally and socially they were equals); and an emperor who tried to assert authority over his equals was taking an important step. Without a state, without any national political unity, the eleventh-century German emperors moved toward the beginning of the politicization of Europe.

What inspired these revolutionary attempts? Who told eleventh-century kings that the rulers of the ancient world had large armies, collected taxes from noblemen, and built palaces to reflect their glory? Obviously, such ideas came from men educated in the classical tradition, from the churchmen who advised the kings. Probably 99 per cent of the literate men in Europe in 1000 were churchmen, and they certainly were the only group capable of rational planning or of urging their royal masters to recapture the grandeur of the ancient world.

THE CHURCH AND THEOLOGY

Broadly speaking, medieval society was divided into two classes of free and unfree, the feudal class and the serfs. Of males of the feudal class, perhaps 10 to 20 per cent were churchmen, and in 1000 their number was increasing at a very rapid rate. It was increasing primarily because the Christian religion was received with genuine enthusiasm: people were truly pious in the tenth century, and they were able and anxious to support the Church and its servants. The ecclesiastical buildings of that period in the "Romanesque" style were much more imposing than anything built in Europe in the preceding five hundred years. Some of these fortress-like structures, with marvelously elaborate sculptures, are still standing, particularly in the Rhineland and in southern France. These were expensive structures, for piety was fashionable in 1000; the European nobility liked priests and monks and were willing patrons of ecclesiastical architecture and clerical pursuits.

Tenth-century churchmen were highly honored and well rewarded, but religious enthusiasm is only one explanation of the increase in the number of churchmen during the Middle Ages. The demand for clerical services increased very rapidly because churchmen were the only literate people in Europe, and thus immensely useful in any task requiring writing. They drew up the wills and charters and tax documents and letters without which aristocratic households and royal courts could not function. "Chapel" and "chancery" were interchangeable terms, and the identification of the religious class with the intellectual class (which included an educated bureaucracy) gave a unique character to western civilization.

By 1000, this elite and growing group of educated churchmen had developed an extremely complex theological system that was in many respects quite unlike the religious beliefs of the common people. There was gross superstition and heathenism within popular Christianity in the tenth century, and many beliefs were tacitly accepted by the Church that formed no part of the faith of educated men. Under the leadership of Pope Gregory the Great at the end of the sixth century, the Church had decided to accommodate and accept the prevailing rural religion with its devils and fertility cults. Contemporary leaders realized that the conversion of the heathen Germans would have to be gradual, that drastic excision of their ancient paganism was neither possible nor desirable. Nineteenth-century Protestant scholars used to denounce the medieval Church for its laxity and tolerance of superstition, but it seems probable that Gregory made a wise decision and that the Church would not have survived with a different, more stringent attitude.

However, pagan superstition was not part of the official theology—
a rich and complicated network of traditions from many sources.
The Old and New Testaments and the patristic writings (St.
Augustine was the most influential of the Church Fathers) were
central strands in medieval Christianity, but other strands were
derived from the classical culture of Greece and Rome and from
the mystical Neoplatonism that developed in Alexandria in the
third century A.D.

Orthodox tenth-century Christians believed in one God in
the three persons of the Trinity: God the Father, God the Son, and
God the Holy Ghost. No one could define exactly how God existed
in three persons (after all, faith is beyond reason) but they were
convinced that He did. God the Father was a combination of a
Roman emperor and the tribal god of Israel, a rewarder and pun-
isher in this world and the next. The Old Testament, with its
emphasis on the power and majesty of God, played a much larger
role in the tenth-century image of God than did the tender and
emotional words of the New Testament. God the Son was regarded as a vehicle or instrument of salvation, and his personality
was not much considered. Medieval artists did not even begin to
portray Jesus as an infant until the eleventh century, when certain
artists in southern France and northern Spain depicted his childhood in their sculptures—but with Jesus as a miniature grown
man, not as a baby. Before that time, Christians could not conceive
of Jesus as a child at all in any emotional or personal sense; in
1000, he was appreciated primarily as the mechanism of human
redemption and as the supreme Judge and Emperor.

Medieval Christians believed that God had to create Jesus to
appear in human form and to suffer because man was too corrupt
to be saved by his own merit. Some men were better than others,
but all would be damned without the intervention of Jesus.
Tenth-century theologians adhered to the Augustinian doctrine of
the corruption and depravity of the human will. The sin of con-
cupiscience begins when the infant suckles at his mother's breast.
Greed, lust, and selfishness are born with man, who would have
to suffer eternal damnation unless part of God accepted punishment for human sin. Jesus Christ took on man's suffering by his
own choice: salvation is an act of "grace," undeserved and freely
given. Men can join in the sacrifice and participate in the merits

of Jesus through the sacrament of the Mass, which gives to each communicant an infinitesimal, but efficacious, share of the glory of Christ. The wafer and wine of Holy Communion are miraculously transformed in substance into the body and blood of Christ, who is present at the altar.

Medieval Catholicism was based on a difficult and complicated theological system, but it was well suited to high ceremony as well as intellectual argument. The sacrament of Communion was performed most impressively in medieval churches, where illiterate peasants and knights who could not have understood Augustinian dogma could appreciate the incense and music and vestments of the Mass. Tenth-century Christianity was a mysterious, sacerdotal, sacramental religion capable of profound appeal to the emotions as well as the mind. Unlike Judaism, it tended to generate art and poetry and music even while it remained open to intellectual refinement—to thought, preaching, and interpretation.

The third face of the Trinity was the Holy Spirit—God's shadow on the world whose institutional form was the Church, the earthly embodiment of a heavenly ideal. This concept, of course, was derived from the Platonic notion of pure Idea, represented in appearance by something less pure. The medieval Church, however, seemed to contemporaries as nearly pure as an earthly institution could be; it represented God, making physical and visible the Spirit that moved men in their hearts. To deny the authority of the Church was to deny God, and the greatest sinner was the heretic who flouted its teaching. The Church used every instrument of culture and communication to put across its indisputable message. Art and reason alike contributed to the mixed-media happening that was medieval Catholicism, where each Mass was a miracle and men waited for the shadow of God to fall across their hearts.

The Intellectual Culture and Its Applications

Trinitarian Christianity was not the only aspect of the intellectual culture of medieval Europe. Another significant aspect was medieval typology—a sort of popularized Platonism. Virtually all medieval thinkers before the twelfth century were Platonists;

reality, to them, was ideal, universal, and pure. They studied the general, universal character rather than any particular instance of phenomena, and they indulged in abstract speculation in preference to empirical analysis. To define kingship, for example, a medieval thinker would attempt to define its ideal nature. He might base his concept upon the image of Charlemagne, whose powers and authority were derived from the nature of *imperium*—even if people three hundred miles away from the emperor had never heard of him and lived untouched by his theoretical powers. This form of thought—deduction from assertions about ideals—had certain advantages. It was sufficiently clear to permit full statements of belief; also, clear ideals can be transformed into goals. A major disadvantage was a weak sense of individual personality. Human complexity was ignored, and people were defined by their status instead of their individual characteristics.

Definition by status fitted in well with the hierarchic principle central to the medieval world-view. It came to Europe from the ancient Near East (with a considerable boost from Platonic philosophy) and was not jettisoned until the Enlightenment, and then only with great difficulty. Hierarchy was the basic organizing principle of the medieval universe, conceived as a ladder with ascending and descending rungs on earth, in heaven above, and hell below. Angels were superior to humans, kings to ordinary people, and those who were closest to God had authority over those farther away. The system was metaphysically justified by the absolute power of God in the entire universe; everything and everyone descended from Him. It was pragmatically justified, after a fashion, by the principle (derived from Roman law) that responsibility and power are inseparable. Bishops and kings were believed to be responsible to God for the social order and the common welfare, and obviously they needed power in order to carry out their mandate. Of course, under the limitations of medieval communication and transportation, and within the molecular, familial organization of society, even very great theoretical powers were not effective over long distances.

Hierarchical social theory was very clear; more important, it conformed roughly with the existing situation and was applicable in the smallest village or the greatest cathedral. In the late tenth and eleventh centuries, the hierarchical theory was widely applied to give order and coherence to what modern historians call the feudal system. In the early Middle Ages there were few formal legal or theoretical distinctions among the various followers or vassals of a lord, but the growing body of ecclesiastical secretaries and advisors to kings and great noblemen gradually extended hierarchical principles to social relations. Feudalism itself became a ladder, and by 1025 (outside of Germany), it was obvious that the relationship of a serf to his lord was entirely different from that of a free man. A knight's homage was freely given (at least in theory; in fact he might be bludgeoned into it) but a serf inherited his status and service dues. The system worked out by eleventh-century churchmen was very complicated, with a great many exceptions to its rules, but its very formulation gave significance to its various ranks. Direct vassals of the king (who were defined by the hierarchical system as possessors of high status and powers) proceeded to acquire such status, and other privileges derived from closeness to the king. By the middle of the eleventh century, every lord knew his exact relationship to the royal apex of the social pyramid, and much of the romantic literature of the twelfth century was concerned with the social ladder.

Such an abstract, formal system naturally came up against certain social and psychological realities. Obviously, some people could not exercise their inherited powers (they were children when they inherited their status and lands, or they were weak, or feeble-minded), while others—strong and brilliant people—were frustrated by inferior rank. There was a substantial increase in the noble population of Europe in the eleventh century, and the hierarchically-structured feudal order was too rigid to expand to include all the younger sons who were excluded from the lands and titles and authority held by their fathers.

Dissatisfaction in landed families took many forms, some of them (such as emigration to the frontiers or overseas) peaceful and constructive. Many noblemen went into the Church, and by the middle of the century, numbers of intelligent and well-educated priests and monks had fallen fairly low on the hierarchic scale. Eventually the Church created good jobs for them, accompanying an enormous expansion of papal government in the twelfth century, but this did not happen fast enough to prevent the formation of a kind of intellectual proletariat. Any system has to take in new people or face reform or revolution, and although the medieval hierarchy was secure and comfortable, it was not free (by our standards) and it was not flexible. Freedom was not the central problem: until the twelfth century, freedom was equated with control—medieval men appreciated stability after centuries of anarchy and violence. Hierarchy appeared to them to be essential to peace, and difficulties arose not with the authoritarian principle of hierarchy but with its inflexibility in practice. Any system, no matter how well designed for a particular social situation, can turn its intelligentsia into revolutionaries if it does not expand to make use of their education and talents.

Another central ideal of the medieval thought-world was *humanitas*—a term which stands for both the classical tradition and the ideals it inculcated. In the third century, the Church chose to preserve the classical curriculum as the basis of education; medieval men learned *humanitas* from the ancient writers. Certain churchmen (Tertullian, for example) denounced classical education as pagan, or aristocratic, or a betrayal of the ideals of the New Testament—yet in the third century as in the twentieth, there were few attractive alternatives. Latin was retained as the language of the Christian Church despite the dubious content of much of Roman philosophy and literature—not surprising, because anti-Semitism was on the rise and Hebrew was not a likely candidate. The curriculum was pruned of some objectionable material, but this was done as superficial excision of passages of Ovid and Catullus, not as a meaningful reinterpretation of classical literature in the light of the Gospels.

Classical education had a significant impact on its students. It inculcated patriotism and respect for order, for the Church, and for book-learning (even learning without immediate use or relevance). The intellectual traditions of Christianity, formed—for the most part—in the medieval world, came from the classics more directly than the New Testament. Jesus, after all, was an extremist, hardly an apostle of the Golden Mean or of the self-reliance, sobriety, dignity, and balance of the noble Romans. The implications of the classical traditions were not, however, entirely conformist —they could be radical as well.

The revolutionary implications within the classical tradition were partly offshoots of its emphasis on human reason, on the ability of the individual to make his own judgments. Classically educated men were sure of themselves and positive in their assertions: indeed, the endless controversies among medieval churchmen reflect that sense of independent judgment, even a tendency to arrogance, contrasting paradoxically with endless professions of Christian humility.

Another radical consequence of *humanitas* was the continuing concern with justice, righteousness, and morality. Medieval men spoke and argued in moral terms: battling popes and emperors ascribed right and justice to themselves, not simply power. Even as late as the fourteenth century, Marsiglio of Padua shocked Europe by asserting that politics was about power and not about right; in the eleventh century theorists of all factions ignored the biological basis of human behavior and the lust for power, and regarded morality as the only recognized motivation for action. Eventually this was bound to encourage criticism of the status quo, when independent-minded thinkers scrutinized their institutions and found them ethically misguided or fundamentally wrong. When it was discovered that men and institutions alike were seldom as moral as they pretended to be, the tension between the moral talk of the Establishment and its actual behavior became critical.

Medieval rhetoric always remained heavily moral, and rhetoric does color, and even produce, behavior. Just as the revolutionary rhetoric of the twentieth century involves everyone, to some extent, in the revolutionary ethos and style, so the character of tenth-century rhetoric made morality the central, indispensable consideration in any political, social, or religious movement.

II. *The Gregorian Reform Movement*

Monasticism in the Eleventh Century

The major focus for discontent with the established system in the eleventh century was not (as some historians have believed) the emerging bourgeois class of the new urban centers. The merchants and townsmen were beginning to become a significant force, but they could not approach in influence the monks who existed at the very heart of the medieval world. Pope Gregory VII (the monk

Hildebrand) sponsored the reform movement that bears his name, but its seeds arose in the monasteries long before 1073, when Gregory succeeded to the papal throne. The Gregorian Reform was much more than the work of one man; it was the culmination of a large and complex upheaval within monasticism itself.

In the eleventh century, the large and important group of monks was enthusiastically admired and lavishly supported by the elite—not primarily because they were learned men (although they were prized as secretaries and advisors to kings and lords), but for religious reasons. Noblemen endowed monasteries and patronized monks very simply because they thought the monks' prayers would help them into heaven. A baron who spent his youth ravaging the countryside and raping the village girls might endow a monastery in middle age in order to speed his term through purgatory. It is generally true that if an elite class supports a nonproductive intellectual group it expects concrete returns—witness the Defense Department's sponsorship of various university research programs, or the mandarins' patronage of scholarship in old China. The services exacted from the monks were prescribed in detail in the foundation charters of the monasteries, which specified the number and nature of the Masses to be sung for the souls of departed noblemen. The aristocrats genuinely believed that the intercession of holy men would reach God and commute their posthumous sentences, and they supported monks in 1000 for the same reasons that noblemen in the thirteenth and fourteenth centuries founded university colleges staffed with priests whose duties included (along with teaching students) the celebration of Masses for the souls of the founders—a custom still perpetuated in the Founders' Days of Oxford and Cambridge colleges.

The monasteries also served as centers of learning (even of radical learning) and as retirement homes for aged members of noble families. Their endowments came entirely from the elite, whose support was so enthusiastic in the tenth century that monasteries proliferated on a grand scale. Their vast endowments were mostly in land, including serfs to work the land, and their huge resources freed many monks from physical labor and frequently even from involvement in agricultural management. Even though St. Benedict founded his first monastery for the purpose of continual devotion and contemplation, his monks engaged in strenuous physical labor as well as prayer. By the eleventh century, however, many monks had escaped physical labor and prayed all day long— and these developed the Gregorian chant in order that they might pray more beautifully. Some monks managed estates; some prayed; others served God as scholars. A group of professional scholars appeared—monks who did nothing but intellectual work and had begun to do it very well. With few students and large amounts of money to support study, these scholars wrote a great deal of history, theology, and law. Their work was not up to the level of the great classical thinkers and writers (no medieval monastic historian matched Thucydides), but their output was impressive.

The Gregorian Reform movement shook the medieval world to its foundations, made ideology fashionable, and remains significant today as the first great self-consciously radical movement in western civilization created out of an elaborate and consistent ideology. For these reasons it is important to grasp the paradoxical motivations of its improbable leaders. The primary drive toward reform arose among the intellectual class of monks, who were well situated to mount the first great attack on the aristocratic establishment of the Middle Ages. Most of the reformers were scholars from the great monastic centers of learning in the Rhineland and in northern Italy—lawyers, theologians, historians, or social theorists. These pampered protégés of the elite attacked the very principle of aristocratic, familial domination of society; they wanted an authoritarian dictatorship of saints, of religious leaders of learning and virtue—of themselves. The monks—creatures of the noble class—were unlikely rebels: Cluny, for example, was not only the monastery where at least two of the Gregorian leaders had been for a time members of the community, but also the grandest, most elaborate and luxurious ecclesiastical institution in all of Europe. (The two radicals thought Cluny was conservative and conformist, but they partook of its resources for a while.)

Classical education, with its traditions of hierarchy and *humanitas,* had produced able and well-educated monks who came inevitably to resent the domination of rough and illiterate noblemen. They believed they could do better themselves, and quite naturally they felt that the best minds should manage the affairs of secular men and lead society toward the kingdom of God.

Perhaps even more important, the monks were worried and

threatened by the appearance of a new group of intellectuals to challenge the monastic monopoly of learning and education. A few great bishops had founded non-monastic schools in their cathedral towns, attracting scholars who were secular clerks— often very ambitious, aggressive, and hungry men. Many of these secular clerks were ambitious cadets of aristocrat families, and the monks feared them as competitors for their position as intellectual leaders of society and advisors to kings and princes. They sensed, perhaps, that now was the last chance for reform—that soon it might be too late for monks to grasp the leadership of the Church and of society. In a sense, then, the Gregorian Reform was a reactionary movement designed to maintain the old monastic dominance against the new scholars. They were correct to fear the new cathedral schools, for these were the beginnings of the European universities.

The monks also had cause to fear that the educational change would destroy their influential political position. In 1000 the monastic intellectuals were definitely part of the power elite, but by 1050 their position was less secure. One challenge came from the new class of intellectuals emerging from cathedral schools. These schools produced not only scholars but also administrators, whose outlook was that of university graduates rather than monks, and whose own careers were of more concern to them than the coming of the kingdom of God. Such worldly and ambitious men found service in the kings' courts—and the kings, who had been taught by monks to strive for *imperium*, welcomed these clever and aggressive new advisors, whose private interests were thoroughly identified with the royal power. Under the tutelage of monks, European monarchs were becoming secular and self-reliant, especially in Germany—and as kings became more efficient and powerful, they had less need of monastic secretaries and advisors.

CONFRONTATION

The Gregorian Reform movement was the first attack on the political and social system that developed in Europe between 500 and 1000 A.D. It was the first ideological revolution in western civilization, and it had enormous impact even though it failed to achieve what it set out to accomplish. The movement tore the

Church apart for twenty years and produced a thirty-year civil war in Germany, substantial fighting in Italy, and vehement quarrels all over western Europe. Like other revolutions, it was not brought about by the uprising of the masses but by the splintering of the elite which occurs when potential rulers (qualified leaders without authority or power) attempt to replace the actual rulers of society. All revolutions are about power even if they are fought in moral terms, and their leaders are always advantaged people. As in any revolutionary movement, of course, individual reformers had particular motives—personal grievances and special problems that were probably as critical as any general factors in producing radical reformers.

By the early 1080s the pope and the German emperor were engaged in open and violent confrontation. Denunciations were almost routine—indeed, the emperor was for a few months deposed and excommunicated in 1075 (the pope won that round). During the subsequent decade, Europe became politicized and polarized. In England and France and the Low Countries as well as Italy and Germany, an outpouring of treatises and manifestoes reflected the widespread passion on the issues of reform, and by 1090 there was probably no literate man and no member of the feudal order (even a petty knight) who was not at least vaguely committed to one side or the other. The rhetoric of the movement and counter-movement was developed to a fine point, and the output of pamphlet material was extraordinary for an age of pen and parchment. In the 1890s a group of hard-working German scholars published about 80 per cent of the surviving materials in three huge folio volumes—about 2200 large pages. Even this probably does not represent more than 30 or 40 per cent of what originally existed, because the survival rate of eleventh-century pamphlets cannot have been very high. What does survive is remarkably cogent and up-to-date political polemic; in their fervor, some of these medieval pamphleteers anticipated political concepts that would not take root for several centuries. They used every argument—philosophical, Biblical, emotional—and after a decade of such rhetoric, confrontation was inevitable.

In order to appreciate the extent of the polarization of Europe, we can compare two out of thousands of statements by eleventh-century churchmen and statesmen. In a letter to Bishop Herman of Metz, Gregory VII asserted (in powerful language) that any good Christian was better than a bad king. Christ hated monarchy, claimed Gregory, and the deference of kings toward popes accords with the natural order of the world. (There are implications of egalitarianism here that did not become overt for more than a century: Gregory summoned forth the goodness of the common man against the evil of the powerful. Faithful Christians are "Christ's body"—bad kings, the devil's body.) The emperor Henry IV responded in similarly violent language, addressing Gregory as "Hildebrand, false monk" and cursing him for his treatment of churchmen (Henry's bishops). The emperor claimed that royal power is derived from God and not from the pope, and he ordered Gregory to relinquish the papacy or be damned. A pope who had attacked the Church through its servants (Henry's clerical advisors) was a false pope with no power to interfere between God and His emperor.

MOTIVATION

The exchange of insults between pope and emperor reflects an important factor in the reform movement—as important, probably, as the dissatisfaction and insecurity of the monks. The emperor's ambitions in the Rhineland and in northern Italy had produced political (even nationalistic) tensions, for in these areas there was no strong political power but merely a group of petty principalities and tiny dukedoms or city-states. When Charlemagne's empire was divided between his sons in the ninth century, its central section became a "Middle Kingdom" without linguistic, ethnic, or institutional unity—an infeasible entity which soon broke apart into political fragments. This made an attractive prospect for an ambitious ruler, and the German emperors were moving in on the Rhineland and on northern Italy during the eleventh century. Quite naturally, they hurt people in the process. Most of the important reformers came from Lorraine, or from Lombardy or Tuscany, where the local aristocrats and high bourgeois were resisting taxation, domination, and exploitation by the German emperor. There is a deep current of anti-Germanism in much of the Gregorian writing; even in the eleventh century, Germans were regarded as tough and mean, and the German aristocrats were considered the cultural inferiors of the gracious and advanced Rhenish and Italian elite. This nationalistic hostility produced much of the emotional motivation of the movement; it seems likely that the great reformers imbibed their hatred of the emperor in early childhood, from families who resented his ambitions, his style, and his very existence.

There was still another factor in the Gregorian Reform movement—one which is in some sense a factor in every revolution. That was the apocalyptic attitude, the conviction that revolution is desirable, even essential, to the establishment of the kingdom of God. Unforunately, we do not have much biographical information about the Gregorian revolutionaries: individual biographies usually reveal what it was that made a man a genuine revolutionary instead of a mere radical or reformer. Certain men, in special periods of history, will *not* compromise, will *not* be satisfied with acceptance into the power structure. Such men divide the world sharply into good and bad, and usually they see themselves as instruments of the good—of God's will, of Providence, of history. Marxism is popular among contemporary revolutionaries partly because it brings apocalypticism up to date: Marx and his disciples secularized the revolutionary conviction that the world must and shall be turned upside down, that destruction of the established order is desirable and essential to the coming of the millennium.

No one has satisfactorily explained the roots of such apocalypticism: Freudian interpretations emphasize the revolutionaries' hostility toward their parents. Obviously this is a generational phenomenon as well as an individual one; it is only when a large group of young people wish to destroy their parents' world that a movement becomes significant. The paranoid mentality (*paranoid* is not used here in a pejorative sense but simply to describe a psychological state) is at the heart of revolution. Revolutionary leaders *must* believe that the men in power are evil, not simply misguided or mistaken, that they cannot possibly reform themselves and must therefore be destroyed. God (or history) commands a revolutionary to act, to destroy the existing order and replace it with something better, whether that be the kingdom of God or the classless society. Like Bolshevik intellectuals and like the bourgeois lawyers and publicists of eighteenth-century France, the Gregorian reformers had comfortable positions within the existing system—much more comfortable than that of the exploited masses (who did not rebel). The attitudes that distinguish revolutionaries from ordinary left-wing politicians are their refusal to rest within the system, their conviction that the rulers of society are truly and irredeemably evil, and their intention to destroy existing people and institutions—if necessary—to prepare the world for the Golden Age at hand.

Twentieth-century historians tend to search for economic and social factors in important movements—particularly revolutionary movements—and there was a socio-economic aspect to the Gregorian Reform. The reformers recognized the existence of a new and important social group in the cities of western Europe (particularly in those of northern Italy, and notably in Milan, which was a seedbed of the reform movement). The merchant oligarchy or upper bourgeoisie of the growing cities had real cause for dissatisfaction with the status quo, as they had acquired wealth and literacy through their own efforts and yet were excluded from the medieval system of noble, peasant, and priest. The aristocratic elite resisted the merchants' drive for political power and social status, and this made the bourgeoisie natural allies of the reformers, who gained their support by preaching to them, showing respect for their ideas and ideals, and identifying their common interests. In cities such as Milan, where the important and lucrative cathedral posts went to aristocratic appointees of the German emperor, merchants and the papacy and reforming monks could agree on the desirability of replacing the cathedral clergy with their own men. Aristocrats (at least those in the imperial camp) were powerful and determined foes of reform, and their bitter opposition was a primary cause of the failure of the Gregorian movement. Aristocratic churchmen perceived the threat to their position and even to their livelihood and effectively resisted inroads by the papacy and its urban allies.

In his famous letter to Herman of Metz, Gregory used a kind of quasi-democratic or egalitarian language that was characteristic of the reformers' rhetoric. These men tended to refer to the *pauperi Christi*, the "poor in Christ"—a deliberately ambiguous phrase designed to appeal to those who resented aristocratic domination. Medieval Christians generally regarded the "Christian poverty" taught by Jesus as humility—an emotional, not an economic state. The egalitarian side of Gregorian Reform was never explicitly developed, partly because the pope needed support from anti-imperial noblemen and rich merchants, but also because no one before the eighteenth century thought in terms of class struggle or economic determination—concepts that clearly did not enter into the medieval world-view. There was a social aspect to Gregorian Reform, but it was more a vehicle than a cause of the movement and it existed in implication instead of actuality.

All reform and revolutionary movements reflect the emergence of new attitudes; they are political aspects of cultural change. Generally they follow the appearance of a new higher culture, which inevitably is soon vulgarized and transformed into a general, popular system: the Gregorian Reform is no exception. The intellectual revolution that is commonly identified with "the renaissance of the twelfth century" began late in the eleventh; it developed, in fact, in part because of the failure of the reform movement. The beginning of the intellectual revolution can be perceived very clearly in the rhetorical style of the monastic reformers, whose words and attitudes challenged the basic intellectual assumption—the dominant intellectual mode—of the early Middle Ages. For five centuries, the foundation of thought and argument had been devotion to tradition. Precedent was more significant than creativity; precedent itself gave force to arguments. Early medieval treatises on any subject from theology to law begin with citations from Augustine or Constantine or Gregory the Great—references to some past accomplishment or quotation from an authority. Kings appealed to custom when they published edicts, and preachers prided themselves not on their own words but on the persuasive use of selected texts.

The Gregorian reformers, and the twelfth-century thinkers who succeeded them, did not abandon the appeal to tradition, but they did introduce two new kinds of argument. They appealed to feeling and to reason: they aimed to arouse a profound response in the hearts of good men through emotional appeal to their deepest religious feelings (the "New Piety"), and they aimed to achieve intellectual conviction through logical persuasion (the "New Logic"). These two styles may appear contradictory, yet they developed side by side; both favor truth over tradition, and both admit the revolutionary possibility that tradition might be wrong. Gregory once pointed out that Christ did not say "I am tradition" but "I am the Word," and this became almost a slogan of reformers who sought the Word in direct revelation or individual reason. Intellectual works built upon citation of ancient texts gave way on the one hand to dialectical argument, and on the other to evangelical prose-poems, and logical reasoning and confessional outpouring alike reflected major intellectual change. The revolutionaries of the Gregorian movement were the first articulate representatives of the new thought-world of the High Middle Ages.

NEW PIETY AND NEW LOGIC

The two new intellectual movements reflected in the attitudes and rhetoric of the Gregorian Reform did not achieve full expression until the twelfth century, but their earliest beginnings can be traced to the generation of the reformers. Historians have named these parallel developments the "New Piety" and the "New Logic," and although it is not entirely clear why they appeared, it is possible to identify certain forces that might have helped to create them.

With the growth of population (especially of the noble class) and the increasing rigidity of the feudal order in the eleventh century—with less available land and more competition for status, frustration mounted, and people began to need escape from intolerable pressure. In any closed, traditional social and intellectual system, those who cannot find satisfaction within its bounds seek liberation from authority and stratification, and in pre-industrial societies such release frequently takes the form of religious mysticism. The mystery religions of ancient Greece and Rome exemplify this principle, as do the Sufism of medieval Islam and the Hasidic movement of eighteenth-century Judaism—a response to the rigid social stratification, economic deprivation, and elitism of the ghettoes of eastern Europe. Also when the Protestant Reformation failed to liberate the masses or even to improve their lot, ordinary people responded by forming evangelical, radical sects which provided release and joy through pietistic religious feeling. The New Piety, then, was the characteristic response to the increasing pressures of a rigidifying society: the evangelical, mystical escape valve.

The development of the New Logic after 1050 is more difficult to explain than that of the New Piety, and it may be necessary to rely in part on the unsatisfactory diffusionist interpretation that new scholarly methods came into northern Europe from Arabic Spain and Sicily in the eleventh century. It is true that scientific and philosophical ideas from the great Muslim centers of learning penetrated Europe at this period, but that does not explain why the northerners accepted and studied the new ideas and methods with such enthusiasm.

Educated northerners (almost all of whom were monks) embraced the new learning and thus developed new modes of thought and argument, partly in response to the contemporary growth of royal power and centralized administration. In some parts of Europe—notably in Germany, Normandy, England (after 1066), and Flanders—the beginnings of statism and of centralized monarchical government were producing an increasingly linear, logical, and ordered political and social system. Law, rather than philosophy, was the first intellectual field invaded by the New Logic, and great efforts were made in the eleventh century to make the law systematic, coherent, and rational. The very earliest dialecticians of the new movement worked in schools of law in Italy and the Rhineland and northern France during the 1050s and 1060s, and only later were their methods applied to philosophy and theology.

In a world of developing political and social order, intellectuals were forced to think hard about the meaning and consequences of law and systematization. Eventually, of course, aggressive eleventh-century kings used and even sponsored their work, but the New Logic in its earliest stages was a spontaneous response to the threat of fundamental political and social change. Just as the New Piety arose from the need to escape social pressure—to compensate for the contemporary loss of opportunities for growth and spontaneity—by establishing an inner source of happiness and joys, so the New Logic arose from the need to understand and work with new political and social phenomena.

It can be argued, too, that both movements fitted well with and even expressed the ethos of the new bourgeois class. An urban middle class had begun to emerge in the growing cities of Europe in the tenth century, and although probably only about 5 per cent of the population of Europe lived in cities by 1100, many of those who did were wealthy, well-educated, and energetic. The old aristocratic order failed to absorb them: the bourgeois could not marry into aristocratic families, nor were they eligible for royal fiefs or high positions in the Church (not even in city churches).

Both the New Piety and the New Logic offered opportunities for non-traditional, anti-hierarchical forms of thought, and the bourgeois stood in need of a system of values or canon of judgment to oppose to the traditional order. If Christian piety instead of noble birth, were the criterion of valuating individuality, then any Christian might be as good as a duke—or better—and his claim to status and power was as valid as that of a nobleman. The Gregorian reformers, including Gregory himself, encouraged (even when they did not explicitly state) the egalitarian view that all men are equal in Christ. Logic and learning suited the bourgeois quest for self-justification and identity by providing sources for all kinds of arguments. From Greek political theory came the concept of community and the Aristotelian view of man as a political being —a part of society as a man and not simply as a member of an hereditary elite.

The bourgeois could not win their "liberties" from the feudal class by fighting—at least not very easily, although they tried occasionally. Neither could they buy their way into the power structure, although frequently they could and did buy political control of their cities. They needed moral and philosophical sanction for their claims, even for their existence outside the traditional order, and these they found in the new modes that appeared in the eleventh century and swept Europe in the twelfth.

Marxist historians, in particular, tend to regard the New Piety and the New Logic simply as expressions of middle-class ideology and reflections of the bourgeois rise to power. Nothing in history is perfectly simple, however, and the bourgeois were not alone in their involvement with the new intellectual movements. Discontented noblemen (younger sons, for example) who suffered from the contemporary shortage of land or could not find places in the hardening feudal order, were intensely interested in new ideas and new ways of living. The most important group in the new intellectual movements was not the bourgeoisie but the monks, who were threatened by the rise of secular power. Monks were still by far the most important group of scholars in Europe, and they wrote the emotional, romantic religious tracts and the political and legal treatises that stirred up the bourgeoisie. However, middle-class needs contributed to the popularization of the new culture even if the bourgeois ethos did not create it, and the new culture became in turn a basis for Gregorian Reform. The reforming monks and their bourgeois allies had to discredit the old order—even its rhetoric and style—in order to persuade men of the value of a new society, and they worked hard to identify the old elite with out-of-date concepts and phraseology and the reform movement with the new culture.

In a professional group sense (because they were monks, and monastic leadership was passing) the reformers were old-fashioned, but as individuals—and particularly in cultural style—they were extremely up to date. St. Peter Damiani, one of the Gregorian leaders, was a leading exponent of the New Piety; another, Cardinal Humbert, of the New Logic; and Gregory VII of both. These men did not depend on evocation of the old-fashioned saints nor adhere to the old-fashioned concepts like theocratic monarchy; they developed a new style and a new rhetoric—the criteria by which most people often judge the attractiveness of a revolutionary movement and its leaders.

III. Militancy and Power

THE NEW CHRISTIAN MILITANCY

In the second half of the eleventh century, a militant attitude appeared within Christianity that was part of the ambience of Gregorian Reform and yet not totally identified with it. The belief that the use of force was justifiable in a good cause, the belief in Christian warfare (even Christian homicide), was not brand new in the eleventh century, nor has it disappeared today: the army still has Christian chaplains. Justifiable violence was an accepted concept throughout the early Middle Ages, and indeed in the ancient world, but it received a considerable boost in the eleventh century. Eleventh-century Christians not only accepted the idea of Christian violence: they acted upon it.

It is not difficult to find in the Bible early expressions of the concept of justifiable violence. Certain passages in the Old Testament reflect their authors' delight in the destruction of the enemies of Israel and of God. The New Testament is relatively pacifistic in ethic, but Jesus himself said "Do not think that I have come to bring peace on earth; I have not come to bring peace, but a sword."[5] (This probably meant that he came to disturb and move as well as comfort men, but it can also be interpreted as a militant attitude.) St. Paul, who came to Christianity from the rabbinical tradition, was not at all pacifistic in temperament. On the whole, the Bible is ambiguous on militancy; the Old Testament appears to condone violence in a good cause and even to relish the downfall of the enemies of God, but the New Testament is divided between the natural pacifism of Jesus and the natural ferocity of Paul.

When Christianity was absorbed into the late Roman Empire, it inevitably took on some of the militaristic character of the environment: the new Christian leaders and teachers were militaristic people. (There is a significant difference between Christian militarism, which admits the use of force as justifiable, or at least not necessarily sinful, and Christian militancy, which demands the use of force to achieve the triumph of the Church and implies delight in smashing the enemies of God.) When the Roman elite became Christian in the fourth century, Christianity became militaristic; it also became (sporadically) militant, and Roman bishops urged their followers to convert the heathen—by force, if necessary—and to destroy their temples or transform them into churches. In the famous controversy over the Altar of Victory, the pagan Symmachus delivered a stirring defense of tolerance and religious liberty but lost the argument to St. Ambrose, who saw no virtue in tolerance of error. Convinced that there was one truth and one way to salvation, the fourth-century Church committed itself to intolerance and force.

The fourth century also produced St. Augustine, whose doctrines were particularly influential in the eleventh century. Gregory VII, for example, spoke and wrote in Augustinian language and imagery, and all of the Church reformers were deeply imbued with fourth-century patristic philosophy. Augustine said very plainly that the Church had the right and the duty to eradicate error, and he even asked the Roman emperor to send soldiers to drive the Donatist heretics back to the Church. He interpreted Jesus' par-

[5] R.S.V. Matthew 10:34.

able of the banquet ("Go out to the highways and hedges, and compel people to come in")[6] as a justification for the use of physical force, and he believed that even forcible conversion or correction was of great benefit to the convert. Imposing the sacraments upon a man may make salvation possible for him—the greatest gift he could be given; further, if he is brought into the Church he can be reached by talk and prayer. Augustine's justification of force was very influential in the medieval Church, and Jesus' text *"Compel* people to come in" was quoted often by ecclesiastics in the High Middle Ages—by the inquisitors, among others.

With a few exceptions, the early medieval Church was militaristic without being militant. In the violent and primitive society of the years between 500 and 1000—a rough blend of Roman soldiers and German savages—the Church was not as aggressive as might have been expected, but force was sometimes used to subdue and convert the heathen. At the urging of his clerical advisors Charlemagne invaded Saxony in the ninth century and killed thousands of heathen Saxons and converted the rest—a wholesale, violent operation that was larger, but otherwise similar, to efforts by other Christian rulers and churchmen. In the eighth century, Europe was invaded by Muslims (Arabs and North Africans) who conquered most of Spain and even invaded southeastern France. They were beaten back to the Pyrenees, but they made periodic forays into Italy during the eighth century. The Muslim faith was regarded as the very vilest kind of heresy. Islam was not accepted as a different religion but as a perversion of Christianity, and slaughter of Muslims was accepted and approved by leaders of the Church.

Early medieval Christians fought heathen Hungarians and Germans and "heretical" Muslims on their borders and indulged infrequently in militant outbursts against Jews, particularly in Spain in the seventh century. On the whole, however, Jews were still respected and protected, welcome at most courts and important in agriculture as well as trade. Early medieval Christians were aggressive against external enemies of Christendom—militaristic, in other words—but they were not militant against non-Christians in their midst.

[6] R.S.V. Luke 14:23.

Through the tenth century, Christianity was a formal and institutional religion and not a moral and inspirational popular faith. Organized as part of the hierarchical, aristocratic system and operated by representaves of the elite class, sacramental Christianity had little evangelical or emotional content for lay society (monks had a different outlook). In the eleventh century, when the New Piety built a high emotional content into Christianity, it became an exciting, participatory religion—and this made militancy possible, or even inevitable. People were excited and incited; they looked for enemies in and out of Europe to kill for Christ. The desire to carry the Cross farther, to purify society of unbelievers, was the underside of the New Piety. Christians were more idealistic, more spiritual, more involved—and their treatment of people outside the fold grew steadily more horrible.

There were three major expressions of the new militancy of the late eleventh century, of which the first was the violence of rhetoric and conduct of the antagonists over the Gregorian Reform. There had been differences between popes and emperors before the eleventh century, but these were mere family squabbles compared to the violent, uncompromising struggle for the world between Gregory VII and the emperor Henry IV, neither of whom showed moderation in language or behavior. Violent rhetoric not only expresses but actually produces violent feelings, and it often leads to violent action. The controversy over Gregorian Reform was not a gentlemanly dispute inside the aristocratic elite, but a fight to the finish among bitter enemies.

The other important expressions of militancy were the Crusades—the holy wars—and the emergence of overt and violent anti-Semitism. All three of these phenomena influenced the character and style of European life and the quality of the Christian religion; they were unappealing but very real aspects of the European intellectual revolution.

THE CRUSADES

Historians used to believe that the Crusades reopened the Mediterranean to east-west trade after centuries of isolation and thus made a critical contribution to the economic and intellectual development of Europe. It is true that the Crusades were inspired in part by commercial motives: from the middle of the tenth century, Venetian and Genoese merchants had aspired to take over certain commercial ventures from the Arabs and Byzantines and to acquire new ports in the eastern Mediterranean. The Crusades helped the Italian merchants in both ambitions, but that does not imply that they opened up the Mediterranean—east-west trade had never completely disappeared, and in the ninth and tenth centuries, long before the Crusades, it was growing fast, spurred on by the growth of the Italian cities.

It is true that the Christian world absorbed a great deal of Muslim philosophy, medicine, science, and literature in the late eleventh and twelfth centuries, but the Crusades did not contribute to this phenomenon—indeed, they probably inhibited it by stirring up religious fanaticism and hatred of Muslims. The intellectual exchange between Christians and Muslims did not take place among soldiers on a battlefield but in the cosmopolitan centers of southern Europe (especially those in Spain and Sicily) where Christians and Muslims lived side by side.

The tangible, institutional impact of the Crusades on the development of Europe was very slight: the institution of monarchy was affected almost not at all, and even the Church (apart from a slight rise in papal prestige) was not much affected by the Crusades in the twelfth century. Eventually two different kinds of crusading movements developed: external Crusades, directed mainly against Arabs, and internal Crusades against enemies within Christendom. The latter—the crusading ideal turned inward—had enormous impact upon the development of European civilization, but this was not fully realized until the thirteenth century.

In the beginning, the Crusades were directed against enemies of the Latin Church outside of Europe, including Greek Byzantine Christians as well as Muslims. Gregory VII was the prime mover of the crusading ideal (as of so much else); he conceived the idea of organizing the flower of European knighthood against the enemy, and by enemy he meant Constantinople as well as Islam, as the Byzantine emperor and patriarch realized. The Latin and Greek Churches had been at odds for many years, partly over theological differences concerning the nature of the Holy Spirit—but these probably could have been settled, as such differences had been settled in the past. More significant was the political disagreement resulting from the Greeks' refusal to accept the supremacy of the bishop of Rome. In the Byzantine view, the pope was just one of the leaders of the Church, coequal with the patriarchs of Alexandria, Antioch, and Constantinople. On the other side, the pope would not accept the authority of the Byzantine emperor—although he dared to defy him openly only after 730. Under Byzantine caesaropapism, the emperor's religious authority made him the head of the Church; in western "papal Caesarism," on the other hand, the temporal authority of the pope made him resemble an emperor.

The official schism of the two Churches began in 1054, when the reformer Cardinal Humbert visited Constantinople as a papal legate and dared to excommunicate the patriarch. Gregory VII hoped to reunify the eastern and western Churches under his own control, partly because he needed the support (and tithes) of the wealthy Greeks of southern Italy. His ambition was to establish a Latin state in Constantinople and reunite the Churches under himself, but he was too involved in conflict with the German emperor to attend to the East. Gregory's ambitions outran even his own great energies; he wanted the world—from eastern Asia Minor to Denmark—to fall under the dominion of the Latin Church.

During this same period, the popes were able to observe the progress of the Spanish *Reconquistà*, which began in the tenth century and did not end until the fall of the last Muslim stronghold (Granada) in 1492. The Muslims had been in Spain since 711, and the Spanish princes after 1000 A.D. came down from their strongholds in the Pyrenees to drive the infidels from the peninsula. In the beginning, at least, the princes were fighting to regain their own lands, and their battles were more political than religious. They frequently allied with Arabs against other Arabs, or even against Christians. Under the influence of the reforming papacy of the third quarter of the eleventh century, however, the *Reconquistà* became more ideological and much more rigid—even fanatic, by the end of the century. Its progress inspired the popes, who observed that the Arabs were less unified and weaker than they once had been. It might be not only virtuous, but clever and feasible as well to attack Muslims—an endeavor supported by God as well as by Christian princes and merchants. Tactically and ideologically, the *Reconquistà* became a model for the First Crusade. It directed the pope's attention away from Constantinople and toward the Muslim world.

The crusading ideal first appeared during the 1070s and 1080s, but the pope's quarrels with the German emperor prevented it from coming to fruition. In 1095, however, Urban II succeeded to the papal throne, and Urban was a perfect sponsor for such an enterprise. He was a typical post-revolutionary conservative—ostensibly a militant reformer like his predecessors, but in fact a compromiser and unifier. Urban recognized the Crusades as a way to reunify Latin Christendom and restore peace, to link papacy and monarchy in battle against a common enemy. He was an extremely clever man, formerly a Cluniac monk and a member of the aristocratic elite—a man who was identified with the reformers but could also restore some of the old image of the pope as the friend of the great aristocratic families. Urban was a practical man, not as ideologically bound as his immediate predecessors; he took into account the interests of the aristocrats, but he also used the new militancy as inspiration for action. The First Crusade was the culmination of eleventh-century militancy, and Urban's cause appealed simultaneously to the pious hopes of fanatics and the secular interests of the aristocracy.

Before he addressed the Council of Claremont in 1095, Urban persuaded Raymond, Count of Toulouse to promise to join the Crusade. Thus insured against total failure, he invited the Christian (particularly French) bishops of Europe to his council and asked them to bring as many lords as they could gather. Then he proclaimed a holy war against Islam in a famous speech that was carefully calculated to appeal to almost every interest of the French aristocrats. They thought of Constantinople as a rich, exciting, cosmopolitan center and Urban persuaded them that it could easily be taken. He anathematized the Turks, titillating his audience with tales of horror and torture and torment by Muslim monsters. He released Crusaders from family obligations and promised the protection of the Church to the families and lands of those who wore the Cross. Cleverly, Urban played on the theme of overpopulation among the French nobility, urging the Crusaders to carve out new estates for themselves on the rich shores of the Mediterranean. He portrayed Jerusalem as an earthly paradise, the center of the Christian world, whose citizens longed for liberation from the enemies of Christ. The pope urged his listeners to undertake the Crusade for the remission of their sins, assuring them grace and offering indulgences to shorten their terms in purgatory.

Explicitly and by indirection, Urban motivated the Crusaders with dreams of money and property and sexual freedom—with the coming of the kingdom of heaven and with amnesty for their sins. His speech was so successful that the audience burst into cries of "Deus vult!" ("God wills it") took up their swords, and left the Council as soldiers of God.

Urban tried to find a crowned head to lead the Crusade, but the German emperor was occupied (he was still in fact fighting the pope), William Rufus of England was not quite sane, and the king of France was totally incompetent. Count Raymond of Toulouse, however, was a dashing representative of the French aristocracy, and the First Crusade was conducted almost entirely by French lords. Duke Robert Curthose of Normandy joined the Crusade largely to acquire the protection of the Church for his vulnerable lands (which he lost, later on, to his brother, Henry I of England). Duke Godfrey of Lorraine was a Crusader, as was Bohemund of Sicily—an ambitious and aggressive foe of the Byzantine Empire. The Frenchmen hoped and intended to take Constantinople as well as Jerusalem, but found that to be impossible. They did take Jerusalem, however, where they established a Latin kingdom that lasted for 150 years. Their success can probably be ascribed to the contemporary political disunity in the Arabic world brought on by the recent Turkish invasion; no later Crusade achieved anything like the success of the First, and most of them were disasters.

In the 1130s, St. Bernard of Clairvaux (the moral, if not the official leader of the Church) preached a second Crusade and persuaded the kings of Germany and France to lead it. Both kings were weak, however, and the Crusaders were cut to pieces by Turks in Asia Minor—by that time the Muslims were united again. An indirect but significant result of the Second Crusade was the divorce of Duchess Eleanor of Aquitaine by the French king (for misconduct during the Crusade), which left her free to marry and take her enormous lands to the English royal family.

The famous Third Crusade of 1188 attracted several monarchs: Richard the Lion-Hearted of England for one, and Frederick Barbarossa of Germany (the best of the medieval German monarchs) who was drowned on the way to the Holy Land. Little was left of the Latin kingdom of Jerusalem in 1188; the Crusade was a kind of relief expedition organized by the pope, but it never developed into a major confrontation. The Germans almost disappeared from the expedition after the death of their emperor, and the English and French kings dissipated most of their energies in fighting among themselves. In 1230, St. Louis of France (Louis IX) attacked the Muslims in Egypt, but his effort was unsuccessful and marked the beginning of the end of the old style of crusading ideal.

The concept of holy war against Islam began to disappear in the late twelfth century, probably because Christians had become more tolerant. Having acquired some knowledge of Islam, they had realized at last that Muslims were not simply Christian heretics —also that the Muslims were tough fighters, and worthy of respect. They no longer regarded Muslims as devils, and they found that they could enjoy the fruits of commerce without conquest. The crusading spirit was then directed toward Constantinople, which was more vulnerable than Islam after the Muslim reunification. In 1204, a group of French knights and Venetian sailors attacked and sacked Constantinople. They robbed and looted and raped, and they established a Latin kingdom that survived for sixty years.

The crusading ideal turned around again in the thirteenth century, when it was directed toward Europe itself and against the enemies on the borders of (and within) Christendom. Crusaders remained active in Spain, and also on the German frontiers where German aristocrats fought the Slavs (even Christian Slavs: the *Drang nach Osten* proceeded even when the easterners were Christians). The concept of holy war was deformed to cover any conflict with the political enemies of the papacy. Even the German emperor and the king of Aragon were attacked by "Crusaders" during this period, and the Albigensian Crusade—an attack on heretics that was also an excuse for the conquest of parts of southern France by northern French aristocrats—is an excellent example of the use of the crusading ideal as a political instrument.

It would be wrong, however, to lay all the blame for this at the feet of the thirteenth-century popes; the concept of the Crusade was always political in some sense, from the very beginning of Gregory's ambitions to conquer Constantinople and dominate the eastern Church. Crusades always were a blend of faith and politics, and in the end the Crusades failed to achieve the papal political goals. Not even the use of "justified" violence for religious and political ends helped the papacy to maintain political supremacy after the thirteenth century.

The most important legacy of the crusading movement was the sanctification of violence in pursuit of ideological ends. This was not a new concept, but it took on new force when the pope and the flower of Christian chivalry acted it out in holy wars. The underlying concept outlived its religious origin, and eventually it was absorbed in the institution of monarchy. When the European kings grew more powerful, in the twelfth and thirteenth centuries, they secularized the concept of justifiable violence and extended it into the political sphere. The defense of the realm and its head became a moral duty, and the state gradually replaced the Church as a holy cause.

The crusading orders, whose members took monastic vows and organized themselves to fight in the Holy Land or to support the Crusaders, combined several major medieval ideals. The Knights Hospitaller served as a medical corps; the Knights Templar as the quartermasters of the Crusades. The Templars were the first European bankers, because the size and spread of their order allowed them to transfer money without transferring specie—a genuine breakthrough in European economic life. They acquired an immense capital by medieval standards, largely because the popes used the Templars as tax collectors and managers of its campaign chest for the Crusades. The third major crusading order, the Teutonic Knights, originated as the German monastic contingent to the Crusades, but they found war in the Holy Land to be less interesting than war on their own eastern frontier. The Knights fought Christian Slavs under the banner of Christ, and extremely successfully—they advanced all the way to Latvia and Lithuania, conquering Prussia on the way. The Knights ruled Prussia until their order was disbanded during the Reformation: the "Junker" aristocracy of modern Prussia was a blend of German lords (many of them descended from Teutonic Knights) and native Slavs.

Anti-Semitism

The third major aspect of the new militancy of eleventh-century Christianity was an outbreak of violent anti-Semitism after centuries of relative harmony between Christians and Jews. It was not a new phenomenon, of course; it had roots in the ancient world —indeed, the central and persistent thread of anti-Semitism in European history raises fascinating and unanswered questions.

In *The Rise of Political Anti-Semitism in Germany and Austria*, the Oxford scholar Peter Pulzer examines significant differences between medieval anti-Semitism and the variety that has plagued Europe sporadically since about 1870. Pulzer feels that modern anti-Semitism developed in industrial, secular society in response to the failure of the liberal democratic system to satisfy the masses in the circumstances of contemporary life. He sees modern anti-Semitism as a social consequence of the failure of liberalism, but medieval anti-Semitism as a religious movement, fostered by the Church and arising out of a completely different social situation. Medieval anti-Semitism was based on religion, and a medieval Jew who converted to Christianity was welcomed—at least in theory—by the Church and by Christian society (a few of the Dominican friars who managed the Inquisition in the thirteenth century were converted Jews). Modern anti-Semitism, however, is based on race, and in the face of virulent anti-Semitism no Jew can escape his identity or expect his children to do so.

Pulzer's theory is quite plausible, but even though he is probably correct that medieval anti-Semitism had mainly religious roots, the anti-Jewish attitudes that developed by the late eleventh century were partly social, or even racial. Jews then were disliked as a people, as a distinct group with distinct, deplorable characteristics. Theoretically they were hated because they rejected Christ, but in practice there was a personal hostility or racism that was similar to that of the Germans in the 1930s.

It is difficult to trace the earliest origins of anti-Semitism, because it is not easy to discover exactly what Romans thought about Jews: the sources are meager. The Jews were just one of the minorities in the enormous, polyglot, multi-racial society of the Roman Empire, and few Romans ever encountered Jews at all. In the first century A.D., Roman rulers probably regarded the Jews of Palestine as stubborn and rebellious people: they were among the rare groups who were not content to live under the Roman aegis. The Jewish royal family and most of the nobility did accept imperial rule, but many others refused to cooperate. These were the religious leaders of the community as well as young, middle-class people who organized systematic subversion and even worked toward revolutionary overthrow of the Roman government. In the seventh decade of the first century, they organized a full-scale rebellion that was effectively put down by the Roman authorities. The Jews were dispersed, their temple destroyed, and since 66 A.D. there have been more Jews in the Diaspora than inside Israel.

Aside from the image of the stubborn rebel, the Romans evidently did have an idea of the "good Jew"—a wealthy, compliant, and assimilated Jew (like Josephus Flavius) who was educated in Roman culture. Right along with this image of the "White Jew" went a contrary image of an unlikeable, devious, conspiratorial Jew—no gentleman. Tacitus mentions Jews in a blatantly anti-Semitic style, and Tacitus was not unique. Roman aristocrats regarded circumcision as a shameful mark of difference, and they could not accept circumcised Jews in their public baths (the equivalent of gentlemen's clubs). When the Roman aristocrats were converted to Christianity in the fourth century, their over-all hostility and contempt toward Jews became part of the emotional baggage of the Christian Church.

However, the real center of ancient anti-Semitism was not Rome but Alexandria, where (as in modern Egypt), there existed a virulence of feeling and a persistent conviction that Jews were genuinely evil. Alexandria was the second largest city in the Empire in the second century; it had a population of perhaps one and a half million, about 300,000 of whom were Jews. The Jews and Christians of Alexandria did not get along well, and not for religious reasons only. The bishop of Alexandria was the political leader of the city (more important than the Roman governor), and the refusal of such a large part of the population to accept his authority placed real limitations on his powers. Alexandrian Christians attacked Jews as Christ-killers and Christian-killers: indeed, it is possible to find in second-century Alexandria almost all of the subsequent motifs of anti-Semitism. The city was a metropolis with the usual urban problems, and Jewish merchants competed with Christians. Any degradation or ghettoization of the Jews tended to favor Christian businessmen, and the Christian merchants learned to use anti-Semitism as a business practice—a process that would be repeated again and again in later centuries.

The anti-Semitism of the Roman Empire was carried into the

early medieval world through Constantinople and Spain, where active persecution, forced conversion, denial of economic and social rights, and various kinds of anti-Semitic discrimination were endemic during the Visigothic Era (fifth to eighth centuries). The Byzantine Church acquired an anti-Semitic outlook through Alexandria, and this was reinforced by economic competition between Christian and Jewish businessmen in Constantinople. In the seventh century, the Byzantine emperor Heraclius I actually gave official support to discrimination and persecution of Jews—not surprising, in a system in which religious dissent was tantamount to sedition. The Byzantine Empire was chronically plagued by heresy, and the state could not afford to allow religious difference. As part of their programs of political centralization, the emperors were more or less obliged to control dissent—and Jews, of course, were arch-dissenters. In the end, Byzantine Jews helped invading Arabs to smash the armies of Heraclius, and this Jewish collaboration with the invaders was particularly important in Alexandria, where Jews helped the Arabs to take the city. Before the eleventh century the Arabs regarded Jews as a legal minority group to be taxed and exploited, but not actively persecuted.

The Christian bishops of seventh-century Visigothic Spain persecuted Jews fiercely; apparently they were determined to isolate them from Christian society. Their motivation is not clear, but it may well be that these rather crude and uneducated men feared Jewish influence upon their congregations. There is some evidence that medieval Jews were not averse to proselytizing, and their religious aggression may have caused trouble (in Alexandria as well as Spain). There was no long or strong Christian tradition in Visigothic Spain, and the illiterate Spanish noblemen may have been attractive targets for Jewish evangelists. The Christian leaders retaliated with persecution, which produced a reaction like that of the Jews of Byzantium; the Spanish cities with large Jewish populations were among the first to fall to the conquering Muslims in the eighth century.

From the eighth to the eleventh century Jews all over Europe were generally left alone to flourish as they could. They were important in agriculture as well as trade, and in southern France they owned land and even became noble vassals of the kings. The Carolingian dynasty was extremely friendly to Jews; there is some evidence that one of the Carolingian princes had a Jewish wife. Some French bishops in the ninth century revived old anti-Semitic propaganda, but to little effect: Jews generally were prosperous and peaceful, and they played a significant role in the new urban development of the Mediterranean world in the tenth century.

After four or five hundred years of peace, virulent anti-Semitism reappeared in northern Europe in the eleventh century. Traditionally, its first outbreaks have been associated with the First Crusade, when Crusaders travelling through the Rhineland and the Balkans on the way to the Holy Land turned on unbelievers along their route. However, the pogroms of the First Crusade actually were outbursts of a militant movement and popular mood that had been created during the sixty or seventy years of the Gregorian Reform.

Certain leaders of the reform were central figures in the revival of anti-Semitism on a literary and philosophic level; their characteristic attitudes are expressed in the works of St. Peter Damiani, the north Italian preacher of the New Piety and the Virgin cult. Two anti-Semitic treatises of Damiani survive, and they are as inflexible in attitude as they are restrained in tone. (The attitudes of religious leaders were often expressed in high-minded language, but when such attitudes filtered down to uneducated people they were expressed in violent and vicious acts and language). The new anti-Semites were jealous of Jewish prosperity, of course, but that was nothing new. More significant was the emphasis of the New Piety on the humanity of Jesus, which led inevitably to contemplation of his passion and crucifixion. If Jews were implicated in the death of Jesus—as, through a plausible interpretation of the Gospels, they appeared to be—then devout and emotional Christians could hardly be expected to befriend the enemies of their suffering Lord.

The ethic of the bloodfeud was still endemic in medieval society. Violent death demanded vengeance by those who loved the victim, and it was not difficult for a preacher to convince an illiterate audience of the need for violent, bloody persecution of the killers of Christ. Furthermore, the Gregorian reformers took an apocalyptic, millennial view of human history and of the development of society. They believed that the kingdom of God would come when all was in order on earth: when the pope ruled the emperor and the Jews had fallen to their proper place. The leaders of the reform did not define that place as the gallows (some of their followers did) but the ghetto. They believed that Christ in his mercy forebore to cut down the Jews, but condemned them to wander the earth until they were judged at the end of time. The Jews served as a reminder to Christians and pagans of the consequence of rejecting the Lord: the Diaspora, in this view, was a pedagogical instrument to instruct men in the fruits of sin. They believed that Jews would fall more and more into subjection and punishment as the millennium drew near; their degradation, in fact, would be a sign of progress toward the kingdom of God—much like the degradation of the bourgeois in the Marxist scheme.

The apocalyptic doctrine of the reformers was extremely successful with violent, illiterate, and pious people who were delighted to find moral justification for beating up the rich. Some eleventh-century Jews were wealthy (although the great majority were poor artisans), and thoroughly detested by workers and peasants and impoverished knights. Those who owed money to Jewish merchants and bankers were glad to have a good reason to beat up their creditors. Medieval bishops preached anti-Semitism on a fairly restrained, religious level, but ordinary people increasingly saw Jews not as religious dissenters but as bad people, exploiters and killers of Christians and of Christ. When anti-Semitism left the pulpit and entered the body politic, it became a personal and bitter hostility that could not be mollified even by religious conversion.

There is some evidence that the Jews were proselytizing again in the eleventh century, and this may have contributed to the strength of feeling against them. They were exceptionally literate, sophisticated people who were acquainted with magnates and sometimes accepted at royal courts, and it seems likely that they would have attempted to persuade others that theirs was an intelligent and rational religion. They may even have had some success: there is a quite reliable story that William Rufus of England told some Jews who had been converted to Christianity that they should return to their faith. It is not unlikely that Christian leaders were concerned about Jewish evangelism.

For these reasons, the anti-Semitic passions of the eleventh century erupted in the pogroms of the First Crusade and into widening attacks on Jews during the twelfth century. In 1215, the Church decreed that Jews must live separately from Christians and wear a yellow star to mark their special identity. They were declared a separate and accursed people, and in 1290 they were expelled from England and France. The entire period of the later Middle Ages was scarred by successive waves of pogroms and persecution all over Europe, and especially in Germany.

THE DISCOVERY OF POWER

During the eleventh century, power emerged as a major aspect of medieval civilization—power as an end in itself, a style, an orientation toward the control of as many people and as much territory as possible. In Germanic Europe of the early Middle Ages, the exercise of power was almost entirely confined within the familial structure of society, and men lacked not only the concept but the will to power as we understand it today. In the eleventh century, however, certain rulers began to act as power men and to try consistently to extend their control over people and territories. These rulers operated without any formulated philosophy of power— such a concept was not articulated until Marsiglio of Padua shocked Europe in the fourteenth century. The power men themselves belonged to the old feudal order and ecclesiastical complex —the world of hierarchy, landed families, and ecclesiastical ideals. It took intellectuals a long time to appreciate the significance of what was happening, partly because the power men started out within the framework of old sacred kingship and social hierarchy, with government and authority seen as means to bring closer the kingdom of God. However, even under the old banners, certain rulers became more concerned with the acquisition of power than with inherited, traditional values.

The "new men" of the eleventh century belonged to two different dynasties, the Salian imperial family, and the dukes of Normandy who became kings of England after 1066. It is difficult to be sure of the exact aims and ambitions of the Salians, for the emperors Henry III and Henry IV were pioneers: they moved forward, but they probably did not fully understand themselves and they certainly did not clearly articulate their goals. These men *can* be interpreted simply as later versions of Charlemagne—theocratic kings, God's anointed—but their behavior belies such an interpretation. Theocratic kings were holy men, sacred creatures who were worshipped but not necessarily obeyed. The early medieval French and Anglo-Saxon kings were saintly men with thaumaturgical powers, and they were also family heads like other aristocrats, whose sustenance came from their family support and family dependents in the form of serfs and soldiers. They lived within their traditions, whereas the power men moved out of traditional sources of strength to seek new areas of control.

The Salian emperors did two new and significant things. They tried, first of all, to build large, private standing armies loyal to themselves and not to some intermediate vassals. They made extensive use of *ministeriales,* serf-knights chosen and trained by the emperor, who became professional soldiers loyal to their ruler. The Salians built castles on imperial land all over Germany and put corps of *ministeriales* in to run them; they apparently envisioned Salian fortresses on every hill in the empire.

Their second major innovation was their emphasis on expanding their family domains—the Crown lands—as a basis for power. The emperors owned no land as emperors, but they gradually built up large family holdings to produce a steady income for the Crown, and that income was used to buy mercenaries to conquer more land. The Salians discovered that expansion within Germany was dangerously threatening to neighboring noblemen, so they directed their efforts to the frontiers and attempted to incorporate parts of Saxony and northern Italy into the family lands. They were not very successful in either place: the free Saxon peasants, who owed no obedience to lords, resisted imperial domination with a vigor that involved the emperors in continual petty warfare. The situation became hopeless after 1075, when Gregory VII excommunicated Henry IV and thus identified resistance to the emperor with resistance to Anti-Christ. The Italians let the imperial armies into Italy but not into their cities, which were strongly fortified, with thick walls and many mercenaries. Despite their failures on the frontiers, however, the Salians accomplished a great deal of significant innovation. They quite systematically engaged in institutional change and organization for power; they were tough and able and aggressive men who could enforce their innovations and make them count.

The Norman ducal dynasty, an equally energetic and talented family, was hit hard in the tenth century by the growth of the noble population. They recovered, and after about 990 they began to see themselves as conquerors as well as administrators. They had an unprecedented concern for the day-to-day details of government —almost a secular interest in the progress of the state. The Norman dynasty used law and even monastic reform for its own ends (a well-run reformed monastery, for example, could pay a larger tax than an unreformed one). William the Bastard (later the Conqueror) greatly improved the functioning of the duchy of Normandy, creating powerful state institutions in a fairly poor land. His motives were thoroughly unidealistic and grasping, but he made Normandy into the most advanced state in Europe despite its poverty and its dearth of cities and of educated men. William instituted the system of liege lordship, under which every Norman vassal took an oath of loyalty directly to the duke that superseded his loyalty to any intermediate vassal. He also instituted the payment of feudal services and dues in precise, stated units, in a businesslike arrangement whereby a lord owed a certain amount of money or service for every unit of land he held. Thus William rationalized feudal obligations, making them matters of written law and not of vague tradition.

After the Conquest, William extended his innovations to England and even improved upon them. He made the feudal bond a source of tax revenue by instituting an inheritance tax (relief) paid by a son on succeeding to his father's fief—and like the Salians, William intended to use his money to hire soldiers to engage in further conquest. Near the end of his reign he commissioned the Domesday Book, an incredibly complete and minute (and historically valuable) record of land ownership and tenure at the end of the eleventh century.

William's second son Henry I (who succeeded William Rufus in 1100) carried on his father's work. He improved the operation of the royal treasury by establishing the Exchequer (the accounting division of the government as well as a tax court), and he established a system of itinerant justices that had a critical influence on the development of the English judicial system. Henry tried at first to put a resident justice in every county town, but he soon ran out of educated men and was forced to send "itinerant" judges in circuit. These men became symbols of the royal power; they were representatives of the king who made decisions—and made them stick—even when the king's armies were far away.

By 1100, the exercise of the techniques of power and the values of the power system were widely accepted. The power men were not idealistic in any sense, nor were they striving to emulate Roman emperors, but simply to build up their own domains and gain greater wealth and control. Even so, many churchmen supported them, and by 1100 several dukes and kings acted on power values; the exercise of power became a central fact of life. Power men worked to develop new institutions and offices to carry their changed ways against the traditional hierarchic, familial system, and they developed a highly optimistic, positive attitude about the nature of the state. Almost inevitably, power-oriented rulers began to want everything, to aim at control over all groups in society. The prime institutional mechanisms for centralized government were mercenary armies and elaborate legal and taxation systems.

Quite naturally, the power men threatened and antagonized a great many people, but they generally were successful even over violent opposition. Their success rested very much on individual personality and contemporary circumstances, however, and the power-style of the German emperors declined in the early twelfth century. (The same thing happened in England between the death of Henry I in 1135 and the accession of Henry II in 1154.) However, power politics revived very strongly at the end of the twelfth century, and devotion to power as an end in itself was central to the functioning of thirteenth century government. The satisfactions of power were legitimized by the Church, which gradually came to accept and cooperate with power men and their values.

The new Christian militancy of the eleventh century developed simultaneously with the new power-style and attitude, and these two phenomena were linked together in a revolution in thought that came to dominate European political and social life in later centuries.

THE BOURGEOISIE

So-called early medieval towns were merely fortresses or government and ecclesiastical centers. In the tenth century, urban life revived in western Europe in a way that had not been seen since the Roman Empire: that is, towns became commercial and industrial centers. The first urban centers were in northern Italy, where a greater town population had been preserved in continuity. Around the year 1000, new urban life appeared, in Flanders, then in southern France, then in the Rhine valley, then in England; so that by the second half of the eleventh century there were urban centers all over western Europe. Even in the middle of the twelfth century, however, the urban population of Europe was not more than 5 per cent of the total population. Even in 1300, it could not have been more than 10 per cent—at the utmost, 15 per cent—and the towns were very small. In the twelfth century, a city like London had between 25,000 and 40,000 people. In the thirteenth century, a city like Florence might have as many as 80,000 to 100,000. That would make it a very large city.

The importance of the bourgeoisie was not numerical. They contributed a whole new economic aspect to life—the commercial aspect—which had a profound effect on the European economy and style of life. Furthermore the bourgeois elite, at least, were literate; they had their own culture and values and were consciously critical of aristocratic power. Their appearance on the scene, although it was largely ignored by the aristocracy in the eleventh century, certainly was not ignored after the first quarter of the twelfth. The feudal nobility had to adjust rapidly and skillfully to the challenge of an educated, non-rural, non-feudal, non-aristocratic group with wealth and literacy on its side, and with certain ideological assumptions that threatened the continued domination of the aristocracy.

Historians used to argue endlessly about why urban life revived or expanded in the eleventh century. Nowadays the argument does not seem really worthwhile, or at least there is no point in isolating one factor among all the others. First of all there was a surplus of agricultural produce, which encouraged the development of local market towns. Then there was the development of international commerce between Italy, which brought in goods from Byzantium, and the East. Merchants, who brought luxury items like silks and spices into western Europe, needed a place to live. In the classic thesis propounded by the Belgian historian Henri Pirenne in the 1920s, these international entrepreneurs gathered around a burg (a fortress) and built their own houses under its walls. They enclosed the area in which they had built, and thus medieval towns developed. In time, new houses would appear in the suburbs outside the walls, and these in turn were eventually enclosed. It is clear, however, that many towns developed as places of local, national, and regional commerce, and that some merchants who engaged only in local enterprise were as wealthy and important as the international entrepreneurs.

Pirenne was right in fastening upon the mercantile aspect of urban life as contributing to its growth, its wealth, and to the status and outlook of the dominant group. Medieval towns were corporations: they were self-governing units which obtained rights to self-government from the feudal lord. Within the commune, among the citizens who were sworn to hang together and protect each other, there was very little actual democracy—not much more than in the surrounding rural areas. From Flanders to Italy, the real power in the towns—the town council—was in the hands of great commercial and industrial families. In Flanders, where wool was all-important, the people who were important in town life were in some way connected with the woolen industry.

Although a clan of self-perpetuating patrician families grew up in the towns, it must be said that townsmen had greater social mobility than countrymen. The control by great families was not so firm, and new families were constantly appearing while old families went under and disappeared. There was instability and social change, but very little democracy. Occasional experiments in democracy were tried, but they never worked—they brought violence, disorder, and suspicion. Too many people lived too closely together: they couldn't trust anyone because they knew each other too well. In any case, by the thirteenth century the towns tended to come under the control of great patrician families who were important in industry and trade. However, these families could rarely agree on how to share power. They joined in factions—what we would call parties, but *faction* is more accurate—and vied for control of the town and its government. The winners often exiled the losers. This went on in city after city in Italy after the twelfth century.

It has been traditional to associate the development of medieval commerce and industry with the development of the guild system. Far too much has been made of the guild, as if medieval commerce and industry could not have been developed without it, and all kinds of romantic mystiques have been associated with the medieval guild. It was simply an association of businessmen. There was nothing very mystical about them, or very romantic. There were two kinds of guilds: the merchants guilds, which were groups of merchants joined in a corporate association to engage in international trade to a specific area or in a specific produce. Certain wealthy members of the merchants guild invariably came to dominate the town government, or disputed for power among themselves.

The craft guild, on the other hand, was an organization of workmen. Medieval industry tended to be household industry. A craftsman with a shop hired day-laborers (called *journeymen* from the French word *journee* or day) and a few apprentices. These lived in his household while they were trained, and he could exploit them ruthlessly. The man who owned the house and the tools, who hired the laborers and recruited the journeymen and apprentices, was called the master. It was a system which depended largely upon hand labor—there was little in the way of machinery, and the craftsmen had to compete for the available market. To reduce competition and to make life a little easier, the masters joined in an industrial guild. They agreed to sell at certain prices, to produce certain kinds of goods in certain seasons, and to fulfill certain rules on the quality of workmanship.

It was the leaders of the merchants guild, the dominant upper bourgeoisie of the city, who urged the craft guilds to become monopolistic and to keep down the free entrepreneur. After all, the leaders of the merchants guild had already made their money. They were not eager to see any great new enterprise or new families. Secondly, they were concerned with peace and stability, with cheap goods, and with keeping the working class happy. Guilds did occasionally provide entertainment, sick benefits, and burial benefits for workers but by and large they were authoritarian institutions subservient to the great merchants and the town council. They needed the merchants to sell their goods and to provide capital, and they were afraid that the town council would exile them or ruin their businesses.

If in its internal organization town life was almost as hierarchical as rural life, there was still room in a practical sense for social mobility. Once a new family had made its money, it could not be prevented from playing an important political role. And if the bourgeoisie were fairly rough on their own kind, if they tried to make city governments into narrow oligarchies, still they were a new group of people who wanted some kind of recognition. They wanted titles and land; they wanted to be summoned to the king's council; they wanted to participate in royal government; they wanted to achieve a full identity and a similar place to that of the aristocracy in the social order. The aristocracy bitterly resisted this intrusion, however, and kings did not realize—at least in the twelfth century and not even very clearly in the fifteenth century—how useful the bourgeoisie could be in their disputes with the aristocracy.

Because they did not achieve equality, the bourgeoisie in the twelfth century began to develop their own ideology. They emphasized, naturally enough, the primacy of wealth over inherited position as a basis of power and status. They believed that power should go to the man who fulfilled his function, who gained his wealth by moving upward, who made a solid contribution. Aristocratic parasites, they said, no longer made any real contribution to society. The bourgeoisie also disparaged churchmen, particularly high, noble churchmen, saying that they were not really disciples of Jesus—they were merely what we would call flunkies and exponents of the prevailing social order.

So in the twelfth century, particularly in northern Italy and southern France, the bourgeoisie developed their own ideology. No matter how undemocratic, how unfair, how exploitative the merchants guild members and the master craftsmen may have been towards the rest of the people in town, certainly they constituted a liberal, revolutionary, subversive force in rural society as a whole. Their work was socially valuable, and they were very unsatisfied with their inferior status. They wanted equality; they fought back; they developed an ideology which denied the whole basis of noblemen's inherited position. The boureoisie said that society was no longer exclusively rural. Commerce and industry were important. Times and values had changed, and it was outrageous that the nobility should live off the power their families had gained at the time of Charlemagne.

The emergence of class-conscious and militant ideals among

the bourgeoisie in the late eleventh and first half of the twelfth century profoundly affected an already extremely complex social-cultural situation. The rise of bourgeois militancy and hostility towards the established ordering of society inserted into the cultural matrix an unprecedented problem for the traditional leaders of medieval Europe, one that in view of their family background, education, and thought patterns they were peculiarly ill-equipped to handle. The incipient class struggle would provide one of the most powerful factors operating toward the crystallization of a liberation movement against the medieval hierarchical order.

Chapter Five
CREATIVITY AND REBELLION

I. Intellectual Expansion

CREATIVITY AND IDEOLOGY

The first decade of the twelfth century marked the conclusion of one period of medieval culture and the beginning of another. The second half of the eleventh century had been an era of ideology and of power struggle for the leadership of Christian society. The twelfth century (especially between 1110 and 1180) was very different. It was a time of extraordinary intellectual creativity: the most original period in the Middle Ages, and in fact in western civilization since the fifth century B.C. It was distinguished by a series of remarkable advances in many aspects of culture, including the first new, non-Platonic philosophy to appear in more than a thousand years.

In the twelfth century there emerged a new consciousness of the self and recognition of the importance and distinctiveness of the individual, marking a significant departure from the group and typological thought of the early Middle Ages. Men began to develop a sense of individual reality and to appreciate the dignity and worth of individual human personality. With the new consciousness came new forms in art and literature; indeed, "Gothic" architecture represented the first really novel and polished artistic style since the triumph of classicism in Periclean Athens.

The twelfth century was also the first romantic era in western civilization, and its romantic themes and motifs still are central in western art. It gave birth to a new educational institution—the university—which survives (with difficulty) today in a form much like that it was given in the twelfth century. Certain political concepts and institutions, particularly the legal systems of Europe and the United States, owe their origin and fundamental character to twelfth-century ideas and implementation.

There have been several periods of fantastic creativity in western history, including the fifth century B.C., the Enlightenment of the eighteenth century, and the brief period of emotional and intellectual flowering at the turn of the nineteenth and twentieth centuries. The Italian Renaissance might be included in such a catalogue (although the thinking of that era was not so original as that of the other three), as might the Scientific Revolution of the seventeenth century. These moments of high creativity are extremely rare: genuinely novel ideas are always rare, and it is difficult to find out why they occur when they do.

Diffusionist theories—for example, the idea that new knowledge from Muslim Spain awoke intellectual inquiry in western Europe in the twelfth century—are fundamentally unsatisfactory because they do not explain why thinkers began to seek new ideas from other cultures. Men do not borrow ideas unless they want something offered by another culture; the intellectual upheaval occurs before the search, and ideas do not simply appear from the outside and transform higher culture by their innate power.

High creativity usually coincides with political and social failure. Usually, such periods follow hard on the intense and debilitating ideological struggles of the final stages of an *ancien régime* which has exhausted its political and social resources and its moral possibilities, a regime of ossified culture without self-confidence. At the point of collapse, a generation appears that insists on returning to first principles to work out a new view of man and society. The greatest cultural achievements of the Athenians were made after the *polis* began to disintegrate, and the Scientific Revolution took place in the atmosphere of political stagnation that accompanied the failure of fervid puritanism. The Enlightenment did not begin until the lassitude of the French *ancien régime* reached new depths of torpor. The burst of creativity at the end of the nineteenth century can be interpreted as a response to the collapse of middle-class liberalism, for despite the high hopes of mid-century liberals, their regime did nothing for either the masses or the intellectuals, and its obvious weaknesses forced thinkers after 1890 to re-explore the very nature of man and society.

The failure of the Gregorian Reform movement to establish a real Christian society produced a crisis in medieval culture. The idealism of the early Middle Ages—in fact the entire justification for its moral values and social framework—rested on the belief that the world was moving toward the full realization of Christianity through the Church. The Gregorian reformers actually tried to implement the ideal—to bring the kingdom of God to earth—but the power elite (the lords and kings and bishops) successfully resisted the pope and the reforming radicals, making obvious their real hostility toward the very ideal of Christian society. The social elite would not subordinate power or family interest to God's will, and their ultimate victory demonstrated the bankruptcy of the moral program on which western idealism had rested since the time of St. Augustine.

The intellectuals of the first three decades of the twelfth century, who had seen the popes exposed as little more than cynical bargainers with kings over the spoils of the Church, could not be held by tradition or moral idealism, or indeed by any public program. With the traditional leaders exposed as corrupt and inept, privatism and quietism prevailed and men looked inward for satisfaction. The City of God had not existed on earth in the tenth century either, but the men of 950 at least believed that they were travelling toward it and that the leaders of Christian society were in the vanguard of the journey. The men of 1150 had no such illusions.

Creative periods in the West are, then, not eras of flourishing political and social ideology, and their great thinkers are forced to begin with a new epistemology and a new understanding of human nature. They must develop a new view of the world and of man before they can go on to debate the organization of human society. Eventually their ideas do produce political and social movements, but not until the thinkers have arrived at some understanding of man and some theory of culture. By the end of the twelfth century a new ideology (or at least an underground liberation movement) was emerging, but it arrived in the wake of a burst of creative philosophical and artistic energy.

The Enlightenment, too, began without any specific social or political philosophy. Voltaire and Montesquieu were interested in basic principles, not in programs, but their successors went on to lead the French Revolution. The new sensitivity and irrationalism of 1900 were inspired by creative work in art and psychology—and not all the social and political implications of that era have been worked out yet. In many respects, westerners still live within the outworn code of nineteenth-century liberalism; the search for ideology to fit the new sensitivity was retarded by the temporary (and false) unity against fascism in the 1940s. The second stage of the rebellion against middle-class liberalism continues still.

Moments of creativity, then, tend to coincide with the bankruptcy of a political and social system that has carried a whole culture and world-view. Such failures generally are followed by periods of political inactivism, of reticence in problem-solving and resistance to sweeping programs, and by a turn inward towards concentration on the nature of man. Serious examination of human feelings and reason often is productive of philosophy and art and literature, and the new intellectual movements in their turn develop into ideologies of rebellion against the old order. This phenomenon is exemplified in the creation of a new culture out of the collapse of the early medieval thought-world as demonstrated in the failure of the Gregorian Reform. Eventually, the twelfth century, too, produced a philosophy and ethic of liberation.

The liberation movement of the twelfth century had a very different outcome from that of the French Revolution, primarily because the old order was able to rescue itself from destruction. The medieval system might easily have gone down, like the Bourbons, before the forces unleashed in the twelfth century, but instead the aristocratic hierarchy managed to come to terms with the new men and the new ideas, absorbing much of the best of the new spirit.

History establishes patterns of development and change, but it does not revolve in deterministic cycles; men in any period are free to create their own history. The *ancien régime* of the eighteenth century made every possible mistake and was destroyed by the forces of liberation, but the bishops and nobles of the thirteenth century (who happened to be bright and effective people) saved themselves—as did the power elite of the sixteenth century who confronted the Protestant reformers. The thirteenth-century Establishment also profited from the failure of the new culture to resolve all its inner tensions: the incredible burst of creative energy of the twelfth century never developed into a consistent and effective social program, and this failure was one important factor in the preservation of the medieval system.

Peter Abelard

At any period of history—even in the twentieth century, when higher education is more widely available than ever before— very few people really understand academic philosophy. The abstract ideas of "professional" thinkers are far too difficult and obscure for most men to grasp, and seldom even interesting to them —and yet the general attitudes of the philosophers are of great social and intellectual consequence. The abstract, systematic philosophy of a period is somehow very close to its "climate of opinion"—to the spirit and assumptions by which people operate —and yet it is difficult to establish a specific connection between academic philosophy and the general culture. It may be that the wider culture affects and colors philosophy, that philosophers reflect and report their intellectual environment. Certain systematic thinkers, however, have had a critical influence on the world-view of an entire generation: John Locke's writings signalled the coming of the Enlightenment, and most of the important ideas of the nineteenth century, from Romanticism to Marxism, had roots within the philosophy of Hegel. For the twelfth century, the intellectual catalyst was Peter Abelard—the most influential philosopher to emerge in the West since the death of St. Augustine.

Abelard had an extraordinary influence on his own generation. He was *the* man of the 1120s—the teacher for whom students flocked to Paris, the subject of controversy and discussion in every intellectual center in Europe—and yet he never became an authority in the Church, and when he died in 1142 his life and career were in ruins and his work discredited. Not long after Abelard's brief heyday, a stream of Greek and Arabic philosophy began to pour into western Europe, making Abelard's pre-Aristotelian terminology and methodology seem old-fashioned even to the next generation of scholars. During his own time, however, Abelard's novelty and brilliance forced thinkers to redefine their basic concepts. The University of Paris emerged as an institution around the magnet of Peter Abelard, and this (academics being what they are) earned him the undying animosity of less charismatic colleagues.

Unfortunately, little reliable biographical data is available on the seminal thinkers of the Middle Ages. Not much is known about Abelard's early life except what he wrote down himself, which may be inaccurate and colored by feeling. He came from a noble family of Brittany, which was then on the frontier of the civilized world: its noblemen were more like the cattle barons of the old West than the sophisticated aristocrats of Paris or Toulouse. However, he was a member of the landed class, and thus he shared that essential self-confidence which marked most of the consequential thinkers of Europe before the nineteenth century. Until very recently, western society was built upon status acquired at birth, and membership in the upper class provided not only sustenance but leisure, and the social and economic security essential to creativity. Thomas Aquinas, Dante, Montaigne, Voltaire—all these men were aristocrats, and their great work could not have been accomplished in any other background. Yet Abelard was on the periphery of the noble class—as a man of the frontier, he was expected to be somewhat extreme and eccentric, and he lived up to that image.

Abelard was educated in the cathedral schools and soon recognized as a genius, brighter than his teachers (most of whom detested him). He became a professor of philosophy at the new university at Paris, and students came from all over Europe to hear his ideas. According to the famous love story (which may be in part a product of his own imagination), Abelard fell in love with and seduced the "niece" (probably the daughter) of a cathedral canon. Heloise had a child, and her "uncle" incited a gang of hoodlums to attack and castrate her seducer. Abelard left the university and became the abbot of a monastery, where he quarreled with the monks, who did not understand his ideas and had no taste for his temperament. He continued to publish his works, but was denounced by St. Bernard of Clairvaux—the self-appointed conscience of the Church in the twelfth century—and forced to recant some of his doctrines. Throughout his life, Abelard carried on an intense and moving correspondence with Heloise, who had been exiled to a convent, and eventually he retired to Cluny, where he died in 1142. These are the "facts" of Abelard's life as the story is known today—largely derived from Abelard's autobiography. They are plausible, but the only biographical certainties are that he was a controversial professor who withdraw from the University of Paris and died at Cluny.

Abelard's philosophical work has many levels, but for practical purposes it can be examined in three aspects—rationalism, empiricism, and voluntarism. In the general meaning of the word (not in its strict, specific philosophical meaning), Abelard was a rationalist: he believed that human reason was the prime road to truth. In the twelfth century, reason was defined as the application of logic (then called "dialectic") to experience and to knowledge in order to gain general truth.

Three sources of knowledge, or bases of truth, are available: reason, feeling, and traditional authority. In the early medieval world (as in other underdeveloped, agrarian societies), the prime basis of knowledge was traditional authority: the past, and the institution that enforced the past—namely, the Christian Church. What the Bible or the Church Fathers said to be true was true; faith was essential to understanding. Reason could be used as a vehicle or instrument to develop and elaborate the pronouncements of authority, but it never was sufficient on its own to find the truth. Feeling was important but secondary, for belief was not derived from feeling. It was revealed by traditional authority; the believer accepted his fatih and then felt happy or sad or awed or solemn about it.

Abelard's major departure from tradition was his conviction that reason could proceed on its own to find truth, that it did not require faith; for him, reason was the prime source of truth. This belief he expressed through his devotion to logic as the chief instrument of inquiry, and through his conviction (and demonstration) that traditional authority was often vague, confused, unreliable, and too abstract to be meaningful. Abelard put the doctrines of faith to the test of reason; using the scientific and philosophical information available to him, he examined revealed truth through logical scrutiny. This is radical, a threatening process at any time, and in the twelfth century (much less change-oriented than the twentieth), it was revolutionary. If the leaders of Church and society had been rationalists themselves, Abelard would have been put to death; indeed, when rationalism did creep into the

Church in the thirteenth century, men were burned for much less dangerous ideas. Abelard probably was fortunate to escape with forced retirement.

Thus if a "rationalist" is defined in a general sense as one who depends on reason as a prime source of truth, then Abelard was a rationalist. However, in the other meaning of the term—the specific philosophical definition—he was an empiricist, an anti-rationalist. In its specific sense, a "rationalist" believes that truth is purely intellectual, that it lies not in particulars but in abstract ideas and general, universal propositions, that it comes to the mind from without by some instantaneous process (such as divine revelation) that does not depend on the accumulation of particular details from experience.

Medieval philosophy before Abelard was built entirely upon the rational Platonic tradition that particulars make sense only in their general character and can be understood only in their intellectual, universal categories—as Plato said, as Forms or Ideas. The early Church adopted the Platonic understanding, which fits very well with any theistic system based on revelation (Neoplatonism became part of Judaism as well as of Christianity). Medieval thinkers conceived of God as pure intelligence or pure spirit, and believed that when men understood things in a general, universal way, they were approaching the mind of God. They believed too that pure ideas or universal concepts were placed in human minds by divine revelation. Men can make sense of the world only through general concepts—by extension, they can understand only through God. Platonism allowed Christians to believe that knowledge begins with revelation, that God implants in human minds the abstract concepts (salvation, Church, monarchy, and so on) that create order out of a chaotic mass of particulars. If God is transcendent, providential, and composed of pure spirit, then Platonic rationalism fits Him very well.

A Platonic philosophic system was bound to become more and more theistic and even mystical, for if the Idea of the Good is approachable only through religious experience, then mysticism becomes almost inevitable. In the fifth book of *The Republic*, Plato spoke of the supreme Idea which is attained only by the "flight of the soul"—a mystical concept. Man gets his intellectual concepts from God, according to medieval Neoplatonists, and he cannot reason without these Ideas. Such a system is somewhat circular (like all theology), but it dominated western thought from the third century A.D.

St. Anselm brought traditional Neoplatonic medieval theology to a peak of refinement around 1100. He preceded Abelard by a few years—indeed, Anselm stands as a transitional figure in medieval intellectual history. In his desire to defend dogma by the use of logic, he was a rationalist—but a traditional rationalist, for he believed that the intellectual concepts of dogma came through divine revelation. Man acquires knowledge through faith (or traditional authority), but to calm any doubts he can and should prove his beliefs by the use of reason. We know that God exists, but we prove His existence to reassure doubters. Anselm defined God in Platonic terms as pure concept—a concept greater than which nothing can be conceived. That definition is the first term of his syllogism proving the existence of God; for the second term he relied again on Platonic definition, stating that the ideas in our minds are real—that they exist, they are not phantoms. In the third term of the syllogism, Anselm stated that God is something we think about (a concept), and therefore He exists.

In his classic "ontological" proof of the existence of God, then, Anselm relied on the old assumption of the reality of ideas. He took a conservative stance on this philosophical issue (although he was much more radical in other matters), but the trend of his time was away from Platonism, and his conservatism produced strong resistance in younger scholars. Anselm's thought on the reality of ideas was not far from that of St. Augustine, and in that he was behind his contemporaries. He was questioned by a young French philosopher named Roscelin who refused to accept the ontological argument, claiming that ideas (even the idea of God) might be phantoms, that we cannot prove that ideas exist. Roscelin eventually became a teacher of Peter Abelard, and was one of the few that Abelard respected.

In modern philosophy, those who believe in the reality of abstract ideas are called Idealists, but in the Middle Ages they were called Realists (because they believed that ideas were real). Anselm's proof was based on the point of view of a medieval Realist or a modern Idealist, and it is an important branch of the great tree of Platonism. The other classic medieval proof of the existence of God—that of Thomas Aquinas in the thirteenth century—rests on Aristotelian thought and not on an understanding of truth as an attribute of universal concepts. The Platonic tradition continues: Hegel worked within it in the nineteenth century, and modern radical political philosophers have roots in it, for they integrate experience in terms of ideals or universal concepts that make sense of particular phenomena. An ancient Platonist, a medieval Realist, a modern Idealist all proceed from confidence in the reality of the Idea.

Going beyond Roscelin, who questioned Anselm's assumption of the real existence of ideas, Abelard adopted the empirical point of view, which is always skeptical about the reality of abstractions. An empiricist believes that the existence of an idea does not give it reality, that we get our knowledge from experience, from the senses—not entirely from physical experience, but from thought and from the learning process itself, which are forms of experience. Empiricism is always critical; it insists on the examination of ideas and of how they are acquired, refusing to accept on faith the reality of concepts.

At certain stages of history, empiricism can be radical or even revolutionary, for it demands that we test such concepts as kingship or priesthood or even deity: who is the king, and how did he become what he is? Empirical movements—refusals to accept ideas or situations on faith or tradition alone—usually appear at moments of tension or during the break-up of an old order; when a traditional order is threatened, empiricism appears. The Sophists flourished while the Athenian *polis* deteriorated, Bacon and Hume worked as the *ancien régime* came to its end. The empirical approach and style of the analytic movement in contemporary philosophy reflects at least in part a response to the crisis of twentieth-century society. (Modern philosophy, however, is much too complex to be dominated by one school or tradition.)

In a negative, critical sense, empiricism can be useful—it can be used to bring down outworn concepts, but traditionally it has failed to offer any replacement. Empiricism (particularly materialistic empiricism) is never compatible with theism, for what can an empiricist use to impose order on chaotic experience? Empiricism is not really a theory or a view of the world but a method or skeptical spirit, and its weaknesses are the weaknesses of modern analytic philosophy, which has not achieved very much. The failings of the empirical approach are demonstrated in the contemporary social sciences, and most clearly in psychological behaviorism, which describes human activities in minute detail without giving its subjects any creed to live by.

Scholars still debate whether Abelard was really an empiricist; certainly he was one by temperament, which was radical enough for his day. (The medieval term for our "empiricist" was "nominalist"—one who believes that ideas are only names, and thus the opposite of a medieval "realist.") Roscelin was an empiricist, but he was a critic rather than a systematic philosopher, and Abelard attempted to build a philosophy on the empirical spirit. He looked at "universals" and decided that they were neutral "states of mind" or intellectual conditions. He never said that universals were phantoms, but he did attempt to examine them in order to discover whether they were true, and that was extreme enough for the twelfth century. Abelard even dared to write a treatise on the Trinity (a sacrosanct concept hitherto regarded as above question by human logic), and although his conclusions were not all disturbing or heretical, the attempt carried the audacious implication that the ultimate truth of Christian dogma was susceptible to rational inquiry. Not satisfied simply to adore the Trinity, he dared to study it.

Any traditional, authoritarian system depends on the acceptance of general concepts that are above examination, and this makes critical investigation itself a revolutionary act. Abelard was the greatest and most influential thinker of his day, and thus his empirical approach constituted a dramatic threat to the stability of the intellectual order. His philosophic legacy was the refusal to depend upon faith and tradition alone; he believed that faith must be buttressed with reason, experience, and human feeling. The desire to justify universal concepts became the spirit of the late twelfth century, and the work of Abelard was crucial in the development of that spirit.

The third major aspect of Abelard's thought—voluntarism—was the basis of his moral philosophy, and here too his ideas were central to the intellectual development of the twelfth century. Ethical systems are either formalist or voluntarist. In formalist systems, certain rules of conduct exist, and good conduct consists in obedience to these. A man who follows the rules is a good man; one who does not is bad. To a voluntarist, however, what is important is not the deed but the intention or the will, and the only good or bad quality in a man is the quality of his will. The same act may be bad or good depending on the circumstances, and an act may be good even though it formally appears to be bad.

Until the twelfth century, Christian ethics (derived from the Judaic tradition) were formalistic. Christians believed that certain kinds of behavior were good by definition, that the Christian code must be followed without question or exception, and that anyone who did not follow it, should and would be punished. To his contemporaries, Abelard's strongly voluntarist line was astounding. He said that it is the intention that counts—that an act based on love was a good act, one based on hatred or selfishness was bad. He favored the ethics of Jesus, he said, who acted only out of love for God and man. (Abelard can be accused of using voluntarism to justify his own love affair, which was damnable in formalistic terms but arose out of love.) Voluntarism, of course, is a threat to authoritarian systems, for if the criterion for good behavior is based on individual will and attitude, then the authorities cannot control people's conduct. (In modern times, the issue has recurred in the dispute over birth control within the Catholic Church, which requires obedience to its moral code regardless of intention or motivation; love is not accepted as a justification for contraception—and the old ethical question has not been put to rest.)

One of the most important developments in the twelfth century was the brand-new recognition of the value of love and individual feeling, including feelings toward other people. Indeed, this became the most revolutionary and significant movement of the century, and perhaps the most controversial. Abelard's voluntarist approach played an important part in the new understanding, and so did the work of one of his pupils—John of Salisbury—who studied in Paris under Abelard and respected him deeply.

EDUCATION

From one point of view, John of Salisbury was a reactionary. He was a humanist who was anti-rationalist and even anti-intellectual, placing little value in the New Logic or scholarship or research. John may have been of peasant blood or of the low nobility; he was orphaned early in life and educated in the Church to be a master of language and the best Latinist of his day. He eventually became a papal secretary, and when he discovered the papacy to be corrupted by greed and power politics, he wrote a very unflattering book about Rome. John served also as a secretary to Archbishop Thomas Becket; he went to the Continent when he was exiled by Henry II after Becket's murder, and eventually became the bishop of Chartres during the early stages of the building of its great cathedral.

John of Salisbury disapproved profoundly of the contemporary development of the universities. Through history, there have been two distinct and different attitudes toward education: one the intellectual, in which education is viewed as a process directed toward the training of minds, designed to fill and inspire as many minds as possible. In the humanist view, on the other hand, education is directed toward the training of character; it should make people act well and train the will (not the mind) by communicating to the young the best ideas of the past. According to John of Salisbury, young people should be brought up in the best traditions of good conduct, molded to serve society. In the twelfth century, John's was the reactionary stand and the intellectual view was progressive, for it looked forward to the new empiricism and to new fields of knowledge, breaking with the traditional indoctrination of the old monastic schools. In the twentieth century it is the humanist approach that is progressive, but the "rightness" of either view reflects contemporary circumstances. John of Salisbury had little influence in his own time, and the drive toward intellectual achievement in education moved forward. Eventually, however, in the Italian Rensaissance his opinions were reinstated, as people began to realize that an education that trains the mind and neglects the will and the character can foster tyranny.

The moral-social, humanist approach was developed in the ancient world, and particularly in Rome, where education was designed to train the young to take over the leadership of the world. Such education can be (and often is) used to buttress an *ancien régime*; that was true in Rome, and again in nineteenth-century Britain, where the playing fields of Eton produced men to take and hold an empire. Such education emphasizes ethics and habitual attitudes, self-restraint and patriotism; it teaches future leaders to write and speak well and encourages them to keep the state going as it has been going.

In the twelfth century, the new radical intellectual class of the universities wanted to re-examine everything (even the Church), to put intellectual achievement ahead of ancient attitudes and codes. John, however, admired Roman education and was concerned about the purely intellectual emphasis that ignored responsibility and moral commitment; he wanted to raise up a generation of good men rather than scholars. Twelfth-century agricultural society was booming, there was new wealth and economic opportunity, and the royal power and its attendant bureaucracy were gaining steadily in size and function. In John's most important book, the *Policraticus* (a study of statecraft), he pointed out pitfalls of power and of big government. Having observed the corruption of the papacy and the brutality of the English king, Henry II, he could see the harshness and amorality of government and power and wealth in the hands of clever and ambitious but amoral men. His solution was an educational system designed to train young men in *noblesse oblige*, generosity, and social responsibility.

Despite John of Salisbury, the emphasis on intellectual achievement continued to deepen and his ideas were not accepted until the Italian Renaissance, when the old emphasis on morality and preparation for leadership was taken up by the ruling elite and adopted all over Europe. In the sixteenth century, the purpose of education became the training of those born to power, to make sure that they did not abuse their birthright. Not only the English public school but the *lycée* and the *gymnasium* developed on this principle, until by the nineteenth century the humanist approach had become entrenched and socially reactionary. Schools inculcated an elitist, genteel style but no longer trained the young in moral responsibility. They provided an inherited elite with a set of language skills calculated to set them apart from the democratic mass. Inevitably, with the growth of democracy, the humanist educational system came under attack. In the United States especially, the schools were denounced for sacrificing intellect to style, for undemocratic prejudice against immigrants and the low-born, for taking educational resources away from the development of the intellect and applying them to the education of "gentlemen."

The educational furor of the late nineteenth century reflected the bitter dispute over this ancient question, and it was settled in favor of the intellectual approach to education—which produced scientists instead of gentlemen and did not attempt to impose a particular style on the young. Educators concentrated on the training of the superior mind (regardless of social background); and the track system was one consequence of the new emphasis on intellect. Contemporary radicals now wish to change again, to return to the concept of a school as a training ground in character and leadership for the new elite—albeit the revolutionary elite. The university again is to become a center of social and political reform, of love and social action, and the humanist educational system of John of Salisbury, of the Italian humanists, and of the English public schools, is to be brought up to date, and to be given the radical moral orientation that John of Salisbury originally envisaged.

Eight hundred years ago, John of Salisbury argued that university teachers should train leaders to serve in the world instead of indulging in endless argument over the existence of universals. In a sense, of course, he was right: scholastic philosophers were arguing the same questions a hundred years after John's death. Academic arguments over universals and similar matters were identified, by fourteenth-century humanists, with reaction, and scholasticism was equated with obscurantism. Yet John already saw scholastic philosophers in the mid-twelfth century as useless time-wasters who discussed irrelevant questions while tyrants and corruption flourished in the world outside. His attitudes are shared by modern student radicals, who see no value in discussing abstract ideas while people starve in Asia, Harlem, or Appalachia.

II. The Romantic Century

ROMANTICISM

The twelfth century may be described as a "romantic" age, a time when romantic attitudes were widespread in popular culture, art, and literature and even began to influence philosophy and theology. The twelfth century was a romantic era, as was the first part of the nineteenth (from about 1790 to 1840). Some students would include the second century B.C. (the zenith of Hellenistic civilization) or the Age of Shakespeare in the late sixteenth and early seventeenth century as romantic eras. However, the later two eras were essentially baroque rather than purely romantic; they were times when feeling was very important in art and literature but did not really affect society very deeply or become a style or a philosophy of life.

When romanticism becomes an acceptable style, contemporary culture is dominated by an emphasis on feeling, which is granted equal (or superior) authority to that of reason or tradition. Jacques Barzun, a profound student of modern romanticism, denies that the nineteenth-century romantics gave exclusive value to feeling. He believes that romantic eras tend to follow (and compensate for) earlier periods when feeling has been neglected or ignored, when tradition and reason alone have been valued. Barzun regards romanticism as a form of humanism, which values *all* aspects of life and *all* sources of truth. Romantics do tend to emphasize a direct emotional response, but not to the exclusion of all else; they express their feelings intensely because this side of human nature has been neglected.

As I see it, romantic eras are eras of individualism, when the emphasis shifts away from the domination of men by society and by community obligations and first place is given by people of the highest sensibility to the individual and his personal quest. These are consciously heroic eras, in which the ideal figure is not a leader of society but a self-sustaining individual pursuing his own dream. Such periods—when love is more important than service or obligation to family or state or even to reform—tend to be anti-social or anarchistic; all human goals and ideals are interpreted in terms of love. Obviously, the romantic ideal is never put into practice by the majority of men—no ideal ever is; throughout cultural history, a small number of leaders and thinkers has made all the difference.

Essentially, the idea of love is a concept of union between the individual and something outside himself, which may be another person, or a force, or a mystery—it may even be a nation, or the proletariat, or the revolution itself. In the Middle Ages, the object of love usually was God or some aspect of the Godhead such as Jesus, or the Church, or the Virgin Mary. (The Virgin was particularly suitable as an acceptable sublimation of sexual feelings and drives.) Love became an accepted way of life in the twelfth century, and the quest for union a valuable pursuit, as it does in all romantic eras of transvaluation, when feeling is given primacy over tradition and authority.

One of the major difficulties of romanticism, of course, is the danger of cheapening feeling in mass culture. When everyone becomes a man of sensibility, feeling is distorted. It is hard (although not impossible) to cheapen reason or tradition, but feeling is fragile; authentic feeling cannot be attained by any describable process, nor can it be attained by everyone. Romantic periods are extremely productive of art and literature, but they also produce a great deal of nonsense and of false sensibility—of phony Bohemianism that imitates the effects of passion without its substance.

Potentially, at least, romantic periods are revolutionary, radical, and even anarchistic. If feeling is the standard of social life, then men will want to organize their communities on the basis of feeling, and this has never been successful. Most often, repression puts an end to the attempts even before they have played themselves out, for such ideals and their implementation inevitably arouse the resentment of the authorities. At the end of the twelfth century and in the early thirteenth, radical romanticism was expressed largely through religious heresy—the only available revolutionary medium—and heretics were cruelly put down. The same kind of thing happened in 1848, when romantic revolutionaries were slaughtered on their barricades.

THE IDEA OF LOVE

A new idea of love appeared in the twelfth century, or at least an old idea in a new form. The Fathers of the Church believed that there were two kinds of love: Christian love, which was good and acceptable, and Greek or pagan love, which was bad. They opposed Christian *agape* (which means thanksgiving) to the ancient *eros*.

The Greeks themselves saw ideal love as the relationship between two human beings who loved the same things, who were devoted to the same Form or Idea. Plato was the great theorist of Greek love, and indeed the supreme spokesman for the pagan idea. He believed that sexual love was the mundane reflection of absolute union in a spiritual ideal, and that sex could never be absolute union, although it was an acceptable lesser relationship. To Plato, of course, the lovers usually were two men, partly because Greece had the kind of military aristocratic society that is not very enthusiastic about women, preferring homosexual love to heterosexual copulation. Also, the Greeks considered the male body more beautiful and better-proportioned than the female, and Greek women were not sufficiently well educated to be suitable intellectual companions for brilliant men—although there were rare exceptions: Pericles, for instance, had a mistress whom he loved very much.

The Christian Church misinterpreted and rejected Plato's ideas of love, and indeed it had rejected sexual love entirely by the second century. The reasons for this are obscure, for it seems unlikely that Jesus was opposed to sex even if Paul was—and Paul's sexual difficulties probably were personal and not philosophical. In any case, by the third and fourth century the Church was totally opposed to homosexual love and hostile even to heterosexual love, except within marriage and for purposes of procreation. This may have reflected the new puritan strain in Mediterranean culture at that time, when even among pagans, puritanism was a part of the intellectual culture of the style-setters. There was a vehement puritan reaction to the sexual mores of the Roman upper class, which by the first century A.D. had become extremely free and extremely elaborate, with strong elements of sadomasochism and an immense, organized system of prostitution. This probably disgusted intelligent observers, especially Christians, who—as Neoplatonists—believed in the separation of body and soul. The Roman emphasis on unlimited physical acts was a denial of the soul, and of the mystical possibilities of the life of the spirit.

The Christians then came up with the concept of *agape*, an extension and perhaps a perversion of a Hebrew tradition. The Jews themselves were extraordinarily free and naturalistic about sex; they did not theorize about it, perhaps because to them the important relationship was that of man and God, not that of man and man, or man and woman. The covenant established a loving union with God, and indeed, the relationship of God and His people resembles a love affair as it is described in the Hebrew Bible. God often was an aggressive, jealous lover, and that relationship was so demanding and so crucial that the Jews never had to worry much about human love—less so than any literate people in history. Unlike the Jews, who regarded human love as something outside the covenant and therefore secondary, the Christians became intensely anxious and excited about the significance of sex and human love in Christian life. Such anxiety has caused untold human misery down through twenty centuries, but it has also produced a creative tension in western society that has contributed to the distinctive culture of the West.

The Church's idea of *agape* was derived from Hebrew covenant theory reapplied to Christian grace, but with an anti-sexual corollary. God chooses to love and save men: He gives love freely and thus breathes life into man. The sacrament of the Mass is an act of thanksgiving, a ceremony of *agape*, the way in which the union of God and man is consummated and grace becomes effective. Through transubstantiation, the Christian can partake of Christ and be reborn. By extension, however, the love of another person detracts from the love of God, because God's love is exclusive. The true Christian devotes himself entirely to God. Absolute virginity is the ideal state, with chastity and celibacy very close in holiness; the only other acceptable state is marriage—but marriage which is consummated only to produce children. Even liberal Catholics realize today that sexual union expresses and creates caring and devotion as well as lust; and some radical Christian thinkers now acknowledge that union between man and woman is the human act closest to union between man and God. But after 200 A.D. Church leaders entirely rejected and denied the moral value of sexual feelings.

This denial of a precious aspect of human nature in a paradoxical way reveals how much Church leaders and thinkers had come to imbibe Roman attitudes—and the very worst, most vicious and aggressive Roman attitudes. For the Roman aristocracy, like the Christian bishops, regarded sexual relations as mere gratification of lust or necessary service to the state and the family. The few Roman writers who dared express an erotic philosophy, who perceived sexuality in terms of love were ignored, ridiculed, or even criminally prosecuted. The wonderful love poetry of Catullus received no recognition as the great literature it is, and we know from his poems how rudely he was treated by the aristocracy, even the women. Ovid's erotic poetry was held to be dangerous to public morals and he was condemned to life-long lonely political exile by the emperor. (Ovid's poetry was greatly appreciated in the twelfth century because he had anticipated some of the erotic attitudes of medieval romantics.) In Roman imperial times (as today) male aggression against women and extreme dehumanizing puritanism are different sides of the same coin, intertwined aspects of the same hostility to human nature. The best that can be said for Christian hostility to sexuality is that it sought to make up for the Roman assault upon women and the deprivation of their dignity by assaulting *all* of humanity, both male and female, and by defaming and repressing as evil the most beautiful thing in human life.

St. Augustine, whose intimations were always better than his doctrines, did try to moderate somewhat the puritanical doctrine of *agape*—to make Christian love more personal and emotional, less abstract, institutional, and exclusively sacramental. Augustine's concept of *caritas*—his view of Christian love—was based on a semi-mystical passion for God expressed not only in the sacraments but in deep personal feeling. *Caritas* was acceptable in medieval monasteries, where eventually it developed into love between brothers—ideally, a loving union in God. Undoubtedly some monks engaged in sodomy (certainly they were criticized for it when the monasteries were attacked in the thirteenth century and finally dissolved in the sixteenth), but it is likely that most often, monastic *caritas* was simply deep feeling, very often expressed in loving relationships between older and younger monks. The sources (often critical sources from a later period) are biased and untrustworthy, but there is no doubt that profound personal feelings did exist among monks, at least by the eleventh century—that the austere theory of Christian love did not precisely coincide with human experience.

St. Anselm is an important transitional figure in the development of the idea of love, and indeed in the intellectual history of the twelfth century, for although he was an extremely conservative philosopher and theologian (a pure Platonist), he was also the first key figure in the new romanticism. Anselm's letters reveal a deep attachment to a group of young monks whose feelings for him and for each other were intense, and at least latently homosexual. The theory of Christian love remained Augustinian, but Anselm certainly recognized the value of deep human feelings. The love letters that travelled among members of the circle of Anselm represent not only their own emotions, but the first clear expression of the new cult of the Virgin, which emerged first in Canterbury in about 1100, when Anselm was the archbishop. By the mid-twelfth century, Mary was accepted (in popular belief) as part of the Godhead, primarily through the monks of Anselm's circle, whose devotion to each other was partially transformed into devotion to the heavenly Mother. As human love became more acceptable in high ecclesiastical circles in the twelfth century, and the cult of the Virgin was preached to the masses, Mary became a vehicle of mystical feeling between God and the individual. In this radical extension of *caritas*, rhetoric and art moved far in advance of theory and Mary was more and more eroticized in art and literature. She was represented first as a human mother, then a genuinely feminine, sexual woman; by 1150, the concept of personal union with God through a highly feminized Virgin was represented in pictures and statues everywhere in Europe.

The Virgin Cult coincided with the new movement of secular eroticism, the acceptance of the love between man and woman. By 1130 the two movements were obviously interacting, and it is difficult to separate one from the other in cause and effect. Obviously, each contributed to the other, and it seems likely that the sequence worked as follows: first, profound homosexual, or quasi-homosexual attachments developed within early medieval monasticism. This was epitomized and legitimized by Anselm and his circle of monks, whose devotion to Mary contributed to the sexualization of the image of Mary in popular belief. The Virgin Cult contributed in turn to secular eroticism and erotic liberation, as it encouraged men—that is, educated men of fine sensibility—to love other women beside the Virgin. Anselm was important as a philosopher, but the ontological proof of the existence of God was far less socially significant than his contribution to the erotic liberation of the twelfth century.

The Liberation Ethic

One of the most critical developments in the twelfth century was the emergence of a liberation ethic—an emphasis on personal fulfillment irrespective of tradition or order or hierarchy. This was an extremely self-conscious attitude which regarded human feelings as legitimate and valuable and accepted the union of human beings (in erotic as well as spiritual relationships) as their highest expression.

Love cannot be ordered or ruled by any authority, and an ethic that gives primacy to love is bound to be radical or even revolutionary. All totalitarian and tyrannical political systems hate and try to repress sexual love. Eroticism is the natural enemy of social conservatism.

Early medieval civilization had been bound by rules of all kinds which operated in a complicated system of traditional obligations and responsibilities and controlled individual human lives. Human beings were seen as types or abstractions—a peasant, a priest, a lord—and when they demanded to be accepted as individuals, confrontation with traditional authority was inevitable. The affirmation of the liberation ethic, involving secular eroticism and human love, was the continuing radical theme of the twelfth century, and this affirmation found profound and beautiful expression in literature and art despite the efforts of entrenched authority to repress and control it.

A movement of personal liberation is not like a political movement, and it is not well recorded except in the lives and private thoughts of individuals; most of our information for the twelfth century comes from autobiography and lyric poetry and adventure-romances. Troubadours and students wrote poems and stories and these supply at least a partial understanding.

It is not certain why the new liberation, eroticism, and self-consciousness became so important in the twelfth century, but one contributing cause may have been the failure of the Gregorian Reform of the previous century. That great ideological movement, which won the loyalty of the best minds and spirits of the period, finally discredited the social system by questioning the moral basis of the old feudal order, and its failure drove sensitive people back into themselves and their private lives. In a positive sense the Gregorian Reform was a failure, but its moral impact was tremendous. The failure seemed to prove that one could be sure only of personal happiness and private satisfaction and not of public causes, that only the love of God and of other people was worth a struggle.

The liberation ethic was encouraged too by the circumstances of life in a period of expansion and achievement in political, economic, and social life. In times of inflation and economic boom and of the successful establishment of social peace and order, human life and society become looser and more free. Eventually, of course, wealth and power and social order conflicted with the liberation movement, but for at least a half a century the optimism and freedom engendered by political and economic success made liberation possible. There were no major wars, and it was possible to make enough money (and have sufficient protection from legal institutions) to live without concentrating continually on the next meal or the next battle. In such times men begin to think about themselves and to want still more happiness; without the continual pressure of famine or anarchy, the law of rising expectations permits the radical vision, which pursues individual happiness and engenders creativity. Romanticism almost always follows the discredit of an *ancien régime*; it is also contemporaneous with an era of peace and prosperity—an opportunity for the young to follow their own ambitions and to search for personal fulfillment without commitment to any political ideology.

In the adventure-romances of the twelfth century, heroes sought personal love and happiness even while they searched for God and for ultimate meaning. In *Parsifal* and other stories, women as well as the Deity are the objects of the hero's quest. The love between man and wife is idealized as the best possible form of human love, and extramarital love is also given value. Divine and human love were intimately intertwined in twelfth-century art and literature, and the union of man and woman was regarded as the closest possible relationship to the union of man and God. This new, radical Christian belief can be viewed merely as a cover for contemporary eroticism, but it seems more likely that it also represented real religious enthusiasm. Many of the romantic concepts arose originally from the ancient Augustinian doctrine of *caritas*, which developed into the splendid search of a Christian knight for God, but Augustine would not have approved of the human love and sex that accompanies the questing knight, and therefore (in the old view) distracted him from serving God.

The values of the second half of the twelfth century were based on a radical philosophy very different from the traditional social thinking of the early Middle Ages, which was founded on the concept of the community. Theoretically, devotion and service to the City of God (in its earthly manifestation, the Church) was regarded as the highest fulfillment of the individual; in practical terms, however, devotion to the family was the dominant ideal. In the twelfth century, on the contrary, the fulfillment of the individual required him to serve himself, to do what made him happiest and follow his own ambitions. The community was transitory, and often simply an obstacle to his personal quest.

One of the most important shifts in attitude of the century was the recognition of women as people to love as well as simply objects of sexual desire and the bearers of children. To love someone is at least to accept that person as an equal. The twelfth century was the first great turning point in the emancipation of women from their previous status of breeding animals and whores, and this was an important aspect of the new consciousness of the individual and his feelings, and of the new appreciation of secular and erotic love.

III. Expressions of the Liberation Ethic

THE ARTISTIC LIFE

Many areas of life and thought were affected by the new consciousness and the liberation ethic of the twelfth century. Among these was literature, and notably the lyric poetry of southern France in the twelfth century and the French and German romances of the thirteenth, in which modern languages made their earliest appearance. The romantic writers had great linguistic ability, and they were learned men who had read and studied everything available. Their chosen form of expression was imaginative literature, perhaps because they were not allowed open advocacy of the secular-erotic life. In this, twelfth-century work resembles nineteenth-century Russian literature, in which great creative minds struggled to express themselves in the teeth of a decrepit and repressive old order. When Gogol wrote *Dead Souls*, he chose an oblique form for his denunciation of serfdom and of Russian society—much like the poets and romancers of the twelfth century, who wrote poems and stories instead of pamphlets and treatises.

The key motif in twelfth-century literature is that of the perilous quest, which indeed is the central theme of romantic writing in any century. The hero liberates himself through the quest and the search; it is how he goes, not where, that matters. Nineteenth-century romantics called this the "philosophy of act," in which happiness comes through the journey itself and freedom is a style of joy and quest. In *Faust* or *Manfred* or even *Moby Dick*, the hero is always moving somewhere, and in the twelfth century he often chose to move toward the Holy Grail—but the *search* for the Grail was essential, and not its recovery. The best examples of the adventure-romances of the period are those of Chrétien de Troyes or Wolfram von Eschenbach (writing in the late twelfth and early thirteenth centuries), whose heroes sought fulfillment through God and human love.

In the Arthurian cycle of romances of knights and ladies, writers found plots that could be used to develop their theme and motif of the perilous quest and the philosophy of act. The twelfth-century writers were noblemen or intellectuals who lived off of noble patronage. They were not saints or fanatics but well-educated and secure aristocrats and gentlemen who wrote well and felt deeply. They were courtiers or comfortable bourgeois, students or professors, and they were very much a part of the contemporary culture. Their development of the romantic themes can be regarded as a very important tributary to the stream of western literature, in which romantic motifs have recurred again and again since the twelfth century.

The historical literature of the early Middle Ages was weak in biography and devoid of autobiography; indeed, there *was* no autobiography between the *Confessions* of St. Augustine and the late eleventh century, and even Augustine's work was closer to homiletics than actual confession. Emphasis on individual lives was regarded as sinful, as it required self-love, which must detract from the love of God. By the end of the eleventh century, however, men began to realize that they could love both God and themselves, and a sense of individual worth and personal quest became acceptable. Indeed, twelfth-century romantics hoped to find God through the pursuit of their own ambitions and in the context of their private lives—the search for the Holy Grail was an excellent symbolic representation of that principle. By the middle of the twelfth century, the idiosyncrasies of individual personality had become intriguing and important, and writers liked to study the lives and work of significant people. The volume and quality of historical writing was very high in the twelfth century, and the best of it was biographical; not since the first century A.D. had so much intellectual energy been devoted to biography and history.

In sculpture and stained glass, the artists of the twelfth century expressed Christian themes in an emotional, romantic style. Their works evoked a personal union between God and man, and the Deity was depicted as a person rather than an abstract principle or power. The madonna and child was a favorite subject, as was the suffering Jesus—and these are characteristic of romantic art, in which women and children and outcasts are favorite figures. Such works express the artists' rebellion against power, tradition, and hierarchy, and a romantic adoration of the underprivileged and of those who were treated unjustly by the authorities—despite the fact that most twelfth-century art was commissioned by the power elite. An artistic ethic contrary to the dogmas of the ruling authority is not surprising in the modern world, but it was new in the twelfth century, when some of the best contemporary art expressed the new ethic.

A new style of life, which probably appeared first among artists and intellectuals and was soon imitated in courtly and aristocratic circles, was based on the new freedom and individualism of the twelfth century. It is difficult to study the development of life-styles, for they are easily and widely imitated and often distorted in imitation, and if they are judged dangerous by the authorities they are repressed, and records obliterated. Most of our information about this aspect of twelfth-century life comes through imaginative literature and not descriptive work. Certainly the style of personal quest, the pursuit of art and poetry and erotic love— the virtuoso artistic style—was widely prevalent in aristocratic courts and universities. "Bohemian" poets were protected and patronized by noble ladies, and university students lived in a style far removed from that of the old medieval monastic scholars.

In the early Middle Ages, even artists and intellectuals served a tradition in which each individual, by devoting himself to his own function, served the community as a whole and its sacred institutions. The Bohemian life is devoted to the self, to personal cultivation, and inevitably it is hostile toward the functional community and at least potentially revolutionary. Radicalism always is part of Bohemianism, and revolutions generally depend on intellectuals and artists to get them started—and yet the personal, Bohemian life is essentially antipathetic to any kind of ideologically committed collectivist program, and intellectuals often are the first to be eliminated by the revolutionary regime.

GOVERNMENT AND LAW

One of the major accomplishments of the twelfth century was the rationalization of government, which had been essentially a local affair until the mid-eleventh century. The great aristocratic families had provided whatever effective government or law existed; the king was generally a figurehead without power outside his family domain. The new, centralized style of monarchy emerged first in England under the Norman kings, about the same time (not so successfully) in Germany, and finally—by the end of the century —in France. The kings provided a political factor in European civilization which had been absent since the fall of Rome in the fifth century.

Remarkable as it seems in the twentieth century, the liberation ethic was expressed in government service. Government itself was radical in the twelfth century, when monarchs were attempting to impose a system of centralized social order upon the ancient baronial hierarchy. Service to the Crown became equivalent to rebellion against the feudal tradition, and it was not the kings themselves (many of whom were interested only in money and personal power) but the radical graduates of the new universities who created the medieval state and worked out its basic mechanisms. Between about 1150 and 1200, civil servants did the actual work of the institutionalization of government, imposing rational principles on aristocratic society. Erstwhile poets and student radicals fulfilled their individual ambitions and pursued their personal quests as administrators and judges for Henry II of England or the German emperor Frederick Barbarossa.

One of the major accomplishments of the centralized monarchy was the institution of a legal system centering on the Crown. This was successfully begun in England in the twelfth century, in France by the latter part of the thirteenth, and eventually even in some of the smaller countries like Aragon in northern Spain. (The Germans were much less successful in this sphere during the Middle Ages.)

The new governments also required their citizens to pay taxes to support the royal courts and the bureaucracy, and they developed effective military machines based on mercenary armies instead of feudal levies. The feudal army was not abandoned ceremonially (or emotionally) until much later, but kings began to use professional mercenaries instead of vassals who fought as a social obligation—although they still were led by generals who fought for the old reasons (because they were noblemen, and war was their job). However, the rank and file of thirteenth-century armies were mercenary soldiers, partly because of the enormous contemporary growth of population. The population of Europe—and particularly of England and France—exploded in the thirteenth century in a manner not seen again until the eighteenth, and many of the superfluous people became professional soldiers.

Like all governments before the late nineteenth century, the new monarchies concentrated on law, taxation, and defense (or aggression); they did nothing about social service, welfare, or education. Kings who were personally interested in education endowed schools and colleges, but the state as such took no part. Indeed, the role of government in European life changed very little between about 1270 and 1870; its basic functions were delineated by the royal bureaucrats of the thirteenth century.

By the middle of the thirteenth century, the royal bureaucrats had instituted legal systems managed by civil servants and professional lawyers—systems which gave many people access to something resembling due process of law. Lords got more justice than peasants, of course, but there was at least a beginning of judicial order, and the little man could hope for more than the ancient, personal methods of redress. Victims (or victim's families) could complain to the king's sheriff or *bailli* instead of their own lords (who might not be able and often were unwilling to help), and criminals faced indictment in the royal courts. It is true that this represented no great advance over the legal system of the Roman Empire, but it was still an enormous achievement, if only because (for the first time in centuries) ordinary people were offered some measure of public protection.

The new laws were based on those of the Roman Empire, and the royal lawyers faced the challenge of finding the old laws and working out the legal process. They had to make law operate in society by convincing or frightening people into following it. All of this required intelligence as well as learning, and patience as well as energy, and by the late twelfth century, a career as a royal lawyer or bureaucrat was a creative role which attracted the best and brightest young people. It was certainly more socially useful and appealing to university graduates than working for the pope, and the best jobs available in 1200 were in the governments of the kings of England and France. The old Roman laws were dug out of archives, introduced into the curricula of the new schools at Bologna and Montpellier and elsewhere, and eventually made the basis of new national legal systems. In their efforts to apply the law in the circumstances of feudal society, the lawyers devised techniques which went beyond those of the Romans. Generally, when Roman law conflicted with traditional feudal practice, they applied the Roman law (which usually favored the Crown).

The Roman law of the Continental countries was based on the principles of equity, rationality, and absolutism. Judges worked for the state (or for the king), and had complete control over what happened in court. Their decisions were made according to general principles, and they used written codes which they altered if they appeared to conflict with justice in a particular circumstance. Judges accepted written depositions from attorneys and attempted to decide the case on the merits of these, but it was their duty to get the truth by whatever means they could find, including interrogation (or torture) of witnesses. This system tended to work well in ordinary civil and criminal cases, but it could be pernicious if ideological questions such as heresy or treason were involved. If the judges were proponents of one ideology and the defendant of another, then there could be little hope of justice—and that is exactly what happened in the papal Inquisition, which was run like any other Roman court.

In the "adversary system" of English common law, on the other hand, judges acted as referees or presiding officers and relied on the opinion of the twelve jurymen who listened to the opposing parties or their attorneys. In the twelfth century, the jury's function was to give evidence as neighbors of the defendant who knew the circumstances of the case and could testify as to the character of the principals. Judges gradually began to accept the jurors' sworn opinions on guilt or innocence, and by the thirteenth century, the jury gave the verdict and the judges advised them according to the law, and handed down penalties (usually hanging). The English common law relied on oral pleading, and it was much less expensive than Roman law, which requires well-educated lawyers to write briefs and well-educated judges to read them. England had no law school of its own in the early period (before 1280) and therefore had fewer law students and judges; the English kings used to send out panels of three judges, of whom only one needed a proper legal education.

English common law worked quite well for ordinary people who were judged by their peers and could stand by their local reputations. It did not work so well with important men or in complex property cases (this is still true, and in fact the English have abandoned jury trial in civil suits in the twentieth century). The common-law courts of the thirteenth century were somewhat more free than the Roman because the judges were not there entirely as agents of the Crown but (theoretically, at least) as impartial arbiters. For that reason, questions of heresy or treason could be handled better in England than on the Continent.

Common law worked quite rapidly in the beginning, allowing the Crown to make money from legal suits and fines while justice was served. By 1300, however, it had become very slow, causing hardship to people with small claims and small property who could not be heard within a reasonable period. Roman law was better in that respect, because English common lawyers (then and now) devoted so much time and energy to the avoidance and postponements of trial. After the Inns of Court were established in the late thirteenth century and began to produce English lawyers in significant numbers, it took at least a year and a half to bring a civil suit to trial.

Despite delays and failures in justice, the new legal systems did give to many people a direct experience of royal government and of a state. Citizens encountered the king through his courts—and almost everyone but the lowest peasants had occasion at some time to be involved with royal justice. By the early thirteenth century, the royal power had begun to impinge upon the lives of ordinary people, and the nature of the monarch himself—whether he was just and well intentioned—made a real difference. The format and operation of the law became extremely important in the rise and fall of families, and family fortunes were decided in court as often as on the battlefield.

Citizens also encountered the king and his servants through the new systems of taxation. Taxation, which forces men to give up some of their own property to someone else, is an unnatural condition, and the great achievement of the royal bureaucrats was to get the *principle* of taxation accepted at all. To be sure, it was accepted mainly because people were forced to accept it by pressure from above, but also because the government did offer people something and made them see that they had to pay for it. The first benefit offered by government, of course, was defense, and kings like John and Edward I of England extorted money from their subjects with fanciful threats of aggression by the French. In a colorful harangue (in French) Edward, in 1294, warned his subjects that the French monarch intended to invade England to suppress English culture.

But the government also had to develop some sanctions or institutional means or justification for its taxes—some mechanism of consent—and this was done in two ways. First, kings made use of their ancient feudal prerogatives as overlords. Also, in the thirteenth century, they began to develop representative institutions to act for the country at large, summoning representatives of the estates to consent to their proposals. In England this system endured to be modified into Parliament in the sixteenth and seventeenth centuries, but on the Continent, the early representative institutions did not survive the age of absolute monarchy.

In the twelfth and thirteenth centuries, then, the ablest young men found idealistic, well-paid, and satisfying work in government and law. It was one of the rare periods when young people could advance rapidly to positions of power—somewhat like the New Deal of the 1930s, which pacified young radicals by allowing them to participate in government. University graduates became much less revolutionary in the generation after Abelard, and between about 1150 and 1270 they moved on to spectacular achievements in the establishment of rationalized government and law. They set up the essentials of legal systems which exist to this day; they organized the transition from feudal to mercenary armies; they established long-term systems of taxation (which, in France, survived until the Revolution). They wanted the central government to be strong because they were part of it, and they were largely responsible for the creation of the mystique of monarchy and the development of a significant sense of national identity. Europeans began to identify their individual ideals and fortunes with their states and their kings, and to look to the Crown for public order.

Probably much more could have been accomplished in terms of economic organization and social justice, but after about 1210 there was much less idealism and more professionalism in public life. This was due in part to the natural trend of the power life, which inevitably becomes less creative and more corrupt when its primary goals have been achieved. The young lawyers and bureaucrats had attained their major objectives by about 1250, and from that time until the nineteenth century, little of significance was accomplished in government. The next logical step was the use of government as a progressive force in society, but apart from interesting experiments in England in the 1530s and some half-hearted manipulation of the economy by the mercantilist powers in the seventeenth century, not much was attempted until the rise of the modern democratic, welfare state.

HERESY AND REACTION

Perhaps the most far-reaching aspect of the liberation ethic was the movement of popular heresy or religious radicalism that provided social outlets for the new freedom and individualism. Medieval heresy has been studied very thoroughly in recent years, but our information will never be complete because most of the documents were suppressed and destroyed by the Inquisition in the thirteenth century. The inquisitors' intent was to remove every trace of heresy from every library and monastery and castle in Europe, and they succeeded quite well, if not fully.

To medieval churchmen, heresy (or "error") meant dissent from the teachings of the Church. In the early Middle Ages, heresies were merely doctrinal differences among the elite. They were harmless to society at large, and heretics usually were allowed to recant and return to life in the community. The heresies of the twelfth century were very different, because they won vast popular support among the new bourgeois class and expressed the disaffection of a significant social group as well as the disagreements of theologians.

The growing merchant class of the cities, and those who depended upon them (at least the top strata of dependents) began to do very well economically, but not very well politically, in the late eleventh century. The townsmen had very little political power: at best, they might have the right of self-government, and that was purchased dearly in royal charters, for autonomy was expensive and had to be bought over and over again. Kings used the merchants' money for their wars and Crusades, but they took no advice from the bourgeois, nor did they grant them any social status. In northern France and England a bourgeois was not even definitely accepted as a free man; his legal status (until the thirteenth century) was equivalent to that of a serf. The Crown had arbitrary taxing power, and even the greatest merchants had to bear not only the stigma of dependence upon the royal will but an utter lack of social acceptance. Aristocrats did not marry bourgeois, and even the wealthiest townsmen were despised by poor noblemen, at least outside of northern Italy and southern France, where urban conditions were much better.

The large majority of the citizens of medieval towns were artisans, some fairly prosperous journeymen in the restrictive guilds, but most only day-laborers who existed hand-to-mouth in good times and often did not survive the bad. The richest merchants were well off, with jewels and furs and large houses, but they were frustrated by their lack of political influence and social status. After the middle of the twelfth century, there was little mobility in the towns, and sons automatically assumed the positions of their fathers. The journeymen were frustrated by economic limitations, and the great merchants by their inability to move still higher. The lowest strata—the proletariat—who constituted perhaps 40 to 50 per cent of the urban population, had no security at all and lived in miserable circumstances.

Medieval cities were unhealthy and unlovely. The necessity for strong, thick walls around the towns made them extremely crowded, and they lacked proper sanitation and adequate housing. There were few possibilities for recreation, and the cities were dark;

in fact they were organized slums, far inferior to the cities of the Roman Empire. Bubonic plague was endemic, and typhoid and typhus thrived on the unsanitary conditions. To make matters worse, the merchant oligarchy of the north (unlike those of the north Italian cities during the Renaissance) were selfish and indifferent to the plight of their fellow citizens; lacking civic pride, they did almost nothing for their towns—perhaps because they were taxed, persecuted, or ignored by the landed elite.

The rich bourgeois could blame their problems on the feudal society around them and the most vulnerable element of that society was the Church. Medieval townsmen held the Church—and its selfish, venal bishops—responsible for most of their frustrations. Many came to regard the Church as a wicked institution usurped by Anti-Christ (the pope) and his myrmidons, rapacious priests who sucked the blood and money of the people and gave nothing in return.

The Church was a scapegoat for bourgeois discontent, but there was enough truth in the accusations to make them persuasive: many priests *were* stupid, slovenly, and vicious, and particularly the urban bishops. Most medieval cities were built around cathedrals whose bishops were members of local aristocratic families who looked on the bishopric as an opportunity to gain wealth for themselves and jobs for their relatives. Most twelfth-century bishops were negligent about pastoral work—rapacious noblemen who cared nothing for the sufferings of the poor.

The popes, of course, should have concerned themselves about the alienation of the Church from urban society, but they were negligent or uninterested. The popes of the eleventh century had aimed at the moral reform of the world and had been defeated, and their successors were disillusioned with reform. In any case, many aristocratic churchmen had opposed either the aims or the methods of the Gregorian reformers: they had not wanted to give up their privileges, or they had disliked the violence and noise of the revolutionary style. Between 1090 and 1120, the great conservative majority of the hierarchy regained control of the College of Cardinals and elected their own people to the papacy. Most twelfth-century popes were either Cistercian monks or canon lawyers. The former (particularly prevalent during the 1130s and 1140s) were men like St. Bernard who were very enthusiastic about reform outside of Rome—about purification and austerity in the monasteries—but for business as usual in Rome. After 1150, however, most popes were lawyers and businessmen to whom efficiency was everything; their major ambition was to build up a system of taxation on Christian churches everywhere and to get a sizeable proportion of their enormous income to Rome. By 1190 they had imposed an income tax on all the clergy, but that was no solution to the problems within the Church and no response to moralistic attacks from indignant bourgeois.

The entire Establishment of feudal society was too powerful to be attacked, but bourgeois critics found it fairly easy to attack the Church. The Church is always vulnerable simply because people can leave it; they can withdraw their financial support, set up their own churches and support their own preachers. When this happens, a social as well as a religious phenomenon occurs, and in the twelfth century this development was closely involved with the cultural liberation movement.

At all times, social radicals use the rhetoric and style of poets and philosophers and artists, and intellectuals and artists tend to borrow concepts in return from social revolutionaries. Radical movements can come from either the intellectual class or from some dissident element in society, or from both together, as in the last half of the twelfth century. The bourgeois began to use the new individualism as a vehicle for attack and action against landed society, and at the same time, certain intellectuals dropped out of their accustomed court and academic circles to lead the discontented bourgeoisie. Radical preachers appeared in the cities, pronouncing a bourgeois ethic and a theology that appealed to the urban middle class. Their theology was innovative and generally evangelical, and they emphasized will and intention over birth and office. What mattered was how a man felt and acted, and a holy man was one who did well and felt right about it. Anyone could be good, and better than a lord, in the religion of the heart.

Such radical Christianity was disconcerting to the Church and the established order, but not strictly heretical. It did, however, identify religion with morality instead of sacramental authority, giving the power and grace of salvation to the individual and not to the Church. As time went on, moreover, the radicals began to denounce the existing institutional Church as an instrument of the devil to ensnare men (instead of the embodiment of God's will). By the 1180s, a radical doctrine of a true counter-

Church of holy brotherhood had become very fashionable in bourgeois circles, and certain ambitious and liberated men (some saints, some frauds) had developed elaborate doctrines around this concept. Joachim, Abbot of Flora in southern Italy, and other radicals composed febrile treatises on the distinction between the inner Church of the saved and the visible church of Satan, working out a complicated philosophy of history. To them the world was in a penultimate stage preceding the Second Coming—the time of Anti-Christ. When things were at their worst, a secret brotherhood of the saved would proclaim the advent of a saviour who would come to destroy evil (in the twelfth century, that meant to destroy the papacy) and inaugurate the kingdom of God.

By 1200, radical preachers were wandering all over Europe, and some of them—Peter Waldo, for instance—attracted large followings. Waldo was not a churchman but a rich merchant from Lyons who formed his own brotherhood and preached to huge crowds in southern France and northern Italy. The new ethic was anti-sacerdotal, personal, anti-papal, and moralistic, depriving the Church of its basis of authority and requiring its destruction before the imminent arrival of the kingdom of God.

The most important heresy was that of the Albigensians, who were concentrated in large numbers mainly in the cities of southern France. (The city of Albi was a center of the heresy.) Their leaders were known as *Cathari* (pure ones) and hence their doctrine as Catharism. The Albigensians have also been called Manichees, because their doctrines resembled those of the ancient Persian Manicheans whose beliefs were derived from Zoroastrianism, the national religion of ancient Persia. Mani was a religious leader of the second century A.D. whose teachings spread through the Roman world, especially in North Africa (even St. Augustine was a Manichean for about ten years). The dualistic theology of the ancient Manicheans and the medieval Albigensians posited the existence of a god of light and a god of darkness and looked upon existence as a struggle for supremacy between God and Anti-God. Salvation required light, or purification—a purely spiritual life of physical abstinence, fasting, and sexual purity. To attain salvation, a dying man could take a sacrament called "consolation" from one of the Cathari and thus join the company of the god of light.

It is not clear whether the Albigensian religion was derived directly from the ancient Manicheans; the Catharist heresy became such a powerful threat to the Church that Albigensian writings and records were rooted out and eradicated by the Inquisition. Our information comes mostly from the reports of the inquisitors, who cannot be relied upon for accuracy. Some scholars believe that ancient Manicheanism spread from Persia into the Byzantine Empire in the early Middle Ages, and thence to the Balkans. There was a sect of Manicheans in Bulgaria in the tenth and eleventh centuries, and it is possible that their ideas travelled into southern France along the Balkan trade routes.

The Cathari were accused by the inquisitors of all sorts of iniquities, from sodomy to wild promiscuity—in fact, of everything from infanticide to race suicide. These accusations have some basis in Albigensian theology, which viewed the physical world as entirely evil. In such a world, what a man did before he took the sacrament of consolation was of little importance, and even the production of a human being (a monstrous combination of spirit and matter) was a bad thing. However, we cannot rely for information about the Albigensians' actual behavior on reports by hostile orthodox Christians.

In the twelfth century, with the emergence of eroticism in conflict with the traditional puritanism of the Christian Church, Albigensianism did offer a means of reconciliation by separating life into two distinct parts—before and after salvation. The Albigensian sexual attitudes provided a possible solution to the contemporary ambivalence—indeed, some scholars believe that Albigensianism was essentially very much like orthodox medieval Catholicism, if not in dogma then in actual popular beliefs. The Catholic Church had never really provided any theory or justification of the sexual drives, or integrated the physical and the religious life. For the most part, medieval men believed that the ideal Christian life was entirely spiritual, and that any physical love (indeed, any close human relationship) detracted from union with God. In a sense, then, the Albigensians only pushed Christian belief a little farther, offering doctrinal justification for popular attitudes. Their ideas were not really contrary to traditional vulgar Christianity; it was their popularity and their institution of an alternative Church that made them dangerous.

Sexual mores certainly cannot explain the intensive repression that pursued the Cathari to the stake. The Church devoted huge amounts of money and energy and military force to the extinction of the Albigensian heresy, and the real reason was not its religious doctrines but its effectiveness. Unlike most popular heresies, Albigensianism won enormous popular support among the bourgeois of southern France. Furthermore, the Albigensians were not just individual evangelical dissenters but a real religious community and thus an unbearable threat to the established Church.

THE SOCIALIZING OF THE LIBERATION MOVEMENT

It was the Albigensian heresy that finally provoked the papacy to reform the Church and revitalize orthodox Christianity —eventually, even, to control and socialize the liberation movement as it affected the religious life. Catharism made the leaders of the Church aware of the dangers inherent in the intellectual upheaval of the twelfth century and the alienation of the bourgeoisie from the Church and established society. By the early thirteenth century, when the liberation ethic had been channeled into popular heresies (the Joachimist, the Waldensian, the Albigensian, and several lesser movements), it became clear that these were essentially socially revolutionary movements against the traditional leadership of medieval society as well as the traditional role of the Church. When the leaders of the old order recognized the real threat to their ancient power, they successfully confronted the "new men" on two levels, employing effective instruments of repression even while they set to work to revitalize the traditional ecclesiastical culture.

Over a period of about seventy years in the thirteenth century, the Church managed to repress or redirect the threatening aspects of the intellectual revolution—its eroticism, romanticism, and anti-sacerdotal individual values. One consequence was the Inquisition (and the Albigensian Crusade), but the other was the flowering of Christian culture into Gothic cathedrals, Gregorian chants, and scholastic philosophy. The Church did use violent repression, but it also tried various other means of controlling and socializing the liberation ethic. Along with political means and physical force, the Church confronted the liberation movement with preaching, learning, and education.

The ways by which radicalism ought to be combatted were demonstrated as early as the 1140s by Abelard's contemporary (and most persistent enemy) the Cistercian abbot St. Bernard of Clairvaux. Bernard—an intensely ambitious and clever French aristocrat—stands as the model of the skillful reactionary in the medieval Church. In thunderous and at times high lyrical sermons, he tried to redirect romantic attitudes back into loyalty to the established order. And this strategy was founded on shrewd psychology: Bernard knew full well that the great majority of radicals really fear confrontation with the power system and established elite, and that there is a very special kind of psychic satisfaction in recasting old authoritarian traditions in the guise of the new counter-culture so that the best of all possible worlds can be gained—the old system supported by radical culture and new romanticism.

Yet it took the narrow, conventionally-minded lawyers who occupied the Throne of Peter a half-century to realize the significance of the strategy that Bernard was proposing. His own disciples in the originally puritan order of Cistercian monks rapidly deteriorated into corrupt land-grabbers and money-lenders, and were not capable of perpetuating Bernard's program.

At the end of the twelfth century the Spanish priest Dominic, working as a preacher against the Albigensians in southern France, revived the Bernardine program of reactionary romanticism, and Dominic's Order of Preachers added other ingredients for the Church's counterattack on radicalism. The Dominicans stressed the importance of academic learning; they realized that the universities should not by default fall to the radicals and they set about infiltrating the theology and philosophy faculties of Paris and other universities so as to give the reactionary position the authority of academic learning. Thus another psychic satisfaction was offered radicals who converted to Romanist loyalty: traditional theology was paraded forth with the support of Aristotelian science. Finally, Dominic and his disciples perceived (and here they had been also partly anticipated by Bernard) that terror and hatred are the reverse mirror images of romanticism and individualism. They advocated the fullest use of political authority and military violence against recalcitrant heretics who had been won over by neither lyrical preaching nor scientific argument. The Dominicans put aside any qualms about branding religious radicals as social subversives;

they summoned to the aid of the Church any king, duke, or baron who would ally with the conservative faction, irrespective of whatever deep-seated propensity to greed, rapine, and self-aggrandisement actually motivated these scions of the aristocracy.

It was Pope Innocent III, a brilliant Italian nobleman and learned lawyer and theologian, passionately loyal to the old authoritarian traditions, but keenly sensitive to the nuances of the new culture, who committed papal resources to the Bernardine-Dominican program in the first decade of the thirteenth century. Innocent understood fully that the papacy and the traditional Church needed a new image. He also sensed that it was too late for the established system to be scrupulous about either methods or allies. When his legates were assassinated by Albigensians in southern France, Innocent did not wring his hands but called out the army, offering his "Crusaders" (greedy and ruthless barons from northern France) the lands and riches of southern France in exchange for the slaughter of heretics, and promising God's blessing on naked aggression disguised as holy war. Innocent did not formally invent the Inquisition (which was not officially inaugurated until 1233), but for practical purposes he sponsored its aims and methods.

Inquisition courts were standard Roman law courts with full power to investigate and try suspected heretics; they used informers, and although they did not burn heretics themselves, they "relaxed them to the secular arm" (handed them over to the state for execution). There was no Inquisition in England, where the kings completely dominated the Church, but in France (whose king wanted to take over Albigensian holdings in the south), it was in the royal interest to support the inquisitors. Repression of the sort practised by the Inquisition in the thirteenth century requires energy and fanaticism based on the genuine conviction that the enemy is the devil. The Dominican friars, who were the main operators of the Inquisition, exemplified this peculiar combination of attitudes and talents.

The Inquisition itself soon became a power style and an end in itself, and it ran out of energy and capacity during the fourteenth century. Inquisitors began to persecute the Jews, in opposition to official Christian policy, which was to leave the Jews—separate and accursed—alone and unharmed in their ghettos. The

Inquisition did not revive as a real force until it became an instrument of the rising Spanish monarchy in the fifteenth century. The liberal Austrian historian Frederick Heer asserts, somewhat too categorically, that medieval society was destroyed by the Inquisition and by repression; that the open and creative world of the twelfth century was closed in the thirteenth, bringing an end to the best of medieval culture.

The greatest achievement of Innocent III and his successors was the redirection and recruitment of the energies of the liberation movement into the transformation of the Church and the modernization of the old culture. The great Gothic cathedrals were built as centers of mass worship; they grew bigger and bigger, and more and more extravagant, with all the lights and music and incense of an overwhelming religious experience. Without much competition from other forms of dramatic entertainment or intellectual stimulation, thirteenth-century churchmen put on a show that could not be rivalled by anything in the daily lives of most men—and they were not niggardly about the expense. Perhaps as much as a quarter of European investment capital between about 1190 and 1250 was spent on church building, and the results were superb. Nothing better in art than the stained glass of Chartres has ever been created.

Men of the thirteenth-century wanted, and got, a religion of personal experience to replace the old explication of obscure texts. The mode of Christian preaching became more naturalistic and moralistic and less elaborate and learned. Sermons were delivered to the masses in the vernacular languages, sermons based on texts and themes taken from the lives of ordinary people. The changes in style were largely the work of the Franciscan monks and their leader, the good saint of Assisi who preached purity, simplicity, and a middle-class kind of optimistic, positive religion. According to the friars, who spoke of an optimistic religion of personal love and bourgeois values, the world was a good and beautiful place. Nor did the Franciscans denounce sexual love and the physical life; they were men of the new culture, and their religion was a romantic and sentimental blend of personal feeling and middle-class ideals. The Franciscans gave the townsmen what they wanted to hear, and the Church took up their ideas and style and put them to work for its own cause.

The papacy controlled the "Order of Little Brothers" very carefully, preserving their popular appeal without allowing them to become wild or radical. The Franciscans were extremely successful and very much loved, and they brought the bourgeoisie back to the Church. Franciscan friars (before about 1250) were men who might have been alienated radicals in the previous century, but they became servants of the established Church instead of rebellious heretics, and they along with the Dominican inquisitors and academics revitalized the old Church until it was acceptable to men of the new culture.

The main trend of the history of the twelfth century was a many-sided, fundamental attack on the feudal and ecclesiastical order of medieval Europe. Such movements tend to occur when the social organization and cultural values of an old order are exhausted, and the critical factor in their failure or success rests not so much in the movements themselves as in the response of the old regime. The French Revolution is the classic illustration of what happens when an *ancien régime* does everything wrong: after the intellectuals of the Enlightenment set the stage for revolution, the French aristocracy and royal government failed in effective action. While the authorities temporized and delayed, the radical intellectuals won support from various social groups and found a social focus for their revolutionary ideas. The Russian government made similar mistakes in 1917; the Bolshevik minority succeeded not primarily through their own efforts but through the lazy, stupid, repressive, and then fearful response of the old regime. In the sixteenth century, Protestant reformers worked very effectively while the Church and the princes hesitated. The radical intellectuals of the Reformation found political and social channels for their revolutionary ideas, and the Counter-Reformation came almost (but not quite) too late to save the Church.

Outright repression of liberation movements is not usually entirely successful. It may eradicate the revolution, but it is bad for social and cultural progress, and the best of the new ideas are lost along with their worst social manifestations. The most successful approach is to combine stern repression with absorption of the new ideas in the old culture, and the *ancien régime* of the late twelfth and thirteenth centuries did this very well despite its late start. Just as the development of the European monarchies diverted the fervor of the radical university graduates of the generation after Abelard into socially useful channels, so the Church found ways to use and absorb the liberation ethic. In the end, of course, medieval civilization did disintegrate when its leadership was discredited in the fourteenth century, but the ancient feudal order managed to counter the liberation movement and survived to support another, late, bright flowering of medieval Europe.

In the twelfth century, the intellectual products of the new universities were extremely dangerous to the stability of the social order and to the power elite, whose authority was based on a specific traditional culture and system of values. Abelard and his colleagues attacked the very foundation of that system in their assault on Platonic idealism, which was much more than just a disagreement among philosophers. No elite can be secure, or even survive very long, in a culture or value system that is not widely accepted by the best minds of the time, and a major struggle followed the period of unrest in the universities which reached its height in the 1130s. The attack on the Platonic hierarchical system imperilled the old order of society, including the Church, and in the latter part of the century the outlook for the old culture was very dark. However, Abelard's intellectual revolution was not successful in the end; it neither brought about radical social change nor destroyed the Church. The liberation movement was aborted or neutralized by repression and absorption, and genuinely revolutionary phenomena (such as the democratic republic established in Rome by Arnold of Brescia, one of Abelard's young students) were rare and short-lived. The liberation movement had enormous consequences in philosophy and science, but it never fulfilled its revolutionary implications, partly because of the effective response of the old regime, but also because of developments within the universities themselves.

Universities attracted and held the best minds of the twelfth and thirteenth centuries; as new and exciting institutions with extensive resources, they were very much a part of the elite world. It was in the universities, eventually, that the movement of critical empiricism (itself a product of the twelfth-century university) was neutralized and rendered harmless to the ancient social and intellectual culture of Europe. The reasons are complex, but certainly they were closely related to the nature of the age—a period of intellectual upheaval, of exciting new ideas and new interpretations. One contributing factor was the gradual decline in the prestige and influence of the faculties of philosophy and theology, which coincided with the rise of the schools of law. Universities are inherently somewhat utilitarian, and as increasing numbers of students prepared for careers in government, the "pure" intellectuals of the philosophy faculty lost their central position. Professional schools are generally somewhat conservative, or at least amoral or non-ideological, and they drew more and more of the best young minds into professional training. The brightest students no longer concentrated on critical analysis of the philosophical foundations of contemporary culture and society, but on learning the rules of the existing system. (There is an obvious analogy here to the professional schools of law and medicine and science in the United States, which take brilliant students out of the agencies of criticism and train them to succeed in the world as it is.) Such minds are lost to revolution and even reform, and this happened in Europe in the thirteenth century.

The work of Abelard was also partially undermined by the great flood of Aristotelian literature into Europe in the 1160s and 1170s. (Abelard himself had not studied much of Aristotle—just enough to inspire his own thinking.) Suddenly, in the next generation, the vast *corpus* of Aristotle as well as works of lesser Greek and Arab thinkers was available to northern Europeans in translations from the intellectual centers of Spain and Sicily and Provence. The radical movement of critical empiricism stood still for three or four decades while the new material was digested and absorbed. Learning itself—learning for its own sake—tends to be conservative, if only because it is not action, and young radicals were distracted by the weight of learning. Students were too busy finding out what Aristotle had said, debating it, and relating it to Christianity, to act, or even to propose action.

Then, too, the intellectual liberation movement was met on its own terms by moderate intellectual alternatives. Important thinkers declared that a safe, sound middle ground could be found —and proceeded to find it. The greatest of these was the Dominican friar Thomas Aquinas, who balanced the new learning and the old culture and said that Christians could have both worlds. Aquinas (d. 1274) was the most successful of the "scholastic" philosophers, but he led a host of colleagues and followers; from 1180 on many scholastic syntheses were published and widely admired.

Aquinas was an energetic, self-confident, and polished Italian aristocrat (teaching at the University of Paris) who dedicated his entire life to a search for compromise and balance. He said that everything was possible—old and new, Church and state, idealism and empiricism; he proposed to take the best of all systems and to use the new as an instrument for the improvement of the old. He intended to keep Church and hierarchy and revealed religion, to revitalize ancient faith without making basic changes. Except for certain ultimate mysteries of revelation (such as the Trinity, which is miraculous and irrational), everything in traditional Christianity was compatible with scientific knowledge. Knowledge, said Aquinas, begins with sense experience and reason: the mind abstracts and builds up general propositions from the data of experience and thought. As a liberal response to philosophic radicalism this was highly effective, for if the world of universals is based on sense experience and reason, then the thrust of critical empiricism loses much of its impact.

Aristotle said that men were political beings, and Aquinas agreed, stating that men lived best in society or a community and that kings and popes and lords ruled by the right of serving human needs. If a king acts in accordance with reason, his rule is ordained by God and men must obey. This doctrine was widely accepted by churchmen and philosophers, who for a long time did not realize its ultimate revolutionary implications. The same doctrine can mean that a ruler who does *not* rule in accordance with reason need not be obeyed. Aquinas was extremely effective and successful in his own day; Thomism is still the official systematic philosophy of the Catholic Church, and his work and its wide acceptance were major factors in the absorption of the intellectual ferment of the twelfth century.

Despite the success of men like Innocent III and Thomas Aquinas, certain warning signals might have been observed by the power elite in the latter part of the thirteenth century. The liberation movement had been absorbed, the Church revitalized, philosophic radicalism neutralized—but the powerful new monarchies had become a significant political factor, and their kings and officers were growing steadily more aggressive and vicious, greedy and reckless. Another danger signal was that the Franciscans—the great instruments of the papacy in the revitalization of the Church—had begun to quarrel among themselves. In the 1250s, one group of Franciscans complained that their brothers were being transformed into bourgeois churchmen. They asked where the religion of love could be found in the thirteenth-century Church, and whether they were supposed to be disciples of the politically ambitious pope or of Jesus Christ. The established religion, they said, was actually turning into the death of Christianity, which required transcendence and sacrifice not found in contemporary churches.

Thomism, too, despite its wide popularity and despite its learning and clever balance of philosophical differences, did not get universal acceptance among thinking men. Certain philosophers (most of them in England) called it nonsense and refused to accept the Thomist solution. Aquinas attempted to synthesize all the high-level philosophical and theological ideas of the twelfth and early thirteenth centuries, but his achievement failed to satisfy some brilliant men—surely an indication that the compromise that marked the absorption and dissolution of the twelfth-century liberation movement would not hold together indefinitely.

Chapter Six
THE CRISIS OF MEDIEVAL CULTURE

I. Decline and Decay

THE CRISIS OF CONFIDENCE

The last period of medieval history per se includes the six or seven decades at the end of the thirteenth century and the beginning of the fourteenth. The years between about 1250 or 1270 and 1325 or 1340 had a special quality quite unlike that of the succeeding era—the one and a half centuries of transition from medieval to modern times which we call the Renaissance or (sometimes) the late Middle Ages. The history of the late thirteenth and early fourteenth centuries is a distinct part of medieval history proper, and its record is one of crisis and upheaval.

Political, social, and economic troubles accumulated very rapidly in the 1270s and 1280s, and by 1300, continual crisis had disintegrated into chaos. Everything went wrong: the very philosophical and moral foundations of medieval civilization collapsed, and although the collapse probably made possible the eventual construction of the modern world, it also produced violence and bitter discord. Any period of transvaluation (transition from one set of values to another) is bound to be violent, complicated, and difficult to understand, and this is certainly true in the context of the late thirteenth century.

Earlier in that same century, the two governing institutions of medieval society—monarchy and Church—had apparently succeeded in absorbing the consequences of the twelfth-century liberation movement. The ruler whom contemporaries regarded as the ideal monarch—Louis IX of France (1226–1270)—ruled over an apparently stable, prosperous, and tranquil kingdom. It must have seemed then that radicalism had been diverted into social and intellectual achievement, that the best of the new ideas and the new culture had merged with the finest traditions of the old civilization.

Although the Age of St. Louis may have been prosperous and tranquil, it certainly was not lacking in critical political and social problems and the king had not been dead long before monarchy and Church alike were in serious trouble. The papacy declined in the fourteenth century to a catastrophic low point from which it never entirely recovered, and by the 1340s there was no viable moral leadership in European society. Every group and institution despised and fought with every other: the bourgeoisie battled the nobility and quarreled among themselves; townsmen and noblemen alike opposed the Crown (and fourteenth-century kings were remarkably stupid and incompetent); for the first time in medieval history, even the peasants rose up against their oppressors. Heresy was widespread, and fourteenth-century heretical movements were even more militant and restless than the popular heresies of the previous century. Furthermore, the collapse of ecclesiastical organization and discipline gave little hope of effective control. The Church was in the total disrepair of the Great Schism, with two popes during much of the fourteenth century, and at one time (in the early fifteenth century), with three. By the beginning of the fifteenth century, the ancient sense of community had virtually disappeared from European society.

The chaos in Church and state did not reach its high point until about 1400, but it began to develop at the end of the thirteenth century—at the very moment when these institutions had apparently accomplished a triumphant recovery of balance, serenity, and synthesis. The important question, of course, is *why* medieval civilization fell apart so suddenly: why endemic social hostility and religious radicalism became open rebellion and heresy, and why and how the revolutionary social, political, and religious movements of the late Middle Ages replaced the peace and accomplishment of the Age of St. Louis and Thomas Aquinas.

The Implications of Overpopulation

There are as yet no definite answers to this question: historians cannot say exactly what it was that brought medieval civilization to its knees. Certainly the rise and fall of the population curve was significant, and the recent attention to the demographic factor in historical causation has made an enormous contribution to our understanding of the late Middle Ages. A rising population curve engenders progress and optimism; with a growing market and an increasing supply of manpower, all kinds of new things are possible. Eventually, however, in a predominantly rural society, the curve rises until there are too many people for the peaceful resolution of social problems; then progress and optimism fail, and this frequently occurs even before overpopulation results in famine. The population of Europe rose steadily, if unevenly, from the middle of the tenth century to the middle of the thirteenth, but in the late thirteenth century its ascent was almost vertical, producing a population surplus far too great for the social and economic resouces of the medieval world.

No reliable demographic statistics are available for the Middle Ages; there are some (questionable) data for England in the late thirteenth century, but it is likely that the population of northern Italy and parts of France rose even more rapidly. No census was taken in any part of Europe until the early nineteenth century, but the late medieval English parish registers and manorial records do provide at least suggestive information on the birth and death rate. The population of England in the late thirteenth century is roughly estimated at something over three million. (It may have been as much as five million—if this total is established it will make a significant difference in the interpretation of late medieval history.) The population of England in 1200 probably was not much more than one and a half million, so that even the lower figure for 1300 (three million) means that the population doubled in a hundred years. Even three million was a large population for a small country, still 90 per cent agricultural: it was no larger in the time of Shakespeare, when urban development and agricultural technology had advanced considerably. (The population did not remain constant from 1300 to 1600: it dropped sharply in the fourteenth century and rose again in the late fifteenth.) In 1700 there were still only five million people in England, but their numbers grew rapidly in the second half of the eighteenth century and reached twelve million by 1820. (The English population stands at fifty-five million today.)

Why did the population curve rise so steeply in the late thirteenth century? Probably the absence of plague was an important factor: plague was (and is) endemic in underdeveloped, pre-industrial societies, so that in a period when it was less virulent than usual, there were more old people, and children survived to raise families of their own.

The population increase had serious consequences at all levels of society—even among the hitherto silent peasantry, whose villages (at least in England, and probably on the Continent) became very crowded in the late thirteenth century. This produced a buyer's market in agricultural labor, allowing noblemen to exploit their peasants more freely than ever. There had been a movement toward manumission of serfs in the late twelfth century, but it now slowed down considerably—not that legal freedom made much difference in the life of the average peasant, whose condition might even worsen if manumission allowed his landlord to force him off the land. It was more significant that agricultural wages did not rise as fast as prices in the thirteenth century (when the price of food, in particular, rose very steeply). The sharp increase in peasant population produced extensive unemployment in the agrarian working class and this in turn led (as in all such agrarian societies, such as nineteenth-century China) to organized crime in the form of outlaw gangs. The English court rolls of the late thirteenth century testify to widespread gangsterism; this is the grim reality behind the Robin Hood legend. The exacerbation of rural suffering and discontent undoubtedly contributed to the peasant rebellions of the later fourteenth century.

In the elitist society of the medieval world, however, an increase in population among the other social classes was bound to be more influential than an increase in the peasantry; the rise in population of the bourgeoisie and petty nobility had very serious consequences. Without plague to dispose of some of their children, these families could not take care of all their sons on the land or in the family business. Their solution, very often, was to prepare them for the learned professions, and there was a notable increase in the number of university students. Many new colleges and student residences were founded in the late thirteenth and early fourteenth centuries, including the Sorbonne (originally a dormitory for students at the University of Paris), and Balliol and New College at Oxford. Large numbers of students were educated for jobs in government or in the Church, but with the limited aims of medieval government (war, law, and taxation), there was not enough work to occupy them all. There was some expansion of royal governments in the thirteenth century, especially in France, but not enough to absorb the energies of all the potential bureaucrats and judges; contemporary kings preferred to spend their money on war and private pleasure rather than the civil service.

By 1300, then, an intellectual proletariat had appeared in Europe—a large group of educated men without jobs, or with dull and meaningless jobs that did not satisfy their ideals or ambitions. There is no doubt that the restlessness of the intellectuals caused serious problems in the late thirteenth century, for unlike their counterparts of the twelfth century, who were absorbed into the expansion and revitalization of royal and ecclesiastical administration, these men were idle and discontented. They were free to speculate, without responsibility, on the problems and failings of government and society and Church, and because they could not achieve their moral aims through their work, they questioned the very bases of the Establishment that employed them. After about 1270 there was continual turmoil in the universities—rabble-rousing, heresy, ugly quarrels between university faculties, and student riots aginst the townspeople and the university authorities. Any radical movement could find support and indeed leadership among dissatisfied intellectuals within and without the university.

The restlessness and discontent of the intellectuals was not produced by underemployment alone, but also by the shift to Aristotelianism in scholastic philosophy. Philosophical movements can have practical consequences if they are relevant to the political and social issues of the day, and the disgruntled intellectuals of the late thirteenth century made a weapon out of the Aristotelian thought on which their education had been based. Their political philosophy departed from the traditional, Augustinian, pessimistic view of the state which had prevailed in European thought since the fourth century A.D. Augustine and his many disciples among medieval thinkers regarded the state, a human institution with human leaders, as essentially and inevitably corrupt. The state was a necessary evil because men were too sinful to live without it; it was a police force ordained by God and His Church to subdue the wicked passions of mankind. Kings, in such a view, were not much more than anointed policemen whose job it was to repress the natural instincts of their fellow men. No one expected the state or its leaders to be just or effective or to help their subjects: on the contrary, citizens were supposed to help, to obey, and even to worship their kings.

In the late eleventh and twelfth centuries, however, the state began to serve the people: to establish law, and to suppress random violence and injustice. In the thirteenth century, the popularization of Aristotelian political thought by Thomas Aquinas and other scholastic philosophers brought the ancient Greek view of political life back to European thought. Unlike Augustine, who believed that only the soul and its membership in the internal City of God were important, the Greeks regarded the *polis* as essential to human welfare, as the fulfillment of the natural law. If man is a political animal who cannot live well outside of human society, then the state is a positive and necessary instrument for the creation of the good life. Aristotle's concepts were elaborated and integrated with Christianity, and students educated in the Thomist view expected their public institutions and their leaders to be active, effective, and beneficent.

The rising expectations of the educated class coincided with a marked decline in the actual character and behavior of the leaders of society; kings and popes alike were notably immoral, selfish, and ineffectual in the late thirteenth century. Popes used their powers of excommunication and interdiction for narrow political purposes until their sacerdotal and political roles were inextricably confused, while kings made obvious their preference for personal glory and private pleasure over public good. (After eighty years of peace, the kings of France and England in the 1290s took their people into a long and exhausting war, ostensibly over dynastic claims of no conceivable interest to the citizens of either country.)

The intellectuals of the fourteenth century were not sufficiently occupied to overlook or ignore the wickedness of the kings and popes, which offended Christian sensibilities as well as the prevailing concept of political and religious leadership. As students, they had been taught to study and criticize the social organization and hierarchy; their Aristotelian education had given them a moral, meliorist attitude that eventually produced not only criticism but militancy and disruption. The phenomenon occurred again in the revolutionary era of the late eighteenth century, when a period of unusually incompetent leadership coincided with a period of under-employment among an intellectual class which had been educated in the meliorist philosophy of the Enlightenment.

DEPRESSION

Dissidence and restlessness certainly were not unknown in the medieval world before the late thirteenth century, but they occurred within the framework of steady economic growth and expansion. By 1280, however—or at least by 1310—the economy began to slow down everywhere except in Italy, and by 1350 even there. The fourteenth century brought rapid economic deterioration, accompanied or produced by social unrest, war, and plague. Investors were reluctant to risk their money in such violent and uncertain conditions, and there was noticeable retrenchment in land development, manufacture, and commerce. Even before the Black Death of the 1340s, Europe was in the grip of its first great depression since the tenth century, a depression that continued until the latter part of the fifteenth century. The boom, the rising population, and the big grain market of the early thirteenth century had encouraged the cultivation of marginal soil in many parts of Europe, and much of this land was exhausted and abandoned even before the critical labor shortage that followed the Black Death. Industrial production declined also: there is evidence, for instance, of distress and dissatisfaction among Belgian textile workers when their guild masters ordered a decrease in production in the early fourteenth century.

Like all depressions, the economic problems of the fourteenth century were caused by overproduction relative to buying power—by the cycle of overspeculation, loss of confidence, and retrenchment (which exacerbates the loss of confidence and sets the economic spiral on a downward course). The thirteenth century boom had encouraged overextension in agriculture and industry, and when political and ecclesiastical turmoil replaced the relative tranquility of the High Middle Ages, landlords and businessmen became frightened. They withdrew land and capital, and their fears and their retrenchment shook the confidence of colleagues, consumers, and dependents. Europe had a proto-capitalist economy in the fourteenth century—a fairly free market despite the restrictive regulations of the guilds—and its business cycle obeyed the economic laws that govern the rise and fall of a free economy.

However, the economy was affected by more complex and special circumstances than the iron laws of supply and demand. The most important reason for the late medieval depression was a basic, critical flaw within the European economy itself, a flaw that operated almost continuously from the thirteenth century to the Industrial Revolution. The essential problem was the deficiency in transportation technology, and the resultant lag between production and distribution. Except during severe labor shortages, production could be increased very simply by hiring more workers, but the costs of distribution were enormous and grew more enormous with an increasing volume of sales. The only roads in Europe were the old Roman highways, progressively deteriorating with each century of neglect. The cost of transportation overland was high, and even in a growing market, the consumers could not afford to pay the freight. Distribution by water was much more satisfactory, but there were not enough rivers to transport goods cheaply to most of Europe; identical goods were cheap to those who lived on or near the Rhine or the Seine and prohibitively expensive to those who lived farther away. Merchants expanded their businesses until their transportation costs grew too large for profit; then they stopped buying goods (causing manufacturers and farmers to lay off workers) and gave up the attempt to reach a larger market.

The problem could have been solved by canals, but canals were not built until the end of the seventeenth century—indeed, the Canal Revolution of the eighteenth century was as important to the European economy as the opening of the railroads to the American. Medieval people had the necessary resources to dig canals (which do not require much more than picks and shovels), but they did not do it because the shortsighted kings, dukes, and bishops who controlled the necessary resources could not conceive of expensive capital projects which, in the first instance, benefitted merchants. Consequently, the limit of medieval capacity to transport and distribute goods inland was reached early in the fourteenth century. Chronic depression plagued Europe from that time on, until the mid-eighteenth century, relieved only by periodic and temporary booms. In the early sixteenth century, for instance, the economy was artificially stimulated by the importation of precious metals from America, which created optimism and inflation. The depression returned after 1580, and its return was followed by the revolutionary unrest of the early seventeenth century.

When depression is severe, as it was in the fourteenth century, people blame their leaders for their suffering; when men are hungry, chronic frustrations easily turn into crises.

II. *The New Intellectual Climate*

CREATIVITY IN ARTS AND LETTERS

The late medieval world was characterized by high quality and voluminous production in art, literature, philosophy, and science. Extensive writings of the period have survived, and the European archives are full of fourteenth-century works, some of which are not yet translated or published in book form. With so much intellectual activity going on, a man had to be very good to stand out above his contemporaries, and fourteenth-century thinkers were very good indeed. They were outstanding in almost every intellectual field except economics: Europe produced no real economic thinking until the early eighteenth century. In the natural sciences, however, late medieval thought was superior to anything in Europe since the time of the ancient Greeks; the medieval scientists came remarkably close to a breakthrough into modern physics.

Craftsmanship in all fields was of high quality: Giotto and Dante would have been outstanding in any era, but even the second rank of fourteenth-century work was very high. Certainly artists and writers profited from the extensive activity and competition in the literary and academic worlds. Perhaps more important, however, was the nature of the times—an era of crisis, when worried people sought answers to fundamental questions about human knowledge, the relation of God and man, the nature of the state and of society. The atmosphere of crisis often inspires important theoretical work on basic problems that are ignored or taken for granted in happier times.

The political and social malaise of the period contributed in another way to the outburst of intellectual effort. When political and social movements and ideals seem promising, active thinkers tend to exert themselves in these fields, and the best minds are lost to art and philosophy. However, when the social and political system is failing and men are disillusioned with public life, the best thinkers turn to the private pleasure of artistic and intellectual effort. Dante's early ambition was to win public office in Florence, and he did not write *The Divine Comedy* until he and his party had been exiled from the city.

Fourteenth-century intellectuals were a varied group with very different interests and points of view, but they shared certain tendencies, including an inclination toward extremism: ideas, once proposed, were pushed further and further to their logical and most disturbing conclusions. In philosophy as well as politics, moderation and compromise were not sought. On the contrary, the period bred angry men with strong feelings, whose violent mood and disgust with compromise encouraged them to mention the hitherto unmentionable. Such heretical or revolutionary ideas as doing away with the Church hierarchy or letting poor men rule themselves, were brought up and discussed—ideas that would have been unthinkable even in the preceding generation.

There was considerable experimentation in subject matter and form during the late thirteenth and early fourteenth centuries, and new areas of thought were opened up and new means of expression were developed. For the first time, the popular culture became a vehicle for high art, and poets searched for forms of expression in which to exercise their fine sensibility and yet make themselves clear to the half-educated. Great literature was taken to the "masses," and literature itself became somewhat bourgeois in the process, adopting forms and styles of the popular culture.

In painting and sculpture, the late medieval period was the most important stylistic turning point between the fourth century A.D. and the end of the nineteenth century. In about the fourth century, the classical form developed by the ancient Greeks (idealized naturalism, in which the human body is represented as the eye would see it if it were perfect) and modified by the slightly more realistic style of the Romans, had given way to medieval impressionism. Medieval artists hoped to portray the world as it exists in the eye of God; theirs was a nonrepresentational expression not of what the eye sees but of what the soul believes, and their style prevailed until the return to naturalism (or classicism) in the late thirteenth century. The new naturalistic style endured (despite temporary revivals of impressionism in the baroque of the late seventeenth century, the Romanticism of the early nineteenth century, and other brief stylistic movements) from the late thirteenth century until the great nonrepresentational revolution which began in France in the 1890s and still dominates western art in the twentieth century.

The crucial shift to a naturalistic artistic style in the late thirteenth century was not the beginning of the great classical, humanist movement we call the Renaissance. That came later (it began in about 1340 but did not really get under way until the early fifteenth century), and was based upon a conscious attempt to imitate the art of Greece and Rome. When the true Renaissance emerged, it gave the existing revival of spontaneous, indigenous naturalism a strong push toward self-conscious, even derivative classicism.

The late thirteenth-century naturalistic movement was not motivated by adoration and emulation of the classics but on something quite different: the artist's attempt to communicate his sensibility to the new men of the period, and particularly to the new bourgeois class. The artists and writers and preachers of the late thirteenth century departed from the typological, hierarchical, highly symbolical and abstruse style that had dominated western art since the fourth century A.D. Symbols were abandoned or made obvious enough to be intelligible to men who could not absorb difficult typology. In a direct and sentimental style, artists attempted to evoke not an intellectual appreciation of a world of traditional symbolism, but an immediate emotional reaction. They wrote and painted in simple language and images, keeping theological codes to a minimum and using obvious symbols and traditional concepts that anyone could understand. Giotto's paintings of St. Francis (executed in about 1300) show the saint in the round as a three-dimensional human being doing real human things— feeding birds, or touching a leper; he is a sympathetic central figure performing recognizable acts. The artist hoped to move the heart and fill the eye with tears, to reduce moral and social problems to individual human terms. The themes and aims of late thirteenth-century art have survived as central motifs of bourgeois art. They dominate nineteenth-century novels and the soap operas and situation comedies of twentieth-century television, which aim to arouse emotional response by the simplest moral demonstration.

The new art and literature of the late thirteenth century owed a great deal to the pervasive influence of the Franciscan friars, who were successfully winning back the alienated bourgeoisie. Franciscan preaching was entirely different from traditional medieval homiletics, which evoked a world of eternal verity in a cool, distant style quite unsatisfactory to the half-educated merchants of the thirteenth-century towns. The traditional sermon, which reminded a man of his Christian duty but did not grip his emotions, required not only self-discipline, but great learning in the entire field of patristic culture. A medieval preacher traditionally began with a quotation from the Bible, then "glossed" the text by citing the various Church Fathers, ending with a homily that was not much more than a formal tag—a reminder or command, not an exhortation. The traditional sermon was a formal textual analysis designed to reveal the vast wisdom of the preacher and of the Church.

Although some Franciscan friars were learned men, they did not use their scholarship in their sermons. Their intention was to convert, not to remind or impress—as in later evangelical movements such as pietistic Protestantism or Hasidic Judaism, the emotional impact was all-important. Franciscan preachers announced the homily at the outset, and went on to convince their hearers to obey it. They told stories of suffering and triumph in "real life" to move the middle-class audience with recognizable scenes, and the dramatic ability of the preacher was more important than his academic credentials. Their sermons were attuned to the ethos and life-style of comfortable, self-satisfied people who thought well of themselves because they had succeeded in a highly competitive society. The townsmen were fairly well educated in a superficial sense, but most of them lacked any power of critical analysis.

To appeal to the new bourgeois congregations, Franciscan preachers adopted a highly emotional, naturalistic style. The new style was impressively successful, and its influence spread to all areas of literature and art in the late thirteenth century. The greatest artists of the era managed to transmute popular forms into vehicles for the expression of individual sensibility, maintaining subtlety and personal vision even while they communicated freely with their contemporaries. The second part of the *Romance of the Rose* (the greatest French poem of the thirteenth century), Dante's *New Life*, Chaucer's *Canterbury Tales,* or Petrarch's letters (and some of his sonnets) reveal the influence of naturalism even while they express the personal genius of the writer. A great artist presents his individual vision of the world, gleaned from his private experience, but his vehicle is the popular literary style and form of his period. Shakespeare wrote box-office drama; Dickens could (and sometimes did) transmute the plots of contemporary pot-boilers into great literature. In a naturalistic period, artists and writers paint and write about "real people" instead of symbols and aim at direct communication of their personal experiences; the great ones are able to raise this personal communication to the level of universal meaning.

Artists and writers shared in the disaffection of the intellectuals of the late Middle Ages, and their work helped to subvert the balance of the high medieval civilization. Any society has a group of values or doctrines that are compatible (or have been made compatible by careful synthesis)—an intellectual middleground, a consensus, on which its culture is based. In the stage of disintegration and transvaluation, the leading thinkers of the new generation begin to resort to one or another of the extremes within the traditional consensus; an important aspect of the disintegrative stage is the drift of the intellectuals toward some extreme point of view. The late medieval intellectuals took a long time to arrive at a direct confrontation with the old culture or to extrapolate the significance of their extreme ideas. Many of them only flirted with advanced notions, but that did not lessen the significance of their radical temperament. Balance and compromise are difficult to maintain, and when an intellectual system gets old and rigid, people get bored with it—to be interesting, one must say something new and different. The late medieval intellectuals were marvelously inventive, but also distinctly irresponsible; they played with new ideas (ideas that led eventually to the polarization of society) without considering their implications, and then were sometimes horrified when those ideas became the bases of violent or revolutionary actions. Making use of the new forms of expression and the popular culture, these men did much to destroy the intellectual consensus on which their civilization was based.

DANTE

Dante was one of the most distinguished literary intellectuals of the late Middle Ages, and certainly he shared in their characteristically inconsistent (even fraudulent) pseudo-radicalism. He took great delight in genteel shock, in expressing outrageous ideas to attract attention—ideas whose logical conclusions he could not accept. All of this fades to insignificance, however, beside his unquestioned mastery of poetic literature. Dante was the true founder of Italian as a literary language, and his poems endure long after his political and religious ideas have been forgotten.

Many critics regard *The Divine Comedy* as the greatest poem of the Middle Ages as well as Dante's masterpiece. Despite his radical ideas, it presents a conventional scheme of salvation based upon orthodox Catholic theology. The poem (supposedly a dream) recounts the poet's pilgrimage through hell, purgatory, and paradise. His guide through hell to the bottom rung of the ladder of purgatory is Vergil, representing reason and classical culture (the supreme embodiment of reason). Reason can assist the soul to avoid evil, but it cannot find the way into a better life.

In purgatory the pilgrim acquires a new guide: Beatrice, representing divine revelation, the Church, the sacraments, and Christian faith. Beatrice, Dante's symbol of ideal beauty, the beatific vision, and the Beatitudes of Christ, was drawn from the poet's image of a young girl he once saw and never met. Certainly his infatuation arose from a high medieval, chivalric concept of love and faith, and this was characteristic of the thirteenth-century Italian bourgeoisie. The wealthy merchants of the Italian towns had money and power, but lacking social status and a sense of self-esteem, they consciously adopted the attitudes and mystique of twelfth-century French aristocratic culture. Beatrice leads the poet through purgatory and the lower circles of heaven, but in the highest part of paradise he is guided by St. Bernard, representing mystical religious experience. Reason allows the Christian to avoid evil; the Church carries him to heaven; but for the final encounter of the soul with God, a mystical experience is essential.

The Divine Comedy is based on traditional, Thomist theology, but Dante did include some of the new and radical ideas of his day, probably in order to keep up with contemporary trends. He placed

Pope Boniface VIII in a low circle of hell—but this was not too dangerous, for Boniface was a radical reactionary and it was very much the fashion among intellectuals to denounce him. It was much more shocking to place Siger of Brabant in paradise, for Siger was not only a well-known professor of philosophy at the University of Paris but an avowed Averroist, a notorious opponent of Thomas Aquinas, and a man condemned by the ecclesiastical authorities.

There was a significant strain of Averroism in thirteenth-century philosophy (it grew still more important in the fourteenth and fifteenth centuries) that was distinctly threatening to the Church. Averroes, writing in Spain in the twelfth century, had separated reason and faith, asserting that science and religion were incompatible, that they said different things. The Christian Averroists contended that Christian dogma was not supported by reason and must be accepted on faith alone. Aquinas, however, based his synthesis on the belief that the Christian could have it both ways, that science supported all of Christian dogma (with a few notable exceptions, such as the Trinity, which were accepted as revealed truth). The Thomist religious Establishment regarded Averroists like Siger as dangerous radicals threatening the very foundations of Christian belief.

Dante not only placed Siger of Brabant in paradise; he also indicated in the prose work *De Monarchia* that he was sympathetic to the Averroist doctrine of collective immortality—and this although the very structure of *The Divine Comedy* was essentially centered upon the Christian belief in personal immortality. Collective immortality is a somewhat pantheistic concept in which individual souls do not survive, although their intellectual energy returns after death to unity with the universal mind. To orthodox Christians, this was an extremely disturbing and heretical notion.

De Monarchia is a didactic work in which Dante asserted his belief that the German emperor should rule supreme in Italy. A strong emperor would have served Dante's personal interest, for his political fortunes depended on those of the imperial party in Florence. Yet, he genuinely believed that a powerful secular state would benefit mankind; his political philosophy was based on the concept of the state as essential to the good life. Dante justified his fealty to the Holy Roman Emperor partly on traditional, historical grounds (honoring the emperor as heir to the great Romans), but this was secondary to his radical pragmatic assumption that a powerful state would contribute to the peace and prosperity of man.

Dante also believed in the worth and integrity of personal experience, and this belief was clearly revealed in his *New Life*. The inner life of experience he regarded as real, and love not as a sin, a snare, or an expression of carnal will, but the most important thing in life. This was radical individualism even for the late thirteenth century, for Dante was not ashamed of his visions of Beatrice—he revelled in them. The contemporary Church maintained the necessity of objective, external obedience to the authority of God and of dedication to involvement in the community, but although Dante gave lip service to the concept of duty, it was the inner life—the secret life of passion—that was most important. Externally, *The Divine Comedy* was a statement of Christian doctrine, and yet it represented one man's experience of Christianity. The doctrine was orthodox, by and large, but the emphasis on the poet's feelings and the individual quest was entirely unorthodox in the context of medieval civilization. To Dante, the religious life was a life of personal experience, and the Christian had not only to obey the doctrines handed down by the Church but to seek and find them. And if he could not? . . .

Dante's individualistic, anti-communal, and anti-authoritarian attitudes harked back to the radical eroticism of the twelfth century; he believed the life of erotic love to be as noble a life as any other. Dante read a great deal of twelfth-century French poetry and he understood the liberation ethic. However, like all great epic poets, he walked the fine line between literary tradition (in his case, medieval romanticism) and personal experience; like Sophocles or Shakespeare or Goethe, he struggled to absorb and synthesize a traditional culture in terms of his own mind and his own life.

Mysticism and Scientism: The English Franciscans

Franciscan friars were extremely popular in England in the latter part of the thirteenth century, and many of the best thinkers of the day joined the order. Even though St. Francis himself had regarded learning as useless in the important aspects of life and an obstacle to the quest for salvation, many of the English Franciscans were brilliant men who tended to go into intellectual and academic fields.

One of the first important thinkers associated with the English Franciscans was not technically a member of the order at all. But Robert Grosseteste, bishop of Lincoln, was emotionally and intellectually a Franciscan as well as the official protector of the English branch of the order. Grosseteste, the first medieval philosopher of science, believed that the processes of nature could be quantified— that natural laws could be expressed in mathematical proportions, and scientific propositions could thus be verified. Grosseteste's ideas mark the beginning of modern physics, which rested on just such a conception of nature until very recent times. Quantification was the principle behind Newton's physics in the seventeenth century, and biology did not really move forward as a scientific discipline until Mendel found mathematical ratios to substantiate Darwin's theoretical work.

Grosseteste probably was assisted in achieving his breakthrough in scientific attitude by Plato, who believed that cosmological processes operated in geometric proportions—and Plato built on the work of Pythagoras and earlier Greeks. The English Franciscans were strong Platonists in the 1250s and 1260s, but Grosseteste was the first to attempt to establish some of the mathematical laws that they knew must exist, and to accomplish something concrete on the basis of the scientific attitude. He worked out a theory of the refraction of light which represented at the very least an early use of the experimental method, if not a major advance in physical knowledge. By the early fourteenth century scholars at Oxford and Paris universities had come very close to what later became the New Physics of the seventeenth century.

The interesting question is why Grosseteste and his successors did not proceed still further, why they adopted the scientific attitude but did not build a solid theoretical or practical science. First of all, they were clerics and not scientists: Grosseteste was a bishop who was too busy in his diocese to spend much time in the laboratory. More important, these men simply did not have the necessary mathematical background to move ahead in physics. Europeans were backward in math until the sixteenth century—well behind the Arabs (who developed algebra), and it is almost impossible to work out the laws of nature with no math beyond

Euclidean geometry. Some fourteenth-century thinkers had an amazingly clear idea of the necessary next step, but that step was not taken until the sixteenth century, when Descartes invented analytic geometry.

Although they could not bring about a Scientific Revolution, the English Franciscans had a scientific, empirical cast of mind that was bound to make them think critically about religious dogma. Empiricism tends to shake the automatic acceptance of inherited belief, and critical thinkers are very apt to turn to dissent or mysticism. Without the authority of traditional dogma, any belief in God must be a passionate belief founded on direct, individual religious experience. The critical temperament was devastating to the thirteenth-century Church, for these scientists were not devout in the conventional sense. They may have had a strong personal faith, but they were unlikely to accept traditional doctrines about God, and they tended to subject the teachings of the Church to close scrutiny.

The Franciscans were particularly inclined to examine and to reject theories of papal supremacy, because (like other radical intellectuals of the day, but with special venom) they bitterly resented the papacy. They believed that the popes had corrupted the order, betraying their mandate from St. Francis to sponsor and protect his brothers. Francis had intended his order to be poor as a corporate body as well as individuals, but the thirteenth-century popes allowed the order to hold property and amass great wealth, willfully defying the wishes of the saint. (Certain Franciscans, of course, went along with the popes: they loved comfort and desired to own property.) The popes disliked the idea of apostolic poverty anywhere in the Church, fearing its effect on popular opinion. The Franciscans were successful and well loved, and if *they* were mendicants (as an order), Christians might demand a similar style of all their religious leaders.

Partly because of their scientific and inquiring spirit, and partly out of bitterness against Rome, the radical Franciscans of the late thirteenth and early fourteenth century damaged or virtually destroyed the Thomistic synthesis. One of their most famous members, Roger Bacon (a disciple of Grosseteste), was a well-known and noisy advocate of the experimental and empirical method. Bacon was not the first empiricist (probably that honor belongs to Aristotle), but he did make Grosseteste's ideas into a program. Bacon was the archetype of the skeptic—tough-minded, undismayed by tradition or authority, and demanding proof of every proposition.

Duns Scotus, a colleague of Bacon's at Oxford in the 1290s, has only recently achieved deserved respect as a great philosopher. The humanists of the fourteenth and fifteenth century regarded Scotus' brand of analytic philosophy as useless as well as impossibly difficult, and they attacked him so violently that his work was severely neglected until late in the nineteenth century. Their ridicule was so sharp that even his name—Duns (or Dunce)—came to stand for stupidity. In fact Scotus was a superb logician, and he applied his logical powers to examination of the proposition at the heart of Thomism. Aquinas, following Aristotle, assumed (but never proved) that the mind can build up general propositions on the basis of empirical knowledge, but Scotus concluded that he was skeptical as to how and whether universals could be established on the basis of empirical evidence.

Scotus' skeptical conclusions were worked into a systematic philosophy by William of Occam, a younger colleague who became the greatest of the fourteenth-century philosophers. Occam was a professor at Oxford at twenty-one, if the accepted dates are correct, and an undoubted genius at any age. He adopted the Averroist position (denied and refuted by Aquinas but fashionable again in the fourteenth century) that the rational power of the mind, working from empirical data, can establish universal propositions with regard to nature but not with regard to God. Man can think rationally and scientifically concerning nature, but not about God; he can discover the natural laws that govern the physical universe, but not universal principles in theology. Occam believed that science was the highest form of rational inquiry, that theology (defined as a rational philosophy of religion) was necessarily specious. Occam himself was a devout Christian, but his faith was based on religious experience and not on reason. Religious knowledge had to come through feeling, experience, revelation, or mystical exaltation. Neither the existence of God nor the validity of Christian morality could be proved; they must be upheld by faith alone. Occam concluded that a man could be both mystical and scientific as long as he was careful not to think mystically about nature or scientifically about God.

William of Occam was the progenitor of two of the major themes of fourteenth and fifteenth-century thought: scientism and mysticism. Eventually, of course, these two movements led in very different directions—toward the Scientific Revolution on one hand, and the Protestant Reformation on the other. The Scientific Revolution did not follow immediately upon the development of the scientific attitude in the fourteenth century, partly because medieval scientists lacked the necessary mathematical tools, but also because scientific pursuits were not yet accepted by society. By the sixteenth century, however, men began to realize that science might produce something useful—advances in weaponry, for example. William of Occam and his disciples were the first philosophers of science, but they were far ahead of their time. Their work was not translated into genuine scientific theory until European mathematics caught up with philosophy in the sixteenth and seventeenth century, nor into practical application and technology until the eighteenth century and the Industrial Revolution.

The logical outcome of fourteenth-century mystical, experientialist, individualistic religion was the Reformation, but for two reasons that did not occur until the sixteenth century. First, the contemporary Church (and particularly the papacy) was at such a low ebb of power, prestige, and moral reputation that it could not confront the religious radicals and force them into a decisive schism from the Church, as happened in the sixteenth century.

A second cause for the failure of the Reformation to occur in the late Middle Ages was the inadequacy of the leadership of the heretical movement. At least two brilliant and energetic leaders inspired the heretical movement—the Oxford scholar John Wyclif and the Bohemian evangelical John Hus—but they lacked the ability of Luther and Calvin to convince a substantial part of the European nobility and bourgeoisie that heresy and counter-churches served the rich man's political and family interests. Wyclif's radical student disciples, the Lollard preachers, played a significant role in fomenting the Peasant's Revolt in 1381 in England, scaring the king and nobility into concluding that heresy implied social upheaval. Hus and the Czech evangelicals of the fifteenth century were also Bohemian nationalists who enjoyed remarkable success in wars with German princes; the spectre of Bohemian puritan legions riding victoriously through central Europe was not conducive to encouraging support for heretical doctrines on the part of the established German landed and urban classes.

Nevertheless, although ruthlessly pursued by kings and nobles, the heretical movement was blunted but not obliterated in the fifteenth century. The English Lollards went underground and in 1500 still had many adherents not only among the peasants but also among the lesser gentry of northern England. A Bohemian Protestant Church had long existed when Luther began his conflict with Rome. And in the universities of the late Middle Ages, the now dominant Occamism provided fertile ground for radical theology. Martin Luther was well schooled in Occamist doctrine, and in the long perspective the sixteenth century Reformation can be seen as the direct heritage of the radical English Franciscans of the early fourteenth century.

POLITICAL RADICALISM

On all levels of European society, a wave of political radicalism began to build up in the late thirteenth century and crested in the late fourteenth. There was widespread interest in communal social organization and even in participatory democracy, which had not existed in Europe since the fifth century B.C. People began to believe that rule from above was not the only conceivable political arrangement, ordained by God for human welfare. On the most practical (and least radical) level, the parliamentary principle emerged, and the idea that kings should rule with the consent of representatives of the people (at least of the important people) took institutional form in many parts of Europe. In every country except England, however, these parliamentary institutions—or Estates —were slowly abandoned or largely neglected after the fourteenth century. England was not unique in developing a representative system in the fourteenth century, but it was unique in preserving that system during the age of absolute monarchy in the sixteenth and seventeenth centuries. In France, for instance, the Estates lost all their power and dignity, and indeed were not even called between 1614 and 1789.

The idea of representative government is not necessarily democratic at all; it is often very aristocratic, and as an aristocratic principle it became important in the Church in the fourteenth century. When it became clear, late in the century, that the papacy could not or would not reform itself or overcome the Schism, various thinkers (centered at the University of Paris) found a possible solution in the conciliar principle. They pointed out that the early Church had relied on councils to settle its disputes, and they developed the idea that the contemporary Church might disentangle itself from Schism and corruption if the popes ruled with the advice and consent of the ecclesiastical leaders. At the Council of Constance in 1414, the conciliar principle worked effectively enough to settle the Schism and establish one pope on the Throne of Peter, but the second part of the principle—that popes should continue to rule with the consent of important churchmen—was ignored and suppressed by the pontiffs. Another important council was convened during the crisis of the Reformation, but it was staged and managed by the pope, as were all subsequent councils until the extraordinary first session of Vatican II in 1962.

Still another reflection of political radicalism was the doctrine of the commune, which was very popular in the north Italian cities. In theory, the communes were self-governing republics run by a council representing the citizens of the town (at least the prosperous citizens), and every institution within the town—even the Church—was subject to the general will of the community. In 1324, Marsiglio of Padua, a radical Italian academic philosopher, propounded the democratic doctrine that social and political order could best be achieved through representative democracy. Marsiglio was the rector of the University of Paris and a great scholar, whose treatise *Defender of the Peace* was about four hundred years ahead of its time. The religious authorities detested his idea that the Church should be taxed and responsible to the state like any other institution, and Marsiglio's work was considered very dangerous. It was effectively repressed until the late sixteenth century, when it became very influential, especially in England, and had an important role in the development of left-wing Protestantism.

Marsiglio's ideas were severely repressed, but they also fell on deaf ears because the Italian communes were not successful and therefore were poor exemplars of his doctrines. Probably the towns were simply too small for democracy, for their jealous, contentious leading families could not endure to share or exchange political power. (Shakespeare's Capulets and Montagues were drawn from real life.) Democracy requires a basis of mutual understanding and consent—if only that the winner of an election be allowed to serve his term without assassination—and the jealousy and violence of the patrician families eventually became too great to be contained within the system. When violence began to hurt business, the townsmen after 1300 extensively gave up their republican institutions and turned to the *podesta* system, bringing in neighboring princes or unemployed generals as dictators to run the towns and enforce law and order.

The Italian communes did not survive, but their failure did not stop the flow of democratic radical ideas and experimentation in fourteenth-century thought. European archives are full of treatises based on remarkably radical concepts—remarkable in the light of the centuries of authoritarianism between theory and implementation. Radical ideas were repressed or abandoned because they did not seem to work, but no political system worked very well in the chaotic conditions of fourteenth-century Europe.

HUMANISM

The other major aspect of late medieval thought was humanism, which was not as influential as scientism, mysticism, or political radicalism in the fourteenth century but became extremely important later. By 1550, every educated man in Europe was a humanist—John Calvin as well as the pope—and this remained true until the late eighteenth century, when Jean Jacques Rousseau became the first significant *non*-humanist thinker in three hundred years.

Humanism is a temperament, or a style, rather than an ideology. It usually is identified with classicism and with adoration of classical models, but its essence is somewhat broader, and can be described as a profound belief in the value of the secular life. This does not mean that the humanists were unreligious or anti-religious; many were devout Christians, but they were also the first dedicated secularists. They maintained their belief in the next world, but they hoped to make the best of this world while they were in it: to live well themselves, and to work toward the betterment of society so that everyone could live well. Sensitive to the environment, they worked hard and gave generously to beautify their cities, and humanists included every aspect of the cultural life (as well as personal comfort) in their concept of the good life.

The humanists depended upon reason, not to establish ultimate truth but as a useful vehicle for the conduct of business and personal affairs and (above all) of social reform. They were moderate and liberal and intensely moral, but their morality was based on reason rather than revelation. Theirs was a Greek morality, a habitual proclivity to moderation, education, and refinement. Like Aristotle, they believed that goodness was a habit, and that young people must be trained in self-restraint and in a habitual preference for and appreciation of the better things of life. They scorned the life of pure intellect and denounced Occamists as "scholastic" (i.e. academic) thinkers whose work lacked social utility. The humanists thought that men knew enough to lead a good life without further intellectual discoveries, and they preferred the active pursuit of social and institutional reform to scholarly disputation over abstract concepts.

To the humanists, education was more important than anything in the world, and they were severe critics of the existing educational system—particularly of the university, for its devotion to abstract research and its neglect of practical work for the improvement of human welfare. They founded their own schools (many were called academies, after Plato) to train the young in proper conduct, appreciation of art, and refinement of temperament. The humanist educators devoted most of their energy and money to secondary schools, believing that adolescence was the crucial age for the absorption of humane attitudes, generosity, and love of beauty. The humanists were the first to regard secondary schools as anything more than a preparation for university entrance, and their schools eventually became the basis of the secondary education system of western Europe. St. Paul's School, founded in London by John Colet in the late fifteenth century, remains an excellent example of a school based on humanist principles. The English public school, the French *lycée*, and the German *gymnasium*, as these institutions existed in the nineteenth century, were all adaptations of the humanist schools. By that time, they had become bastions of aristocratic privilege, perpetuating outmoded codes of behavior and style, but their later history does not detract from the truly innovative and distinguished contribution of the humanists to European education.

In education as in other fields, the humanists were as good as their word: they actually founded and managed academies instead of merely contenting themselves with the production of theoretical treatises on education. Their schools did fine work, too, in spite of their elitist character. For several hundred years, the aristocrats and upper bourgeoisie of Europe were taught dignity, self-respect, social commitment, and the appreciation of fine art. The great advances in European cultural achievement between the fifteenth and the nineteenth centuries were supported by aristocratic and bourgeois patrons who had been educated for just such a role: they bought paintings, took musicians into their courts and palaces, and subsidized the work of poets and playwrights. It is unfortunate but undeniable that the extension of cultural opportunities to a wider audience has not raised the level of cultural achievement, nor have artists enjoyed a rise in status or security since they began to depend on the open market instead of aristocratic patrons.

The humanists cultivated a temperament, and their temperament was of a particular and limited kind: it was often non-intellectual, sometimes anti-intellectual, and almost always elitist. Politically it favored beneficence and intelligence by rulers, and rarely questioned traditional forms. However, the great cultural centers of the western world owe many of their finest aspects to the humanists. Because they believed that the secular life is the only life men can know, they worked to make it beautiful and valuable, and their concept of beauty and value fostered dignity and style while allowing for, and socializing, money and power. To realize such a vision, they knew, education was essential, and the education of the young was their special province. Twentieth-century educators and reformers hope to make available to all men what the humanists made available to the elite. If this can be accomplished, it will immeasurably enhance the quality of human life.

III. Social Groups and Ideals in Late Medieval Europe

We have seen that during the eleventh and twelfth centuries the feudal aristocracy in western Europe came under challenge from groups in society who put up different values, different forms of wealth, and different skills against those of the traditional warrior

class. The aristocracy bent under these attacks, but in the end—
and this is of great importance for European history—they controlled, rebuffed, or absorbed the new groups. Threatened by a
new culture, by economic change, and by new groups striving for
wealth and influence, the old nobility readjusted, reformed, and
reinvigorated itself. This is the prime reason why descendants of
the feudal nobility were able to exercise leadership in European
society in the fourteenth, fifteenth, sixteenth, and seventeenth centuries—long after the waning of the intensely rural, underdeveloped, illiterate, violent, and disordered conditions in which
feudal institutions had been developed. The men who had come to
the top in the feudal military world stayed at the top, but they
changed. With somewhat different values and education, the old
feudal families became the European aristocracy. There is no development in European history more important than this perpetuation of the feudal aristocracy by its remarkable resilience, its
adaptation, and its absorption of new cultures and new groups.

During the twelfth century the aristocracy was harassed by
the bourgeoisie, by the students, by the bureaucrats (who were students grown up) and by the king. At the end of the twelfth century
they began to fight back by altering their composition and even
more their ideology. Feudal society polarized into two separate
groups: a few great aristocratic families and a mass of ordinary
knights. The great families had the wealth, the time, and the power
to play a role in political life, and they bore the brunt of hostility,
resentment, and ideological onslaughts by the bourgeoisie, students, and bureaucrats. It was these great aristocrats who had the
incentive and the leisure to develop a new ideology to justify their
continued leadership. They took up the functional theory of social
groups which had been propounded by the bourgeoisie and the
university students—namely, that each group in society must fulfill
its function, that nothing is given to a man simply by inherited
status. The high aristocracy of the late twelfth and thirteenth centuries developed their own functional theory; they believed that the
aristocrat, who had the most independence, the most wisdom, the
most learning, the most freedom and time to engage in political
life deserved therefore to hold high political power—that was their
first argument, but it was only a minor one.

The main argument was that the aristocrat, who was a superior type of person, should have a superior type of power. Their position, they said, was earned by the superiority of their minds, not simply by their great-grandfathers' good luck. They held power by inherited tradition and deserved it because they had the independence, education, and wisdom to rule. They were the natural rulers of society, not through inheritance but through superiority—certainly superior to the bourgeois, immersed in his accounts and in the grimy stock-taking of diurnal business life. Certainly they were more experienced than the volatile undergraduates, and more public-spirited, tolerant, balanced, and national in outlook than the bureaucrats, who were too busy trying to improve their own position to view the good of society as a whole.

This is a very important argument. It was used right down to the twentieth century to justify the dominance and special privileges of gentlemen in government and society. The argument first appeared in the twelfth and thirteenth centuries in response to the triple onslaught of the bourgeois, student, and bureaucrat. Of course the great aristocrats were highly educated, and this argument was not merely a desperate response but was based on their understanding of classical political theory. The great man shall rule and others shall follow, in Plato's idea of the republic. The aristocracy wished to emulate Plato's philosopher-kings, who not only ruled but deserved to continue to rule. Certainly the bourgeoisie could not be compared to these very fine gentlemen, with their fine fastidious tastes.

Indeed the aristocracy was extremely impressed with itself, and in some ways it was very successful in rebutting the onslaught. In the thirteenth century, some of those people who might have been expected to be critics of the social order were deferential; there was little real opposition from the English bourgeoisie, for example, in the thirteenth century. The aristocracy did so well that it believed it could never fail, and during periods of imbalance or impotence in government in the thirteenth and early fourteenth centuries the nobles stepped in. This happened in England on two occasions when the barons took over the government for a few months.

Thus the aristocracy reconstituted itself in ideology: it became a group of blue bloods—of very special people. The way they ate was special; their way of life was special; their pattern of ideals was special. They were convinced that they ought to continue to dominate society, even in the face of threats from new groups. Noblemen should run the government, displacing the university men. On the occasions when aristocratic government was attempted, the weaknesses of the aristocratic mind were demonstrated. Noble government never worked, because these fine gentlemen with their breadth of vision had just that—breadth, but not much depth. They lacked intensity and the ability to get at the heart of problems, to sit long hours and deal with boring tasks in the public interest. That was the kind of service the bureaucrats had given the English king.

Aristocratic government tended to lead to civil wars. It was weak government; it was mismanaged; the aristocrat had too high an opinion of himself to cooperate with others. In England and France in the fourteenth and fifteenth centuries, when these newly-literate, educated, ideologically motivated aristocrats took over the government, the result was chaos and social disaster which discredited aristocratic rule. They tried to assert traditions of feudal power against the centralizing work of the government and against the educated bureaucracy. They did succeed in taking over—but were unable to operate the government once they had it. Their efforts revealed that although the aristocracy could do many things, it could not run the government well for any period of time.

The thirteenth century was very disappointing to the bourgeoisie, as in a sense were the fourteenth and fifteenth. They saw the rejuvenated aristocracy taking over certain parts of bourgeois culture—literacy at least—and developing a philosophy which was a direct response to bourgeois functionalism. The aristocracy had its own functionalism and the bourgeoisie made little progress. Indeed, as the leading oligarchic mercantile families fell out with one another, the cities became violent and disturbed. By the end of the thirteenth century, at least in Italy, the bourgeoisie very often had to call for a dictator, a *podesta* (often a nobleman) to rule the city. Many cities north of the Alps—particularly in the Rhine Valley—abandoned their independence and asked for rule by a king or his administrator. The communal movement failed, and the bourgeoisie was discredited with it.

Nevertheless, something very important did take place in Italy in the fourteenth century; the bourgeoisie began to ape the aristocracy. The Italian bourgeoisie believed themselves capable of living the lives of aristocrats; they felt that they had the necessary education, greatness of soul, fastidious taste, and wealth. The high Italian urban bourgeoisie of the fourteenth and fifteenth centuries imitated the ethos and the style of the French aristocracy. This was helpful in asserting their equality in European life, but it did not go very far. It was a personal, familial solution to the class struggle, not a social and corporate one. Certain families went aristocratic, demonstrating their equality and their right to be respected. The Medici family of Florence, who began in the thirteenth century as merchants and bankers of obscure circumstances, were marrying their offspring into the French royal family by the sixteenth century. A French queen and a pope of the sixteenth century were Medicis, which was very good for the Medicis but demonstrated social mobility rather than class emancipation.

In the late twelfth and early thirteenth centuries, the bourgeois were self-conscious as a class. They were resentful of being held down, they felt equal or perhaps superior to the nobility, but were unable to make any headway against the centralizing power of the state and the rejuvenated aristocracy. What happened then in Italy, and to a lesser degree outside of Italy, in the fourteenth and fifteenth centuries was that certain families of the bourgeois became aristocrats themselves. They accumulated great wealth, pursued education, and patronized the arts. In two or three generations they were accepted into the European aristocracy at the highest level. But the bourgeoisie as a whole remained outside the landed aristocracy. Younger sons of the bourgeoisie sometimes entered the royal bureaucracy and rose to be great ministers with aristocratic titles, but they did so as educated individuals and not as bourgeois. If a young man went to the university at the age of fourteen, broke away from his family and ended up as minister to the king, his was not a bourgeois triumph but an example of individual mobility.

Thus there was in Europe at the beginning of the sixteenth century a remarkable perpetuation of aristocratic leadership, despite the challenge presented by new, powerful social groups and despite notable failure of aristocratic government in the fourteenth and fifteenth centuries. Historians have not been able to explain the inability of the bourgeoisie to advance to important political positions. Certainly their numbers were small compared with all of rural society, but they were as numerous and as wealthy as—or wealthier than—the aristocrats. It was a moral failure, a failure of nerve, that held them down. Individualistic and rather selfish, they pursued family and private interests. They could not visualize themselves clearly as a class nor develop a consistent social theory.

Economic change vitiated bourgeois self-confidence. At the end of the thirteenth century, just as the struggle between the bourgeoisie and the aristocracy became intense, Europe entered the long depression that lasted to the middle of the fifteenth century. The sharp decline in international trade and the many bankruptcies in businesses and banking houses in Italy, caused by economic as well as political factors, undermined bourgeois class consciousness.

The great aristocrats were affected by the depression of the late Middle Ages, but they were able to compensate for it by seizing power, by gaining control of government and siphoning money from its treasuries. The aristocratic involvement in government helped to compensate for the decline in profits from land, and although they messed up the government, they did make profits out of their intervention. The bourgeoisie suffered a terrible malaise, a failure of nerve, in the depression. Banking houses failed; industry was no longer profitable; cities stopped growing for the first time in three hundred years. The long depression for which the bourgeoisie could not really compensate, helps explain their political impotence in the late Middle Ages. Just at the point when a great confrontation between the bourgeoisie and the aristocracy was apparently inevitable, the bourgeoisie backed off. Instead of demanding class emancipation and social reorganization, the wealthier bourgeois was satisfied if he could make it into the aristocracy. If he could not, he remained a mute dependent of great lords and kings, hoping that his son's humanist education would abet his progeny's social mobility.

European cities of 1500 were centers of wealth, of ingenuity, of learning, and of civilization, yet the real power still lay in rural areas. Society was no longer exclusively rural; commerce and trade were very important, but the managers of industry, trade, and banking had no real political power. In Italy they had less power in 1500 than they had in 1300, because they had surrendered their power to great lords and to a society in which the old lords of the countryside continued to be leaders. It was a remarkable case of archaism and traditionalism. The political impotence of the bourgeoisie, its failure to achieve emancipation or even a clear identity as part of the hierarchic social order was one of the most significant and—one might say—unfortunate developments of the late medieval world.

In the late Middle Ages the peasantry improved its position, due largely to a labor shortage brought on by the Black Death. Perhaps half of the peasants of Europe got wiped out in the middle decades of the fourteenth century, but those who survived were very well off. The agricultural labor shortage fostered the peasant manumission that took place on a large scale in western Europe in the fourteenth and fifteenth centuries. Serfdom had disappeared in those countries by 1500, and the peasants had become small landholders. Many small peasants holdings were enclosed by capitalistically-minded lords and the peasants driven out altogether, but the old serf class was gone.

However, just as serfdom disappeared from western Europe, it became increasingly important in central and eastern Europe. This was remarkable, because in eastern Germany, for instance, during the twelfth and thirteenth centuries, peasants were brought in from the west with guarantees of freedom. They came as immigrants on the basis of the promise of freedom, but their freedom was abolished in the fourteenth and fifteenth centuries, while peasants in the old manorial parts of western Europe achieved manumission. Serfdom was imposed on the peasants of central Europe through the control exercised by the knightly, aristocratic class over the government; here the lords used their political power to achieve a social reorganization to suit their own interests.

Western European peasants benefitted greatly from the labor shortage of the late Middle Ages, which produced full employment, allowed them to force manumission from the lords, and encouraged their general prosperity. Nevertheless, the peasant was still very much subject to tremendous fluctuations in the agricultural market. The lord could use the force of government against him—he could force him off the land and replace the old agricultural economy with capitalist grazing lands. This began to occur in England in the early sixteenth century, and there were similar developments in Spain in the late fifteenth century. The peasant, in spite of his new freedom and prosperity, became subject to the fluctuations of a capitalist market as well as to the traditional aristocratic control over wealth, the political order, learning, and the Church—the exponent of moral power in society. We must not romanticize the effects of the manumission of the serf, because it was accompanied by an increase in the number and variety of aristocratic weapons.

The group in society that probably suffered most in the depression of the late Middle Ages was the lesser nobility. In the twelfth century a polarization had taken place between great lords and lesser ones. The lesser lords were bothered greatly by declining agricultural prosperity, by land going out of cultivation, and by peasants' demands for higher wages. They tried very hard to prevent sweeping changes, without much success. Many of the lesser lords in England and France in the fourteenth and fifteenth centuries were themselves forced down into the ranks of the peasantry. It was a very difficult period for the lesser lords. In England they became known as the gentry. The gentry were people who were known to associate with peasants, whose culture was usually not much above the peasant level, whose vision was narrow, and who were constantly harassed by the great lords on one hand and by the dissident and rebellious peasantry on the other.

Historians still do not fully understand the significance of one aspect of the social history of the late Middle Ages—that is, peasant and industrial proletarian rebellions. In several of the cities of Flanders and Italy there were strikes, all sorts of civil commotions, and in some cases outright rebellions. In England there was a peasant revolt in 1381 that the government put down only with luck and violence, and in the same period in France there was a similar rebellion known as the *Jacquerie*. However, these early proletarian uprisings came to nothing. They flared up; the government and the aristocracy (very frightened) grabbed their weapons and put down the peasants and the workers in indiscriminate massacre. Then for thirty or forty years things would be quiet, until they flared up again and the cycle repeated itself.

It is very hard for historians to make anything out of all this, and by and large they have not done so. In the first place, we are really not sure that these were the first rebellions. Perhaps there were uprisings back in the eleventh century, when the polarization of society gave good cause for them, which were ignored by the churchmen who kept the records. Either they were too stupid and ignorant to understand what was going on, or they were too clever to perpetuate knowledge of these occurrences. But even if these fourteenth-century rebellions were the first, they had no immediate significance. They were the wild, savage cries of people who were acquiring for the first time some literacy and some leadership, mainly from the lower ranks of the clergy. Clergymen (both Franciscan friars and parish priests) were appearing who had some idea of individual freedom, individual conscience, and social justice.

The rebellious groups lacked any real plan of action, and the best that could happen to them was that they might be recruited into one of the great aristocratic factions. This happened in Florence, where the Medici enlisted dissident workers in order to frighten other factions. In that way the workers were brought into political life, although in a very subservient and cynical fashion. However, that was the best that could happen; generally, however, these rebellions frightened the rulers of society but had no fundamental effect upon social structure or economic organization.

The central social facts of 1500 are the perpetuation of aristocratic dominance, the failure of the bourgeoisie to achieve emancipation and equality despite their great wealth, and the continuing tension between the university-educated bureaucracy and the aristocracy. This social pattern was reinforced by the still widespread acceptance of the aristocrats' theory that theirs was the only group whose values deserved recognition, by the subservience of most churchmen to the hierarchical order, and by the continued exploitation of the peasantry despite legal emancipation.

The feudal warrior class, which came into existence after the fall of Rome, had become civilized over the centuries. This European aristocracy succeeded remarkably well in meeting the challenge of new social groups, and there is an amazing continuity in medieval European society with reference to its dominant class. One class appeared; it continued to rule; it changed and became more civilized; it was challenged and absorbed part of the culture of the challenging groups; but it remained the dominant group in European society at the end of the Middle Ages.

Epilogue
BEYOND THE MIDDLE AGES

Hegel, the most provocative and brilliant philosopher of history in the past two centuries, summed up a good part of his whole theory in the aphorism "the Owl of Minerva takes flight when the shadows of night have fallen": we only understand the history of a particular era when it is all over; we perceive the meaning of the past in retrospect.

To fully understand the meaning of the Middle Ages we have to inquire when the Middle Ages ended, and by what criteria can we mark the end of the Middle Ages; what are the fundamental differences between the medieval and modern eras? If we can answer these questions, then the significance of the Middle Ages will be brought more clearly into focus.

The word *modern* is not a colorless or indifferent term. It is a word that connotes a positive value, and when applied to society, it is a word which is generally used in a favorable way. Historians have used *modern* to refer to their own or recent times and have done so in a way that implies that their era is one that is exciting and important, and in most instances they have claimed that the modern era is superior to all previous ages of historic development. Writing in the early twelfth century in England, the monk Eadmer set out to write "A History of Modern Times in England" and since then many historians have undertaken the task of writing a modern history. Modern history, then, is the history of a period in which we are still involved—a period in which the passions and the problems of the present day are at work, an era in which the institutions of our society and the concepts and values by which we live are predominant.

There are three schools of opinion as to when modern history begins, and three schools of opinion, in accordance with this division on chronology, as to the nature of the contrast between medieval and modern civilization. These three schools of interpretation of modern history may be listed as follows: (1) the Renaissance and Reformation interpretation or the humanist school, (2) the modernization-industrialization interpretation or the economic school, (3) the neo-humanist interpretation which could be designated the anti-industrial or New Left attitude to modern history.

I. The Renaissance and Reformation Interpretation

The first interpretation of the period and nature of modern civilization to make its appearance was the Renaissance interpretation, and it was one that universally prevailed until the twentieth century. Indeed, this interpretation has only undergone severe challenge and a diminution in its canonical quality in the last four decades. The roots of this interpretation go back to the ideology of the Italian humanists of the fourteenth century. These scholars, products of the high bourgeoisie of northern Italy in the fourteenth century—writers like Petrarch—were in rebellion against medieval culture. They regarded medieval culture as abstract, rigid, authoritarian, lacking in humane values and respect for the feelings and values of the individual.

The humanists were also motivated by a class bias. The wealthy merchants and bankers of Italy were very well educated, or at least their sons were, and they deeply resented the fact that the power elite of Europe, the feudal and ecclesiastical aristocracy, refused to accept them on terms of equality or even to recognize the existence of a bourgeoisie as a significant part of the social order. Because they were hostile and resentful of their treatment at the hands of the feudal-ecclesiastical hierarchy, the middle-class humanists were driven to develop a philosophy that consciously claimed to (although in reality in many ways did not) reject the medieval culture of the thirteenth century.

The humanists were men of very great learning and they were able to use their devotion to classical literature as an integral part of their ideology. They projected an elaborate scheme of historical development. This interpretation first of all posited that the culture of the ancient world of Greece and Rome was centered on the citizenship of free men and the values of public service in an autonomous political community. This may be a rather fanciful or at least romanticized view of the actualities of Greek and certainly of Roman life, but it is what they believed and there is some plausible grounds for believing it.

The humanists presented the Roman Empire as a unity of flourishing city-states which in turn were dominated by public-spirited and well-educated citizens. In other words, as so often happens in historical interpretation, the Italian humanists saw the Greeks and the Romans as men much like themselves. They viewed the period of the second century A.D., the height of the Roman Empire, as a golden age for mankind, and they believed that history entered a dark age with the conquest of the Roman Empire in the west by the German barbarians in the fifth and sixth centuries. The culture that then succeeded classical civilization was initially, and to a degree it was always essentially, a barbarian culture which went against the finest achievements and the highest ideals of the free individual and the untrammeled mind that had existed in the ancient world. Therefore the culture which provided the value system of the feudal-ecclesiastical hierarchy that the Italian bourgeoise had to fight against was the culture that had originated in barbarism and in the destruction of the greatest of all civilizations, that of classical antiquity.

The humanists of the fourteenth century and their successors in the fifteenth century in Italy and then, also by the fifteenth century, like-minded scholars and ideologies in northern Europe, proclaimed a liberation from "the dark ages," from barbaric "gothic" culture. They advocated a return to the culture and value system of classical antiquity. In other words, they proclaimed a "renaissance," a rebirth, a recovery. This interpretation of western history posited three ages, that of the ancient, the medieval, and the modern worlds, and the modern world in this view came about through a cultural revolution—through a return to fine Latinity, through an appreciation of free intellectual inquiry, and through the recovery of the classical forms of naturalistic art in which the real shape of the human body was appreciated and portrayed. This cultural revolution was effected in their own day, the dawn of modern history, the first post-medieval era.

It is not easy to posit a whole history of civilization purely in terms of intellectual and artistic development, and with the Reformation of the sixteenth century, this modernist interpretation, as propounded by the humanists, was given an additional force and made more elaborate. It is important to note that, in any case, many of the leading Protestant reformers, among them the friend and associate of Martin Luther, Phillip Melanchthon, and John Calvin himself, were heavily steeped in the humanist tradition. Some Protestant reformers, like Luther, were not in a full sense humanists, but they certainly had imbibed humanist learning; and in the early stages of the reform movement before Luther's decisive break from Rome, the reformers had been heavily involved with Erasmus, the Dutch scholar and the leader of northern humanism. Consequently the Reformation interpretation of history, as was the case with Protestant reform itself, was a continuation of Renaissance humanism, and the Reformation interpretation, as was similarly the case with Protestantism itself, greatly broadened and intensified the attitude and the social philosophy of the humanists.

The interpretation of history presented by the Protestant reformers also posited a return to purity. The humanists had said they were returning to the purity of classical culture; the Protestant reformers, beginning with Luther, claimed they were returning to the purity of the "apostolic Church," that is, to the earliest Church, the Church of Jesus and his immediate disciples. The Protestant reformers believed that life in the spirit of Jesus and his first disciples was a life of humility, a life of poverty both spiritual and material, a life of purity and love, and that this was the real Church, the true Church, the model of what the Church should be. This view, then, contended that as the Church spread in the Roman Empire, as it gained a vast number of adherents, and as above all it gained the support of the Roman emperor himself beginning in the early fourth century, the Church was absorbed into the power structure of the Roman Empire and changed its value system and above all its form or organization. The organization of the Church changed from that of a simple priesthood of all believers in which leadership was given to those with the charisma of the greatest purity to that of a leadership by a sacerdotal hierarchy which had all the trappings of Roman power, as the papacy transformed itself into a perpetuation of Roman authoritarianism. The Protestant reformers announced that the modern Church was one that disavowed

Romanism, rejected involvement in the corruptions of Roman imperial majesty, and, as far as was humanly possible, went back to the simplicity and purity of the earliest Church.

This thesis, when actually applied in religious life, created many problems: above all, it made Lutheranism a potentially revolutionary doctrine in social as well as religious life, and after the German peasants in 1525 took Luther too seriously and undertook a kind of communist movement against the nobility, Luther qualified his doctrine of the apostolic poverty and simplicity of the Church. Nevertheless, in terms of historical interpretation, Protestantism, like Renaissance humanism, propounded the idea of the great post-medieval return, the recovery of purity, the bridging of the centuries.

The Renaissance and Reformation interpretations both believed modern history involved a rejection of the intermediate medieval world and a return to ancient purity; in the case of the humanists a purity of classicism; in the case of the reformers a purity of apostolic Christianity. It can be seen how easy it was for John Calvin to be both a great humanist and a great reformer. Although ultimately there is a certain kind of disparity between humanist and Christian ideas, nevertheless these two value systems can live with one another and did in the sixteenth century, so that the humanist and the Protestant views of history both demanded the rejection of medieval culture and medieval institutions. By the end of the sixteenth century, the interpretation that dominated historical thought until the twentieth century had been elaborated—modern history begins with a revolt against medievalism and return to a golden age in the past, a golden age of culture and a golden age of religion.

Some additional formulations of this modernity thesis posited upon an idea of return are possible. The most important of these was adumbrated in England in the sixteenth century when a constitutional theory was propounded that inaugurates modernism through the medium of political revival. The parliamentary legislation put through by the government of King Henry VIII in the 1530s separating England from Rome claimed that in sundry old chronicles it was stated that the king of England was an "emperor," that is, he had the *imperium*, he had the absolute power, the sovereignty of a Roman emperor, and he was not subject to any foreign potentate, including especially the pope. It is implied in this view of history that an English king was sovereign at one time in some vague medieval past, but the pope had usurped authority over him, and now the English king was reasserting fundamental rights and returning to his sovereign status and the re-establishment of the complete independence of the English people. In England therefore, in additon to the return to the classicism of the humanists and the return to pure Christianity of the Protestant reformers, there was enunciated the idea of the return to royal supremacy, royal sovereignty, and English national independence.

This modernity thesis, as developed between the fourteenth and the end of the sixteenth century, shaped all subsequent historical thinking until very recent times. In the eighteenth century it was shrilly taken up and elaborated by the *philosophes* of the French Enlightenment who detested the clerics in their society with frenzy. They applauded the Renaissance, they detested medieval superstition, as they called it, and they regarded the modern world as beginning with the Renaissance.

In the early nineteenth century in Germany, modern academic historiography was developed principally under the leadership of historians at the University of Berlin of whom the most famous and the most significant, in the context of this discussion, was Leopold von Ranke. Ranke was much more sympathetic to the medieval world than the Enlightenment *philosophes*. Nevertheless, when he came to examine the development of Europe in the fifteenth and sixteenth centuries, as he did in several works of great learning and insight, he accepted the modernity thesis that had been established in the sixteenth century. Ranke did not enthuse at length about the humanist revival, but he did place great emphasis on the Reformation as the beginning of the modern world. Ranke himself, as a conservative German Lutheran of the nineteenth century, did not regard the Reformation as a return to the purity of the apostolic Church. But in his view, what the Reformation accomplished was the destruction of the unity of Christendom, thereby opening the way for the rise of the sovereign states, the great modern national entities. Ranke significantly contributed to the development of the modernity thesis along the lines of the Renaissance and Reformation interpretation by secularizing it, or more specifically, by politicizing it.

Modern history is national history in Ranke's view. It is the history of the great powers, of the post-medieval European state system. This state system came into existence in the sixteenth century, making use of the kind of secular and realistic political theory propounded by the Italian humanists like Machiavelli and of the experience in international diplomacy and the forms of the modern-type government that had been worked out in the Italian city-states in the fifteenth century. Thus Ranke, writing in the second quarter of the nineteenth century, took up the modernity thesis and gave it a secular and strongly political form, and this new view had an enormous impact on the writing of all European history in the following hundred years.

In the century after Ranke it became conventional to regard modern history as beginning around 1500, and to see the Italian humanist revolt against medieval culture as a kind of advance warning of modernity. The Reformation was usually viewed as decisive not because it brought men back to the purity of the Christian faith—academic historians customarily did not deal in such sentimental terms—but rather because it destroyed the unity of Christendom and it opened the way for the great powers and the European state system. In this way it is significant and rather peculiar that that element of the modernity thesis which in the sixteenth century had been the least prominent, namely the doctrine propounded in England on the sovereignty of the English king, predominated in Ranke's interpretation and in the view of his followers and adherents from 1840 to 1945. It was this English political view of the nature of modernity, a political categorization rather than an intellectual or religious one, that generally prevailed in academic historiography.

Nevertheless, the most dynamic and in some ways the most persuasive explication of modernity along the lines of the Renaissance and Reformation interpretation, did make considerable use of the humanist thesis and of intellectual criteria. This dynamic and persuasive view was presented by one of Ranke's disciples, Jacob Burckhardt, a Swiss scholar, in his famous book, *The Civilization of the Renaissance in Italy*, published in 1860. In this work Burckhardt takes up Ranke's modernity thesis on the great difference between medieval political and modern political life, namely the movement from universality and idealism to national particularism and *realpolitik*, but he combines this with the whole humanist philosophy. Burckhardt brought together the political categories that Ranke had so strongly emphasized with the intellectual and cultural revolution view that had been worked out by the humanists themselves during the fourteenth and fifteenth centuries.

Therefore Burckhardt believed that the modern world began with the throwing off of the "veil" of the medieval group value systems and the rediscovery of the individual and of individual self-consciousness, a rediscovery that was aided and partly inspired by the study of classical tradition. Burckhardt's book is one of the very few works of nineteenth-century historical scholarship that is still read and studied today. In the nineteenth and early twentieth centuries the criterion of modernity was more political, and Burckhardt was not at the center of the prevailing interpretation. But in the past three or four decades historians have felt political history to be too narrow, or they simply have become bored with it. Burckhardt's interpretation of modernity, which supplemented Ranke's political categories by re-emphasizing the humanist criteria, has been found to be more pleasing to twentieth-century tastes. The views of Ranke and Burckhardt still command strong support among academic historians. In 1966 the American scholar Cyril Black, in his study of "the dynamics of modernization," presented what was essentially an updated version of this interpretation of modernity: Black's key categories are political and intellectual.

The Renaissance and Reformation interpretation of modernity paradoxically received strong support from Roman Catholic scholars in the nineteenth and early twentieth centuries. Alone among historians, the Roman Catholic group naturally looked upon post-medieval modernity as a bad rather than a good thing. Indeed, one of the heresies that Catholics were supposed to avoid in the early twentieth century was the heresy of "Modernism," which was a movement within Catholicism in the first decade of the twentieth century that sought a coming to terms with modern culture by Roman Catholicism. This was suppressed by the papacy. Until the Second Vatican Council, modernity and Modernism were condemned by the Church, and Roman Catholic scholarship placed itself out of the whole value system of modern thought by going on the assumption that modernity was a bad rather than a good thing. Nevertheless, with regard to the question of when modern history began, Roman Catholic scholars were in agreement with Protestants and secular liberal writers. They agreed that it began in the sixteenth century with Luther and the Reformation, and they were very eager to attribute this beginning to Luther and the Reformation because they disliked the modern world so much.

Catholic scholarship of the late nineteenth and early twentieth centuries was severely partisan—a mixture of parish passions with Irish and Italian prejudices—and it vehemently claimed that the only good era of history was the medieval because it had been dominated by the Church and that bad things triumphed in the world when the Church's unity and domination of Europe was ended. This had occurred with the Reformation; indeed, there was no doubt among Catholic scholars that modernity was a product of the Reformation and began in the early sixteenth century. The only difference between Catholic and other scholars on this problem was the Catholics said this coming of modernity was a very bad thing, and other scholars said that actually this was a very good thing because it was assumed that the modern national state, modern individualism, and modern secularism were values and systems that were much to be applauded; they viewed modernity as liberal, beneficent, and rational.

II. The Industrialization Interpretation

The second school of interpretation of the idea of modern history has come to the fore and gained prominence in academic circles largely since the second world war. The beginnings of this interpretation, however, go back to the nineteenth century, although at that time and even in the early twentieth century this interpretation had very little support in academic circles.

This modernization-industrialization or economic interpretation of the beginnings and nature of modern history certainly can be traced back to Karl Marx. Marx wrote a great deal about history, although as a matter of fact his mind was too categorical, too full of the structures of English economics and German philosophy for him to undertake the precise research into the complexities of human development which is required for sound historical interpretation. Nevertheless, Marx was a very great social thinker, undoubtedly the most original and provocative social thinker of the past hundred and fifty years, and grounded as he was in the German philosophy of Hegel, which in turn was a philosophy that stressed development, Marx had very important things to say about history. To put it another way, the whole Marxist philosophy is in a sense a theory of history, and although Marx's understanding and knowledge of the complexities of social change were deficient, his general historical vision was an original and important one and has exercised an enormous influence in the modern world, on historians as well as among radical movements and theorists of various kinds.

Following Hegel's dialectical philosophy of thesis, antithesis, and synthesis in history, Marx saw a dialectical progression through the course of European civilization. Marx begins, as the members of the first humanist school of interpretation do, with the consideration of the medieval society. This he regarded as a feudal society; that is, a world which was entirely rural and in which there are two classes, the lords and the peasants. Now, according to Marx, in the late Middle Ages and in the sixteenth and seventeenth centuries a new class came to the fore. This class was the bourgeoisie, the urban middle class who made their living as capitalists and stood outside of feudalism. The bourgeoisie was the harbinger of a new society, a new system of values, which culminates in modern industrial society. In the Marxist view, beginning in the late Middle Ages and the sixteenth and seventeenth centuries the bourgeoisie undermined and eventually overthrew the power of the lords. The bourgeoisie introduced a new kind of production, namely urban industrial production, and by the mid-nineteenth century the bourgeoisie had become the dominant class in society. Coinciding with this rise of the bourgeoisie, there is the development of an industrial proletariat, and in the next stage of society the proletariat will come under the leadership of the Communist party, or the Communist revolutionary group, overthrow the bourgeoisie, establish the dictatorship of proletariat, and prepare the way for a truly socialist society.

Marx was working within the context of the assumptions of nineteenth-century historiography, and it is evident that he was strongly influenced by the belief that very important things happened in Europe around 1500. But to him the important thing that happened was not the rise of humanist values, the Reformation, and a European states system—these were merely secondary derivative matters—but rather a change in the means of production and the rise of a new class to power.

In the late nineteenth and early twentieth centuries, scholars and social philosophers who were loyal adherents to the Marxist system tried to take his abstract schemes and work out a detailed historical thesis to justify Marx's paradigm. They tried to show how in the sixteenth and seventeenth centuries the bourgeoisie did indeed come to power. They tried to show that humanism was part of the ideology of a new self-conscious class. They were very interested in showing that Protestantism was originally, or at least ultimately, the ideology of the rising bourgeoisie. It was claimed that Protestantism came, by the seventeenth century, to allow capitalist endeavor as a legitimate calling in life, and thereby Protestantism accommodated itself to the new economic situation in Europe, which Catholicism failed to do.

A group of English scholars, beginning in the early twentieth century with R. H. Tawney, took the lead in trying to academicize the Marxist paradigm and to show how the triumph of the bourgeoisie was actually the dominant theme of the period of the sixteenth and seventeenth centuries. It was even claimed that the political developments of the period actually were directed by this reaching for power on the part of the bourgeoisie. On the Continent, it was claimed that the new absolutist state came to dominate over the aristocracy through monarchial alliance with the bourgeoisie. This latter thesis, many times proposed, has never been worked out by any scholar in detail, although as late as the 1950s the very distinguished Sorbonne historian R. Mousnier gave it his authoritative support.

Marx's most prominent disciples in the western world among academic historians have been Englishmen, and it was with regard to English history that the theory of the triumph of bourgeois capitalism as the real process of modernization taking place in the sixteenth and seventeenth centuries has been most fully developed. Tawney, writing originally just before the first world war and in a famous essay published in 1940, argued that the triumph of the urban bourgeoisie, allied with rural capitalists among the English gentry, overthrew the Stuart monarchy in the 1640s because the Stuarts were loyal to old-fashioned medieval paternalistic values which tried to protect the peasantry against the depredations of ruthless capitalists. This thesis has been recently elaborated by the Oxford historian Christopher Hill. The Marxist thesis was given further respectability by the British scholar Lawrence Stone who presently holds a distinguished chair at Princeton University. Stone's celebrated book, *The Crisis of the Aristocracy*, provides a sophisticated Marxist scheme in which it is not so much the bourgeoisie rising out of their own ability and aggressive instincts, but the failure of the aristocracy to maintain their status and the undermining of the ancient habits of deference, that brings down the framework of the old feudal society and makes possible a more rationalized middle-class form of social life.

The first propounding of an economic view of modernity was, then, made by Marx, and this was worked out by his recent disciples in the 1950s and 1960s. If we follow the interpretation of the Marx-Hill-Stone school, the question arises as to when actually a modern society comes into existence. The answer would seem to be: not fully until the Industrial Revolution of the eighteenth century, but already in the 1640s in England the bourgeoisie had achieved at least a short hold on power, and Protestantism early in its development had become a stalking-horse for aggressive capitalism. Consequently, in the Marxist interpretation of modernity, it would seem that modern history does *not* begin in a full-fledged way in the sixteenth century, as held by the Renaissance and Reformation school; rather there was a progressive or evolutionary development beginning with the intrusions of mercantile capitalism and bourgeois effectiveness in the late Middle Ages and the sixteenth century. Then with the takeover of Protestantism by capitalist values and the political importance of the bourgeoisie in the seventeenth century, the modern world slowly emerges, but is not fully established until the Industrial Revolution of the eighteenth and nineteenth centuries. The complexity and sophistication of the Marxist interpretation is obvious, and it considerably expanded—beyond what the Renaissance and Reformation interpretation had provided —the categories that comprise post-medieval modern history.

In the Marxist interpretation there is a kind of half-love and half-hate attitude toward the modern era. The Marxist view, of course, condemns a great deal of what happens in modern history. Modern history means the exploitation by the bourgeoisie of the proletariat, and modern society, therefore, is fundamentally an immoral society which will be superseded by communism, or the Labor party, or the welfare state, depending on how radical the degree of Marxist revolutionary zeal inspiring the particular historian. In all cases this modern era is a most imperfect one, a fundamentally immoral one, and must be superseded. Nonetheless, this modern bourgeois era is seen as a necessary, creative, historical stage and a progressive advance beyond the feudal medieval period that preceded it.

The Marxist school, therefore, has affinities with the Renaissance and Reformation school, which stresses the tremendous superiority of humanism, Protestantism, and statism over medieval culture and political and social organization. Marxists are not as enthusiastic as proponents of the Renaissance and Reformation school with regard to the change from medievalism to modernity, because in their (somewhat romantic) view the medieval world did provide some kind of paternalistic protection for the poor, the unemployed, the miserable, and the sick which under the ruthless capitalism of the seventeenth, eighteenth, and nineteenth centuries was abandoned. Still, the Marxists regard the feudal world as one that was basically pre-modern, irrational, and unprogressive, and in any case it was inevitably doomed. Whether one regrets it or not, medieval society had to be superseded because of inevitable and necessary economic change in the direction of industrialization.

To the Marxist historian, then, the triumph of the bourgeoisie, beginning in the sixteenth century and reaching its culmination in the nineteenth century, was a process of the modernization and rationalization of a society which nevertheless contained within it a moral defect that in turn will be corrected in the post-modern period, the utopian era of the future. In the socialist era or the communist era, the modernized and rationalized qualities of bourgeois capitalism will be retained but will be applied in the interest of society as a whole by some kind of beneficent ruling group, whether they are British Socialists or Russian Communists.

The criterion of modernization as equivalent to the development of an industrial society has been applied in historical study during the past three decades, and especially since the second world war, by western scholars who are not Marxists and in fact in many cases are vehemently anti-Communist. The adherents of this non-Marxist but economic school see as the most important development in all of history the emergence of an industrial society. They are not very much concerned with the appearance of a middle class per se, but rather with the whole process of change which produces the factory system, extensive urbanization, tremendous population growth, and enormous acceleration in technological change. This school, which is a subdivision of the industrial-economic interpretation of modernity, designates as the most important single development in history the Industrial Revolution of the eighteenth and nineteenth centuries. It began in England, and in the nineteenth and twentieth centuries this Industrial Revolution has been carried to nearly all parts of the world, and is in the process of being universalized.

It is held that those societies which do not experience this industrialization are pre-modern and are doomed to medieval misery or extinction. The only means to social survival, the only way of beneficence, the only way of coming to terms with the possibilities of human life is to experience the process of industrialization and urbanization that began in England in the eighteenth century and in Germany, France, and the United States in the nineteenth century. In this view, the modernizing, rationalizing social process was carried to Russia, Japan, and other countries in the late nineteenth and twentieth centuries and must be applied everywhere in the world if we are to achieve post-medieval peace, ordered humanity, and beneficence.

It is necessary to discriminate carefully between the Marx-Tawney school and the non-Marxist industrialist interpretation. For the Marxist school, the modern era begins to glimmer around 1500, and with the advance of Protestantism and the triumph of the English bourgeoisie in the civil wars in the 1640s, modernization was pretty well on its way, although not until the Industrial Revolution of the eighteenth century did it attain its full form. This modern era is viewed as socially an advance over the pre-modern era, but it is morally imperfect and will be superseded by a post-modern social era.

The non-Marxist industrial school of historical interpretation places the beginning of the modern era precisely in eighteenth-century England. Before that there had existed in Europe a society which had extremely slow technological progress and very slow population growth in which occasional spurts of population were often wiped out by famine, plague, and war; a society which continued after 1500 to be dominated by traditional medieval aristocratic values, whether Protestant or Catholic does not really make much difference; a society in which the values were hierarchical—that is, it was assumed that a small elite would have most of the benefits of the world. Therefore the ideology that prevailed in the seventeenth century was substantially still medieval. In this industrial interpretation, humanism was not very important, because it did not fundamentally change men's social attitudes.

Beginning in the eighteenth century, this interpretation contends, there appeared a mass democratic society, self-perpetuating industrial change, tremendous urbanization, a fantastic population growth incomparably greater than anything that ever appeared in the world. The population grew faster in Europe between 1750 and 1850 than in all preceding centuries of human history. In this century a thorough change occurred in the social environment and wholly changed the possibilities of life. There was a longer life expectancy; there was mass education; there was an emergence of a wide and universal suffrage and of genuinely democratic government and genuinely mass culture. Conseqeuntly, the eighteenth and nineteenth centuries are the true beginning of the post-medieval modern era. Modern history begins around 1760 in England; it becomes very widespread throughout western Europe and the United States by the second half of the nineteenth century, and this process of modernization is now being applied throughout the world.

In this non-Marxist industrial view, the modern era is in a sense the ultimate historical era. Although modern industrial society is faced with grave problems, such as runaway population booms especially in Asia and Latin America, this is the only kind of rational society possible, the only kind of real progress over whatever previously prevailed in the world. Basically there was scarcely any progress, this view holds, between the way men lived in Egypt in 2000 B.C. and the way they lived in England and France in 1700 A.D. English society of 1700 A.D., almost as much as Egyptian society of 2000 B.C., is "the world we have lost." The whole style of life, the whole circumstance of life, has undergone a revolution in the past two hundred years. This is the best we know and this is the best we ever hope to know and the best that all society should strive for.

The Marxist and non-Marxist industrial interpretation have very much in common in that they both find the criterion for modernity in economic and technological progress and attendant social change. But there are fundamental differences between the two schools. The Marxist view is fairly conservative in its dating in that it tends to agree substantially with the Renaissance and Reformation interpretation, holding that the sixteenth century begins the modern era, or at least announces it, if it does not fully develop modernity. On the other hand, the non-Marxist industrial school does not think anything very important or novel happened in Europe in the sixteenth century: the Reformation was a purely religious matter, a squabbling among priests, and it is really not until the eighteenth and nineteenth centuries that any fundamental change takes place in the circumstances of human life and the post-medieval modern era is inaugurated. The Marxist view is very appreciative of the significance of the bourgeois triumph and the lapsing of aristocratic control in favor of middle-class domination. Yet it is very critical of the many aspects of bourgeois life that effect the exploitation of the proletariat, and it sees the modern era not as an infinite point in history but a finite stage that will and must be superseded. The non-Marxist industrial interpretation sees nothing beyond this present stage of history and it seeks to apply it throughout the world.

Many scholars have been involved in the development of the non-Marxist industrial interpretation. The first scholar who probably can be said to have suggested this view was the English social theorist and historian, Arnold Toynbee (the uncle of the famous philosopher of history of our day), who wrote in the 1880s and who first identified the Industrial Revolution of eighteenth-century England as an enormous turning point in history. Yet Toynbee was still to some extent conditioned by the moral and somewhat pejorative attitude toward the Industrial Revolution among late nineteenth-century English intellectuals. Toynbee's moralism has been strained out and a completely favorable and deterministic attitude toward the Industrial Revolution as the necessary and only possible road for all of mankind has been worked out by many historians and theorists in the twentieth century. Pioneers in developing the interpretation in the 1930s and 1940s were the English economic historians Sir John Clapham and T. S. Ashton. Since 1945 a host of scholars in the United States and Britain has clarified and elaborated the non-Marxist industrial view of modern history. These include the British historians R. M. Hartwell and Peter Laslett, the American historian David Landes, and particularly the American economic theorist W. W. Rostow.

It is a very fascinating reflection on the complexities of modern institutions and social theories that, although this industrial school in the United States and England is decisively and at times vehemently anti-Communist, there is a certain similarity and parallel between this western industrialist interpretation of modernity and the Stalinist attitude toward social change. Stalin fully believed in the need for industrialization in Russia, and to achieve it he was willing to sacrifice the happiness of a whole generation of the Russian people, to allow the death by famine of millions of people, to use the secret police to destroy in the most ruthless fashion any opposition to his regime, and to exercise the most authoritarian and savage kind of political rule. The purpose of all this—unless we assume that Stalin was completely mad and there does not seem to be any evidence that he was—was his passionate belief that Russia had to pass very rapidly to the stage of modernized industrialization if it was to survive and achieve prominence among the nations of the world. In order to achieve this end, great sacrifices were deemed necessary on the part of the Russian people.

The non-Marxist western industrialist interpretation of modern history in a kind of peculiar way resembles the Stalinist ideology. No primary value in society or in history is accorded to tradition, religion, intellectual life, values. In this view of modernity the only really important thing that can happen in history is the achievement of the rationalized, industrial, and bureaucratic state, although for this purpose all ancient values of the orient, all tribal modes of African life—all medievalism—must be sacrificed. This view is very critical of the societies which preserve their old religion, their old values, their old political forms which impede the achievement of modernity. In this view, unless the process of modernity takes place in these societies, their situation will be pathetic. The only way to live is the modern way, the way of change in Eng-

land and the United States and other western industrialized societies, and a failure to achieve this is social disaster and almost a
moral stigma.

There is a distinct conflict of values between the Marxist and
non-Marxist industrialist interpretation of modernity. The Marxist
view retains overtones of criticism of industrialism that prevailed
among humanitarians and utopian socialists in the nineteenth century—industrialization, while it produced modernity, at the same
time engendered a great increase in man's inhumanity to man. It
liberated man from medieval ruralism, but it imprisoned him in the
modern factory. Hence the Marxist conclusion is that modernity
is by no means a moral good, but rather an amoral necessity which
must be superseded at some future time by a more beneficent society. Marx's own view of history postulates some future date for
the withering away of the state, some kind of anarchic golden age
in the future. The young Marx was very much influenced by early
nineteenth-century romantic anarchism, and although he later
condemned the anarchists and the utopian socialists, a strong utopian, humanist current was embedded in his doctrine, except that
the utopian anarchy was put off to a post-modern era.

The western non-Marxist historians who place the beginning
of the modern era in the eighteenth century and see this as the only
road for mankind, entirely reject this moral dissent from modern
industrial society which Marx never abandoned. They are strange
bedfellows with Stalin, who also believed that industrialism was
the only road a society in the twentieth century ought to follow.
Stalin gave lip service to Marxist-Leninism, but he was in fact a
ruthless kind of economic realist with no ounce of utopianism or
romanticism or even beneficent humanitarianism in his being. With
no vision of any kind of beneficent world, he declared that all of
Russian society must sacrifice itself to the point of mass murder for
the achievement of modernity.

The western industrial theorists and interpreters of history
have a very similar view. Nothing is really important in history
except economic and technological change and no society can really
say it is progressing anywhere until it experiences what Rostow
calls a "takeoff" to an industrial society, to the point of self-sustaining economic growth and population expansion which he sees as
being the critical turning point in the history of any society. Just

as Stalin did not care how many novelists, poets, and musicians had to be shot by the secret police, or sent to Siberia for opposing his ruthless schemes for modernization, so the modern industrialist historians, although vehemently (sometimes fanatically) anti-Communist, agree with Stalin in that they do not see any great value in a new Petrarch, a new Confucius, even a new Gandhi in Asia or Africa. The only worthwhile change they postulate is a new technology and a new urbanized life.

This interpretation has become very strongly fixed in the historical view of the academic world in the past two decades, and there is good reason for this ascent to orthodoxy. This interpretation of modernity has gained adherence because of the dominance of anti-humanist, scientistic, and collectivist attitudes among history faculty in British, French, and American universities. This view also apparently fits in very well with the circumstances and problems of the recent and contemporary world. Most academic historians, the great majority of whom in the United States are not Marxist, would subscribe to this industrialist view of modernity because it seems to be the shape of the modern world—this seems to be the way our own society takes form. Historians draw their assumptions and categories from the reality of life that they see before them. There is no other way to develop one's assumptions as to what is important in history. Although in the sixteenth century, the nineteenth century, or the early twentieth century, intellectual and religious values and the shape of political institutions seemed crucial, nowadays these aspects of the past are dismissed as mere "superstructure." The only significant difference, it is held, lies between industrial and underdeveloped traditional societies. The problem of underdeveloped societies has become a great theme for discussion and debate in the past twenty years, and it has come to dominate all historical thinking and particularly our understanding of when the post-medieval era began and what the nature of modern history is.

III. The Neo-Humanist Interpretation

The third interpretation of the beginnings and the nature of modern history only began to make its appearance in intellectual circles in the United States and in western Europe in the second half of the 1960s, and it is at present not much more than a social philosophy. It is a point of view which has received very little transcription into a precise historical formulation and has yet had a small influence upon historical scholarship. But in the writings of some very young scholars of the New Left in the United States there is a glimmering of this attitude being transformed into a working historical assumption. Because of the strong influence this attitude toward modern society has had on the student generation in the late 1960s, this view will in time be transformed into actual historical interpretation. It will be bitterly resisted by the prevailing generation of scholars, but in time it will come to take its place as a plausible view and the basis for a legitimate school of historical interpretation.

This third approach to modern history may be termed the anti-industrial and neo-humanist approach. There are certain affinities between this attitude and both the Renaissance and Reformation school and the Marxists. The affinity with the Renaissance-Reformation school lies in the fact that the anti-industrial and neo-humanist school takes as its criteria not materialistic institutional forms, but rather the values of men, the way men live, the happiness that men achieve in the world. This is in a sense a long throwback to the old humanist thesis that when men in the fourteenth century in Italy saw themselves as individuals rather than members of a group—as was strongly emphasized by Burckhardt—a fundamental change and a great upheaval took place in the history of European civilization. This new school today also thinks that men's feelings about themselves, their self-consciousness, and their personal values are the essential things in any society. Rather than the external forms, it is the inner man that counts and this places the new interpretation in parallel with the oldest school of interpretation of modern history.

The new interpretation also has affinities with pre-Stalinist Marxism and actually with Marx himself—"the young Marx" who was heavily moralistic and romantic, who saw industrial society as imprisoning men and alienating them from their real human nature, and who envisioned a post-modern society in which men would be liberated. It is with this aspect of pristine Marxism that the new anti-industrial attitude in social and historical thought is allied, and to some degree it is directly inspired by the "young Marx." In so far as the Marxists differ with the non-Marxist industrialist interpreters of modern history over the question of whether our present society is the last stage or the best stage of social change, and in so far as the Marxists project yet another stage when man's humanity will be liberated from the rigid, abstract authoritarianism of the industrial order, there is a close alliance between Marxism and the new radical thinkers.

Indeed there is some direct inspiration here, because the most vehement exponents thus far of this new attitude have been writers among the so-called New Left who reject Stalinism with its mechanistic, totalitarian subjection of men to the industrial order and want to liberate men from modern society. These men of the New Left have indeed been inspired directly by the early writings of Marx in which utopianism, moralism, and humanism is much more pronounced than in his later writings. The new attitude is to a degree an offshoot of the earliest form of Marxism. It has sometimes been viewed as merely a resurgence of a pristine Marxism against the later Stalinist perversions and against the western counterpart to Stalinism, as reflected in the economic school's subjection of man to the needs of industrialization and rational modernization.

Merely pointing to affinities with the young Marx would be a narrow view of the new radicalism, because this attitude also constitutes a return to Renaissance humanism in which the most important thing that happens in history is the assertion of individualism and the primacy of individual values. Although the vehement exponents of the New Left have not been very conscious of the ultimate ancestry of their program, their ultimate intellectual progenitor is indeed the old humanist school which claimed that the fulcrum upon which history turned in the fourteenth and fifteenth centuries was a radical philosophy of individualism and assertion of the moral superiority of the individual against the dictates of a corporate authoritarian order.

If we consider this matter further, the neo-humanist, anti-industrialist attitude is one that in a peculiar way is actually very close to the interpretation of modernism that prevailed in nineteenth and early twentieth century Catholicism. This Catholic interpretation condemned the modern world as materialistic, as putting business above divine values, as placing pragmatic social dictates above man's conscience. The new interpretation, the new radical philosophy, similarly condemns modern society and modern economy for its dehumanization, deprivation of human personality, its compromise with moral standards, and its subversion of the primacy of conscience. Of course, in a fundamental way, there is an unbridgeable disparity between the old Catholicism and new humanism. The latter view does not wish a return to the authority of papacy over conscience—they find the authority of conscience in themselves. But Catholicism itself is undergoing enormous changes at the present time and has been since the Second Vatican Council and there has developed a radical movement in the Church which has definite affinites with the New Left. This new radical Catholicism is likely to support an interpretation of post-medieval history similar to that now propounded by the New Left. For radical Catholicism also condemns modern society for its materialism, its compromises, its dehumanization and alienation of the individual, and its corruption of conscience. In so far as radical Catholicism does not return to medievalism, it will have the same attitude to the modern era as that of the New Left, namely that the modern era is an intermediary stage in the history of civilization—that it is in many aspects immoral, in many aspects not an improvement over what had gone before, and in many cases a decline from what had gone before and a stage in society which must be superseded.

The new radicalism, and its concomitant neo-humanist interpretation of history, also draws inspiration from Freud's analysis of the repressive effects of modern civilization on the human psyche, especially as interpreted by neo-Freudian thinkers like Norman O. Brown and Herbert Marcuse. Whereas Freud tended to want to help men adjust to repression, the neo-Freudians want to rearrange civilization so as to release man's spontaneous capacity for love.

Finally, the new interpretation is bound to become very widespread and to gain adherence in the non-western world, in Asia and in Africa. Indeed this new interpretation does take certain inspiration from, and has certain affinities with Maoism, which presumes to speak for the non-western societies. Although in some ways Mao is a disciple of Stalin, there are other ways in which he is not—Mao is a bifurcated, awkward, inconsistent thinker or possibly has been made so by circumstances of Chinese society. Although for a long time Mao Tse-tung, like Stalin, seemed to wish to sacrifice everything for the purposes of Chinese industrialization and seemed to regard modern secularism and modern material industrial society as the only possible model, his later attitude seems to be quite different. Whatever may have been his original view (or perhaps he was misunderstood in his original view), it does appear that Mao has rejected the Soviet Union's trend toward the kind of balanced industrial order that prevails in the West, and with it, the modern world. There is in Mao still some of that anti-materialistic, anti-rational attitude that is characteristic of Chinese culture, particularly of Confucianism. This attitude brings Maoism in some ways close to the New Left and to the attitudes of the younger student generation in the West, and it is really for this reason Maoism has achieved a certain fashionability among this generation. Castro also appears to be a holdout against monolithic modernization and industrialization.

One does not, however, have to be a Maoist or a Castroite to reject the industrialist interpretation, the industrialist philosophy, the Stalinist attitude—far from it. All of the so-called underdeveloped societies, such as Africa, Latin America, and India, have experienced very mixed success in trying to achieve industrialization. They will probably more and more question whether the only trend of history, the only road their society can pursue, is the course of post-medieval western history since 1760. They will consider whether they have to engage in a so-called rational allocation of resources while abandoning their own old social values and structures in the interests of this supposedly finite stage of history. Partly because their traditions will reassert themselves as nationalist ideologies, and because the road to modernization is turning out to be very difficult in these underdeveloped societies, as a recent study by Gunnar Myrdal shows with respect to Southeast Asia, the non-western societies will reject more and more, one suspects, the industrialist interpretation of history as a kind of authoritarian ideology that betrays the best traditions of their own cultures. Must these underdeveloped societies try to imitate the post-medieval West, which probably they can never do fully, while depriving themselves of the best things in their own historical development?

These underdeveloped societies, when they begin to reflect upon history, will reject the whole industrialist interpretation of modernity, or they will at least conclude that this form of modernity is a partial, very limited kind of modernization. They will seek other roads to modernity, other ways of coming to terms with modern technology, even by rejecting a good deal of modern technology in the interest of traditional values. The underdeveloped societies are bound, therefore, to take a neo-humanist attitude to history, or at least what in western terms would be called a neo-humanist attitude. They will put primacy upon values rather than upon social organization and the dictates of an economic order.

This radical neo-humanist interpretation has scarcely been dignified by scholarship, but generally historians are among the most conservative of academic groups, and it usually takes a decade, sometimes a whole generation, before new social ideas begin to become operative assumptions in historical interpretation. This neo-humanism is likely to become a central idea in our time, and it will condition historical thinking. It is likely that in the 1970s, and certainly in the 1980s, the industrialist interpretation will no longer be a universal one, but will be vehemently opposed.

For the moment one can only suggest the outlines of what this neo-humanist, anti-industrialist interpretation will be. We will not call it necessarily a New Left interpretation because, as we have seen, it can be supported by many people of other persuasions than what we think of as the New Left. Neo-humanism is a term which embraces also all sorts of anti-materialistic, anti-corporatist, anti-authoritarian, and anti-western attitudes, and emphasizes conscience, personal feeling, interpersonal relations, mystical communion, and all the spiritual values and individual drives that are possible in any given society. The terminology is at best awkward, because it is hard to define a term for an intellectual movement before that movement has fully developed and all its implications and directions are evident. Nevertheless, this is likely to be a very important movement and to be applied in leading historical interpretation; it will require us to re-examine the whole of modern history, and even pre-modern history. One can only at this point suggest what this interpretation is likely to be.

If the supreme value is individual happiness and the goal of society is the way in which men can live as full human beings, in which every aspect of their being can achieve its fullest realization, then not only is communist industrial society condemned along with western capitalist industrial society (as by Marcuse), but we see that the distinctions which were often made between pre-modern and modern societies are not fundamental. If the criterion of history is individual freedom, then it is very questionable whether there is any post-medieval modern period at all; that is, whether any fundamental change has occurred in history with regard to the degree of individual freedom that men have achieved. We might conclude that men escaped certain tyrannies and miseries existing in the pre-industrial world and these were replaced by new forms of terror.

In industrialized society men have had opportunities to make a good living, to have material comforts, to travel, to be educated, and to exercise a political franchise. Because these changes have taken place, however, does not necessarily mean that men are any more free than in pre-modern society. What they have gained in one respect, they have lost in another. In industrialized society they have lost a certain kind of enjoyment of nature and participation and closeness to nature that existed in pre-industrial society. Industrial society brought material benefits to the masses, in a sense mass culture, but on the other hand—particularly through technology and population expansion—it made life more difficult. Life became noisy, the air became polluted, the cities congested, and the struggle for existence in some ways more severe and more competitive than in the pre-industrial world.

It is very hard to gauge these things accurately, and whoever expounds this view is immediately accused of a romanticization of the medieval world as a pristine golden age and of a refusal to recognize that pre-industrial society was exploitive, filthy, and violent. This is a very important criticism, but be that as it may, the radical view claims that what men have gained in one respect they have lost in another, and so that the sum totality of change with respect to the criterion of individual freedom has been very small. Only change in technique and in social organization has occurred, *only institutional change*, but not in the psychological circumstances of life.

All the other schools of modernity think men have progressed one way or another, whether political, religious, intellectual, or economic, but the neo-humanist school, with its criterion of human freedom, asks whether any human liberation has been achieved. Where is the great liberation that took place because of the Renaissance or Reformation, the coming of the modern state, the Industrial Revolution, and mass consumption society? Are men in truth more free than they were in classical Athens, in first-century Rome, or in thirteenth-century Paris?

This is a very plausible argument and a very serious one. It forces us to re-examine all our criteria for the course of western history. If we take a kind of psychological interpretation, if we say that the real problem is the repression of the individual's freedom, of individual spontaneity, the repression of love, then where are we in history, how far has humanity advanced? We still have war; we still have authoritarian regimes; we still have police states. We still have regimes which are based on repression and terror and certainly upon physical compulsion rather than upon cultivation of the best instincts of men and through liberation of their spontaneous instincts for good, for joyous harmony. Therefore if we say that the point of discrimination in history, the fundamental category, is that of liberation from repression, history has not changed very much and the orthodox academic criteria of modernity seem empty and false.

History, in this view, appears to be a series of changing techniques and strategies of repression and hatred, of bigger and better wars, of more elaborate police states, of more red tape and bigger bureaucracies, but not any kind of fundamental change in the degree to which men achieve the best potential of their nature, expressed in "little nameless unremembered acts of kindness and of love." Man's search for freedom and spontaneity, happiness and beauty remains frustrated. Man remains alienated from his humanity. In this view, modernity lies in the future. We have never achieved the modern age, we have never escaped from medievalism.

If, then, we take up this latest kind of social thinking which has certainly inspired the new generation of students in the universities, and some of their teachers—although it probably will take a long time before it penetrates into the crust of academe—then we must reconsider the whole nature of our historical thinking, the whole nature of what we are doing, the whole course of what the world is all about, and we will see that in a moral and psychological sense we have made very little progress beyond the Middle Ages.

What we see is that the whole of history is a series of repressions, more subtle and elaborate repressions, more intense and effective forms of hatred and dehumanization by the engines of the state, the industrial order, and all kinds of authoritarian regimes. If we take this kind of social philosophy seriously, and I think it will be taken seriously in historical thinking, then we must reconsider the whole course of history.

With regard to the problem of modern history, we would find that there is yet no post-medieval modern history, that the past is a continual succession of authoritarian and dehumanizing regimes throughout the whole history of the West, and in studying history we have merely been examining the techniques of repression. Once in a while there has been a voice in the wilderness. Once in a while there has been a cry of the heart. Once in a while (as in the twelfth-century liberation movement) there has been some movement toward liberation against power, against the chains that bind men in the social order. But these individuals who cry out are destroyed and forgotten and the movements are in turn suppressed, driven underground or savagely exterminated. This bleak picture is really the essence of history; and historians, from this point of view, are merely experts on the techniques of repression and corruption of human nature. There is no medieval as against modern history.

If there is substance to this view, we would have to reorganize and recast our whole way of historical thinking. History would become much more topical, much more categorical, much more comparative. That is, we would see no fundamental periodization, no fundamental breaks in the past, and following this assumption we would be studying the way in which all the oppressive regimes operated and compare the techniques and strategies they employed. And the truly post-medieval modern era—the escape from the limitations of the past, the escape from disorder, the truly rationalized world—would still lie in the future.

The historian, in this view, would have to be as much a prophet and advocate as a scholar—history would be a prescriptive as well as descriptive discipline. By studying these repressive regimes of the past, he would be trying to find ways to supersede the dehumanizing institutions that presently exist in the world. The historian would have to suggest ways in which liberation can at last triumph and the individual can at last become free against the haters, the warriors, the pharaohs, the emperors and kings and lords, the Stalinists and the fascists that have prevailed since human society began and still prevail today.

SUGGESTIONS FOR FURTHER READING

I. The Patristic World

Andras Alföldi, *The Conversion of Constantine and Pagan Roman Culture* (Oxford: Clarendon Press, 1948)

Charles N. Cochrane, *Christianity and Classical Culture: A Study of Thought and Action from Augustus to Augustine* (London: Oxford University Press, 1944)

Gerhart B. Ladner, *The Idea of Reform* (Cambridge: Harvard University Press, 1944)

Ramsay MacMullen, *Constantine* (New York: Dial Press, 1969)

Henri I. Marrou, *St. Augustine et la fin de la culture antique* (Paris: L. de Boccard, 1938)

Arnoldo Momigliano, *The Conflict between Paganism and Christianity in the Fourth Century* (Oxford: Clarendon Press, 1963)

Theodore E. Mommsen, *Medieval and Renaissance Studies* (Ithaca: Cornell University Press, 1959)

Anders Nygren, *Agape and Eros* (Philadelphia: Westminster Press, 1953)

Jean R. Palanque, *St. Ambroise et l'empire romain* (Paris: L. de Boccard, 1933)

George L. Prestige, *God in Patristic Thought* (London: S.P.C.K., 1959)

Frederik van der Meer, *Augustine the Bishop: The Life and Work of a Father of the Church* (London and New York: Sheed and Ward, 1962)

Harry A. Wolfson, *The Philosophy of the Church Fathers* (Cambridge: Harvard University Press, 1956)

II. Benedictine-Germanic Culture

Cecil Delisle Burns, *The First Europe; A Study of the Establishment of Medieval Christendom, 400–800* (London: Allen & Unwin, 1947)

Erich L. Caspar, *Geschichte des Papsttums*, 2 vols. (Tubingen: Mohr, 1930)

Hector M. Chadwick, *The Heroic Age* (Cambridge: Cambridge University Press, 1926)

Pierre P. Courçelle, *Historie littéraire des grands invasions germaniques* (Paris: Hachette, 1948)

Heinrich Fichtenau, *The Carolingian Empire* (Oxford: B. Blackwell, 1947)

Louis Halphen, *Charlemagne et l'empire carolingian* (Paris: A. Michel, 1949)

Roger P. Hinks, *Carolingian Art* (Ann Arbor: University of Michigan Press, 1962)

Fritz Kern, *Kingship and Law in the Middle Ages* (Oxford: B. Blackwell, 1956)

David Knowles, *The Monastic Order in England* (Cambridge: Cambridge University Press, 1949)

Robert Latouche, *Les Grands invasions et la crise d l'occident au Ve siècle* (Paris: Aubier, 1946)

Wilhelm Levison, *England and the Continent in the Eighth Century* (Oxford: Clarendon Press, 1956)

Edouard Salin, *La Civilisation merovingienne, d'àpres les sepultures, les textes et la laboratoire* (Paris: A. et J. Picard, 1959)

Theodor Schiefer, *Winfrid Bonifatius und die Christlichen Grundlagen Europas* (Freiburg: Herder, 1954)

Philibert Schmitz, *Geschichte des Bendiktinerorderns* (Einseideln-Zurich: Benziger, 1960)

III. *Romanesque Culture*

Paul Alphandery and Alphonse Dupront, *La Chretiente et l'idée de croisade* (Paris: A. Michel, 1959)

Marc Bloch, *Feudal Society* (Chicago: University of Chicago Press, 1961)

Carl Erdmann, *Die Enstehung des Kreuzugsgedankens* (Stuttgart: Kohlhammer, 1965)

Henri Focillon, *L'An mil* (Paris: A. Colin, 1952)

————, *The Art of the West*. Vol. 1 (London and New York: Phaidon, 1969)

Kassius Hallinger, *Gorze-Cluny* (Rome: Studia Anselmiana, Fasc. 22/23, 24/25, 1950)

Ernst H. Kantorowicz, *Laudes Regiae, a study in liturgical acclamations and medieval ruler worship* (Berkeley and Los Angeles: University of California Press, 1958)

Gerhart B. Ladner, *Theologie und Politik vor dem Investiturstreits* (Darmstadt: Wissenschaftliche Buchgesellschaft, 1971)

Jean Leclerq, *The Love of Learning and the Desire for God* (New York: Fordham University Press, 1961)

Ernst Sackur, *Die Cluniacenser in ihrer kirchlichen allgemeingeschichlichen Wirkamseit bis zur Mitte des Elften Jahrhunderts* (Darmstadt: Wissenschaftliche Buchgesellschaft, 1968)

Percy E. Schramm, *Kaiser, Rom und Renovatio* (Leipzig and Berlin: B. G. Teubner, 1929)

Richard W. Southern, *The Making of the Middle Ages* (New Haven: Yale University Press, 1965)

IV. Reform and Expansion

R. R. Bolgar, *The Classical Heritage and Its Beneficiaries* (Cambridge: Cambridge University Press, 1964)

Arno Borst, *Die Katherer* (Stuttgart: Hiersemann, 1953)

Marie D. Chenu, *Nature, Man, and Society in the Twelfth Century* (Chicago: University of Chicago Press, 1968)

Ernst R. Curtius, *European Literature and the Latin Middle Ages* (New York: Harper & Row, 1963)

Joseph de Ghellinck, *L'essor de la littérature latine au XIIᵉ siècle* (Brussels: Desclée de Brouwer, 1955)

Alexander J. Denomy, *The Heresy of Courtly Love* (Gloucester, Mass.: Peter Smith, 1965)

Peter Dronke, *Medieval Latin and the Rise of the Love Lyric* (New York: Oxford University Press, 1966)

Etienne H. Gilson, *The History of Christian Philosophy in the Middle Ages* (New York: Random House, 1955)

————, *The Mystical Theology of Saint Bernard* (London and New York: Sheed & Ward, 1955)

Herbert Grundmann, *Religiose Bewegungen im Mittelalter* (Hildesheim: G. Olm, 1961)

William T. Jackson, *The Literature of the Middle Ages* (New York: Columbia University Press, 1960)

William P. Ker, *Epic and Romance; Essays on Medieval Literature* (London: Macmillan, 1908)

Stephan G. Kuttner, *Harmony from Dissonance* (Latrobe, Pa.: Archabbey Press, 1960)

Clive S. Lewis, *The Allegory of Love; A Study in Medieval Tradition* (New York: Oxford University Press, 1967)

Roger S. Loomis, *The Grail, from Celtic Myth to Christian Symbol* (Cardiff: University of Wales Press, 1963, and New York: Columbia University Press, 1963)

Erwin Panofsky, *Abbot Suger on the Abbey Church of St. Denis and Its Art Treasures* (Princeton, N.J.: Princeton University Press, 1948)

Jefferey G. Sikes, *Peter Abelard* (New York: Russell & Russell, 1965)

Gerd Tellenbach, *Church, State, and Christian Society at the Time of the Investiture Contest* (Oxford: B. Blackwell, 1940)

Allan Temko, *Notre-Dame of Paris* (New York: Viking, 1955)

Christine Thouzellier, *Catharisme et valdeisme en languedoc á la fin du 12e au debut du 13e siècle* (Louvain: Nauwelaerts, 1969)

Philippe Wolff, *The Cultural Awakening* (New York: Pantheon, 1968)

V. Consolidation, Reaction, and Alienation

Morton Bloomfield, *Piers Plowman as a Fourteenth Century Apocalypse* (New Brunswick, N.J.: Rutgers University Press, 1962)

Marshal Clagget, *The Science of Mechanics in the Middle Ages* (Madison: University of Wisconsin Press, 1961)

Marie D. Chenu, *Toward Understanding Saint Thomas* (Chicago: H. Regenery, 1964)

F. Copleston, *Aquinas* (Baltimore: Penguin, 1967)

Alistair Crombie, *Robert Grosseteste and the Origins of Experimental Science 1100–1700* (Oxford: Clarendon Press, 1962)

Georges de Lagarde, *La Naissance de l'ésprit laïque au déclin du moyen age* (Louvain: Nauwelaerts, 1970)

Stewart C. Easton, *Roger Bacon and His Search for a Universal Science* (New York: Columbia University Press, 1952)

Johan Huizinga, *The Waning of the Middle Ages* (London: E. Arnold, 1924)

Josef A. Jungmann, *The Mass of the Roman Rite: Its Origins and Development* (New York: Benziger, 1955)

Gabriel LaBras, *L'âge classique, 1140–1378* (Paris: Sirey, 1965)

H. C. Lea, *A History of the Inquisition* (New York: Russell and Russell, 1958)

Gordon Leff, *Heresy in the Late Middle Ages: The Relation of Heterodoxy to Dissent* (Manchester: Manchester University Press, 1967, and New York: Barnes and Noble, 1967)

————, *Paris and the Oxford Universities in the 13th and 14th Centuries* (New York: Wiley, 1968)

Clive S. Lewis, *The Discarded Image* (Cambridge: Cambridge University Press, 1957)

Henri Maisonneuve, *Études sur les origines de l'inquisition* (Paris: J. Vrin, 1960)

Emile Mâle, *Religious Art in France, XIIIth Century; A Study in Medieval Iconography and Its Sources of Inspiration* (London: J. M. Dent, 1913, and New York: E. P. Dutton, 1913)

Benjamin J. Nelson, *The Idea of Usury, from Tribal Brotherhood to Universal Otherhood* (Chicago: University of Chicago Press, 1969)

John T. Noonan, *The Scholastic Analysis of Usury* (Cambridge: Harvard University Press, 1957)

Heiko A. Oberman, *The Harvest of Medieval Theology, Gabriel Biel and Late Medieval Nominalism* (Cambridge: Harvard University Press, 1963)

Hastings Rashdall, *Universities in the Middle Ages*, 2nd ed. (London: and New York: Oxford University Press, 1942)

Durant W. Robertson, *A Preface to Chaucer* (Princeton, N.J.: Princeton University Press, 1962)

Rudolf Stadelmann, *Vom Geist des Ausgehenden Mittelalters* (Stuttgart-Bad Cannstatt: Friedrich Frommann, 1966)

Fernand van Steenberghen, *Aristotle en occident, les origines de l'aristotélisme parisien* (Louvain: Editions de L'Institut Superieur de Philosophie, 1946)

Otto G. von Simson, *The Gothic Cathedral; Origins of Gothic Architecture and the Medieval Concept of Order* (New York: Pantheon, 1962)

Karl Young, *The Drama of the Medieval Church* (Oxford: Clarendon Press, 1967)

INDEX

DATE DUE

DEC 13 70			
DEC 15 '76			
17 Dec DE 13 '77			
SE 28 '82			
DE 6 '82			
JUN 20 '89			
JUL 6 '89			
GAYLORD			PRINTED IN U.S.A.